Operational Expert System Applications in the Far East

Pergamon Titles of Related Interest

Titles in the Series
Cantu-Ortiz/ OPERATIONAL EXPERT SYSTEM APPLICATIONS IN MEXICO
Lee/ OPERATIONAL EXPERT SYSTEM APPLICATIONS IN THE FAR EAST
Liebowitz/ OPERATIONAL EXPERT SYSTEM APPLICATIONS IN THE UNITED STATES
Liebowitz/ PROCEEDINGS OF THE WORLD CONGRESS ON EXPERT SYSTEMS
Suen & Shinghal/ OPERATIONAL EXPERT SYSTEM APPLICATIONS IN CANADA
Zarri/ OPERATIONAL EXPERT SYSTEM APPLICATIONS IN EUROPE

Other Book Titles of Related Interest
Crespo/ REAL TIME PROGRAMMING
DeCarli/ LOW COST AUTOMATION COMPONENTS
Mladenov/ DISTRIBUTED INTELLIGENT SYSTEMS
Mowle/ EXPERIENCE WITH THE MANAGEMENT OF SOFTWARE PROJECTS
Reinich/ LARGE SCALE SYSTEMS
Rodd/ ARTIFICIAL INTELLIGENCE IN REAL TIME CONTROL

Journals
ANNUAL REVIEW IN AUTOMATIC PROGRAMMING
COMPUTER LANGUAGES
COMPUTERS & ELECTRICAL ENGINEERING
COMPUTERS & GRAPHICS
COMPUTERS & MATHEMATICS WITH APPLICATIONS
COMPUTERS & OPERATIONS RESEARCH
COMPUTING SYSTEMS IN ENGINEERING
ENGINEERING APPLICATIONS OF ARTIFICIAL INTELLIGENCE
EXPERT SYSTEMS WITH APPLICATIONS
MATHEMATICAL & COMPUTER MODELLING
MECHATRONICS
MICROELECTRONICS & RELIABILITY
NEURAL NETWORKS
PATTERN RECOGNITION

Operational Expert System Applications in the Far East

Edited by

Jae Kyu Lee
Korea Advanced Institute of Science and Technology
University of Southern California

Riichiro Mizoguchi
Osaka University

Desai Narasimhalu
National University of Singapore

Daniel S. Yeung
Hong Kong Polytechnic of Hong Kong

PERGAMON PRESS
Oxford • New York • Seoul • Tokyo

Pergamon Press Offices:

U.K.	Pergamon Press plc, Headington Hill Hall, Oxford OX3 OBW, England
U.S.A.	Pergamon Press Inc. 395 Saw Mill River Road, Elmsford, New York 10523, U.S.A.
KOREA	Pergamon Press Korea, Room 613 Hanaro Building, 194-4 Insa-Dong, Chongno-ku, Seoul 110-290, Korea
JAPAN	Pergamon Press, 8th Floor, Matsuoka Central Building, 1-7-1 Nishishinjuku, Shinjuku-ku, Tokyo 160, Japan

Copyright © 1991 Pergamon Press Inc.

All Rights Reserved. No part of this publication may be reproduced, stored in a retrieval system or transmitted in any form or by any means: electronic, electrostatic, magnetic tape, mechanical, photocopying, recording or otherwise, without permission in writing from the publishers.

Library of Congress Cataloging-in-Publication Data

Lee, Jae Kyu.
    Operational expert system applications in the Far East / by Jae Kyu Lee.
    p.   cm.
    Includes index.
    ISBN 0-08-041440-0. -- ISBN 0-08-041439-7 (soft)
    1. Expert systems (computer science)--East Asia. I. Title.
QA76. 76.E95L44 1991
670'.285' 633--dc20   91-25727
                                                                                      CIP

Printing: 1 2 3 4 5 6 7 8 9 10 Year: 1 2 3 4 5 6 7 8 9 0

Printed in the United States of America

The paper used in this publication meets the minimum requirements of American National Standard for Information Services -- Permanence of Paper for Printed Library Materials, ANSI Z39.48-1984

Contents

Preface ... vii

PART 1 Steel Industry

Chapter
1. Application of an Expert System to Blast Furnace Operation ... 1
   Taichi Aoki, Mamoru Inaba, Takashi Sumigama and Masaaki Sakurai
2. An Expert System for Large Scale Fault Diagnosis in Steel Manufacturing ... 11
   Tatsuro Hirata and Etsuro Minami
3. Prediction of Blast Pressure in Blast Furnace Operations ... 34
   Sang-Ho Yi, Young-Soo Hong and Hoo-Keun Lee

PART 2 Electro-mechanical Industry

4. An Expert System for Elevator Design ... 43
   Hirokazu Taki, Tsuneyoshi Katsuyama, Hidekazu Tsuji, Akihiko Naito, Motonori Yoshida and Kihatirou Ohnishi

PART 3 Power Industry

5. Alarm Based Operational Guidance System ... 54
   Seiichi Terunuma, Hiroshi Takatsuto, Megumu Yoshida, Hiroki Yamamoto and Tomoko Kaneko
6. Diagnosis System for a Gas Turbine Air Conditioning Plant ... 64
   K.P. Chow, K. Chui and S.S. Lo
7. Diagnosing Steel Structures at Hydro Power Stations ... 79
   Takao Terano, Shouichi Matsui, Hideharu Nakamura and Kousuke Yamamoto

PART 4 Automobile Industry

8. DIAS2: A Diagnosing System for Automobiles with Electronic Control Units ... 96
   Suk I. Yoo and Il Kon Kim

PART 5 Oil Industry

9. UNIK-PCS: A Crude Oil Delivery Scheduling System ... 109
   Jae Kyu Lee, Yong Uk Song, Min Soo Suh and Han Seong Yun

PART 6 Paper Industry

10. A Scheduling Expert System for Paper Production ... 122
    Shoichi Kojima, Hiroatsu Hara, Nobuo Matsuda, Yoshitatsu Mori, Michiaki Nishimura and Yasuhiko Yasuda

PART 7   Air Line Industry

11. Cockpit Crew Scheduling and Supporting System   133
    Kiyoto Onodera and Akira Mori

12. Knowledge-Based Approach to Airport Staff Rostering   143
    K.P. Chow and C.K. Hui

13. Practical Application of a Connectionist Expert System—
    The INSIDE Story   162
    Ho Chung Lui, Ah Hwee Tan, Joo Hwee Lim and Hoon Heng Teh

PART 8   Construction Industry

14. Development of Expert Systems Supported Construction Planning
    for Shield Tunneling Method   176
    Satoshi Okuide, Yasuhiro Kitagawa, Minoru Harada and Zenichi Igarashi

PART 9   Investment Industry

15. Application of K-FOLIO at Lucky Securities: BRAINS   186
    Jae Kyu Lee, Hyun S. Kim, Seok C. Chu, Jung C. Shin, Suhn B. Kwon,
    Woo J. Kim and Kee Y. Gwag

    Author Index   201

Preface

Expert systems are no longer toys for the entertainment of researchers. Recently, expert systems have been developed extensively for industrial applications.

Since a particular industry, company, and functional domain determines the features of the specific expert system, it is not easy to theorize on the development paradigm in compact, universal laws like the *law of gravity*. The process of developing Expert Systems seems an art form that can be aided partially by tools.

Under these circumstances, one of the most useful sources of information—although it may not be a perfect one—is the experience of former developers. With this thought in mind, we selected 15 operational expert systems from the many that are found in the Far East. We covered Japan, Korea, Singapore, Hong Kong, China, and Taiwan, even though we could not include all appropriate cases from these countries at this time. We anticipate that other excellent cases will be included in following editions.

The cases may be organized from a number of perspectives. We classified them first by industry, and then by functional domain. The selected cases feature the steel, electromechanics, power, automobile, oil, paper, airline, construction, and investment industries. The covered domains are control, diagnosis, prediction, design, emergency management, scheduling, configuration, and portfolio.

We are grateful to all the contributors. Both case authors and readers worldwide should benefit from this publication through the two-way exchange of constructive comments. We hope this book will serve as a helpful forum and as a catalyst for more challenging theoretical research and greater industrial payoffs.

Jae Kyu Lee
Korea Advanced Institute of Science and Technology and
University of Southern California
Riichiro Mizoguchi
Osaka University
Desai Narasimhalu
National University of Singapore
Daniel S. Yeung
Hong Kong Polytechnic of Hong Kong

Application of an Expert System to Blast Furnace Operation

TAICHI AOKI, MAMORU INABA, TAKASHI SUMIGAMA,
AND MASAAKI SAKURAI

Process Control Dept., Fukuyama Works, NKK Corporation 1 Kokan-cho,
Fukuyama-city, Hiroshima-prf, 721, Japan.

1. INTRODUCTION

NKK FUKUYAMA WORKS is an integrated iron and steel works which produces various kinds of steel products from raw material such as iron ore, coke, and other auxiliary material. The blast furnace produces pig iron from the raw material, and the pig iron is sent to the refining process. The refined steel is rolled into various products, as shown in Figure 1.1.

NKK has been trying to apply Artificial Intelligence (AI) technology to the various production process in the works since the early 1980s. Among the applications, the blast furnace expert system is the first case in the world of applying AI technology to real-time process control. NKK has been expanding the applying area and developing various AI application systems for various processes. Among them, the blast furnace expert system, the first application, is discussed in this chapter.

2. THE BLAST FURNACE PROCESS

The blast furnace is situated at the up-stream of the process in the works as shown in Figure 1.1. Figure 1.2 shows the concept of the blast furnace. The raw materials, mainly coke and iron ore, are charged alternately at the top of the furnace, while at the bottom, the hot air (approximately 1000 degrees centigrade) is blown in. On the other hand, the iron ore, charged at the top, slowly descends toward the bottom, being heated and deoxidized by the gas coming from the bottom. The iron ore melts into molten pig iron and is discharged out.

All of these activities are carried out simultaneously and continuously. Consequently, the blast furnace is a complicated chemical reaction process, having three different phases (solid, liquid, and gas) at the same time. The process has a long time delay; it takes about 6 to 8 hours to get from the top as iron ore to the bottom as molten pig iron.

3. NECESSITY OF THE EXPERT SYSTEM

In a blast furnace daily operation, "stabilization" is required rather than "optimization." In order to stabilize the furnace condition, various models had been tried and developed. Some developed the models using statistic methods. Some of the models arrange various sensor data and provide alarm information when an index goes out of a certain appropriate range. But even though the above-mentioned models have been developed and the output has been taken into account, operators decide their operational actions by judging the in-furnace conditions with criteria based on their heuristic knowledge, especially in the following three subjects. Thus, those subjects have been taken as the target of the expert system.
(1) Abnormal furnace condition predicting.
(2) Thermal condition control.
(3) Burden distribution control.

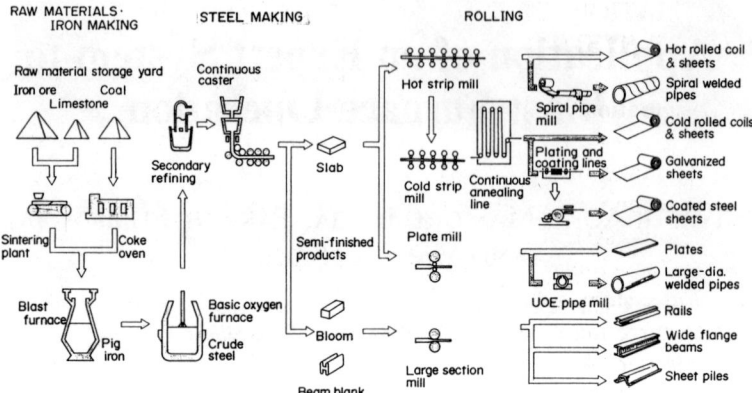

FIGURE 1.1. Fukuyama work process flow chart.

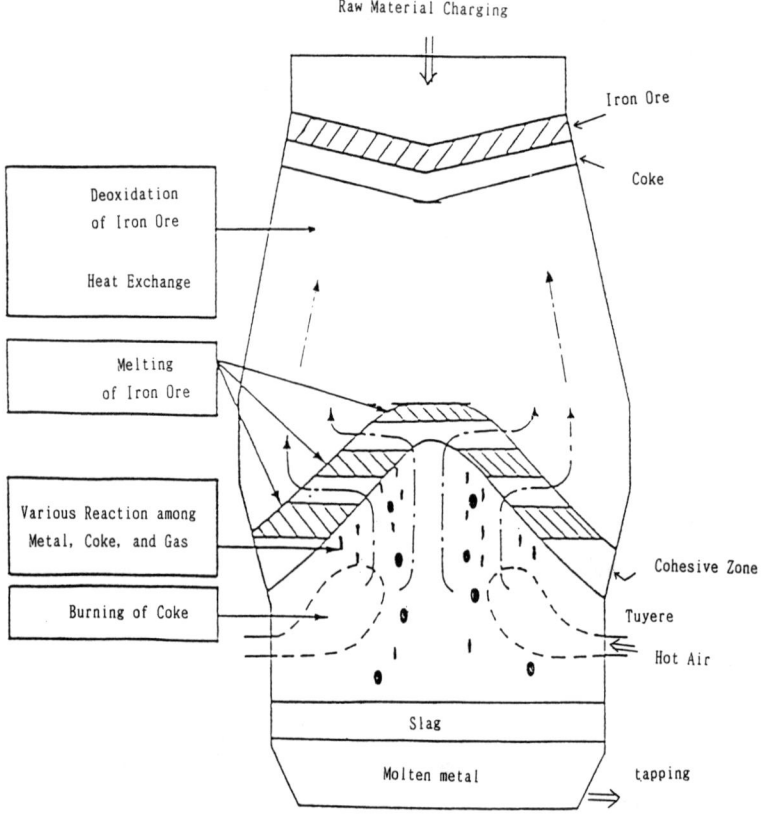

FIGURE 1.2. Concept of blast furnace.

4. CONFIGURATION OF THE EXPERT SYSTEM

4.1. General Configuration

It is very difficult to make an application system only with AI technology. With the co-operation of various system engineering technologies as well as AI technology, an integrated application system is realized.

This system has three main parts in structure: process computer, AI processor, and distributed digital controller, as shown in Figure 1.3. The process computer collects sensor data and pretreats them to make fact data for reasoning. The AI processor gets information from the process computer and plays a role of reasoning, using the knowledge base. The reasoning result is sent again to the process computer. And based on the reasoning, the set points for the control are sent to the digital controller, and are controlled automatically.

This system is a part of a total blast furnace operation system and constitutes a part of the total computerization system in the steel works, connected to the business computer and other process computer systems such as the energy control system and the lower stream process control system.

4.2. Pre-treatment of the Sensor Data

In an on-line real-time expert system, the data for the reasoning cannot be gotten by interactive operation. All of the fact data must be prepared at the start of the reasoning. The sensor data should be pre-treated and processed so that the fact data should be prepared.

In this system, the pre-treatment has two stages in function. The first stage is to remove the fluctuation which has little relationship with the process tendency, and then smooth the trend data. The second part is to extract the characteristic fact data from the time series data.

1. *Smoothing the trend data.* Some of the measurement data obtained from sensors contain some pseudo-periodic fluctuations caused by some disturbance, which has little

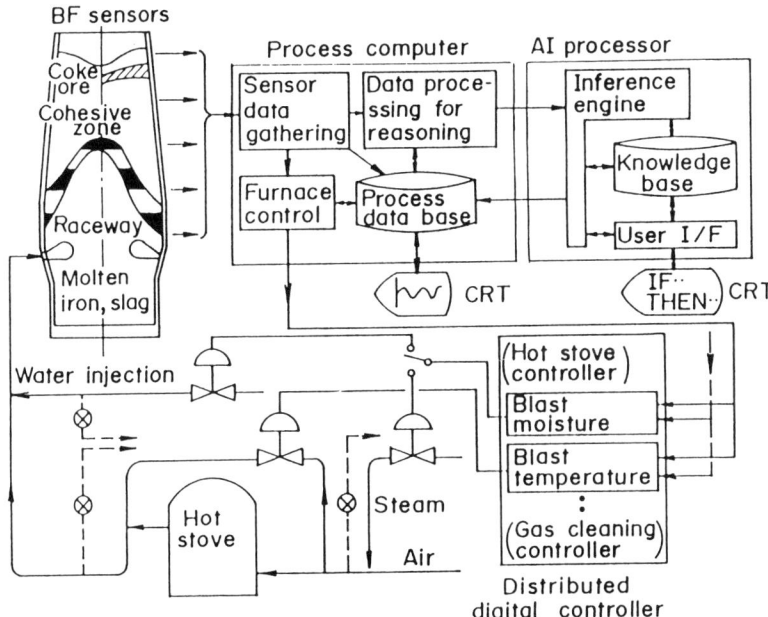

FIGURE 1.3. Configuration of the Expert System.

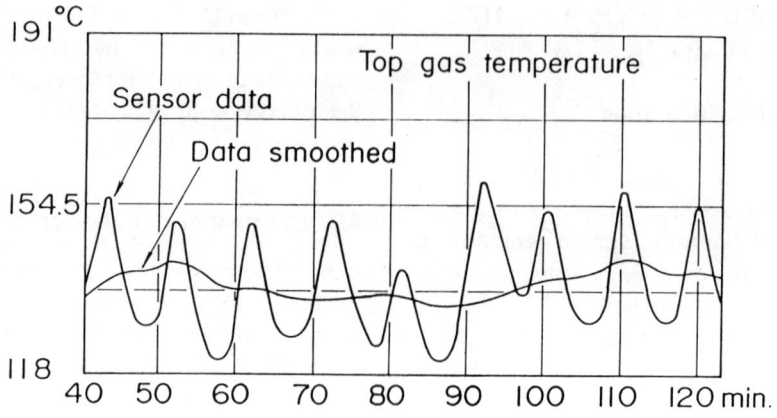

FIGURE 1.4. Example of data smoothing.

relation with the object. The fluctuation has a time constant of 10 to 20 minutes. On the other hand, the thermal condition tendency has a longer time constant. Thus, higher frequency composition should be removed from the data. Figure 1.4 shows an example of this smoothing. It is done by a statistical processing technique on the time series data. Even with the same sensor data, the smoothing method and time constant differs for each sub-system, just as the operators' viewpoints differ. And smoothed data are sent to the AI processor or the next pre-treatment stage.

2. *Extracting the fact data.* When an event fact data is necessary, it is extracted by the second stage pre-treatment. The treatment is provided to catch a peculiar phenomena. Figure 1.5 shows an example. Fluctuation, or integral value of the time series sensor data, is considered based on many years' operation experiences.

The operators can do such pattern recognizing activity, only giving a glance at the trend graph on the CRT. But the expert system itself is not good at such activity. In this system, the process computer plays a role of

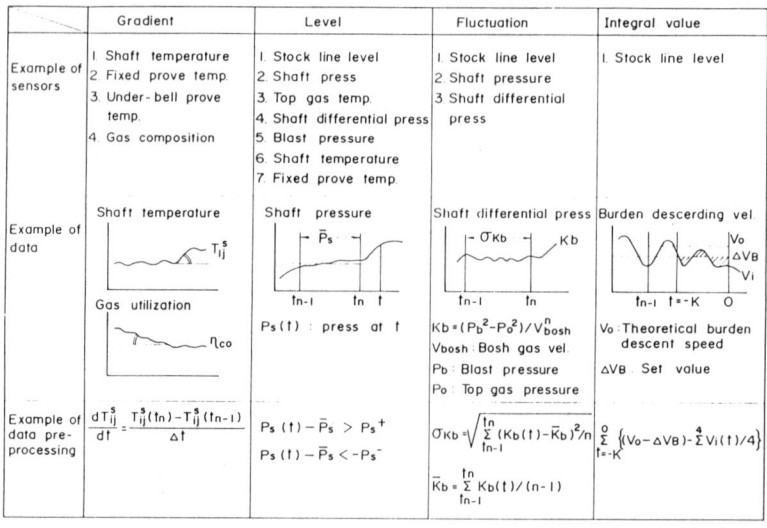

FIGURE 1.5. Example of fact extracting.

Blast Furnace Operation

this pre-treatment with the conventional system engineering method.

4.3. Composition of Knowledge Base

4.3.1. General Composition. The knowledge is described in the form of "production rule," "frame," and "LISP function." Among them, the production rules (if-then type) are mainly used. The frames and LISP functions are referred from the production rules.

The advantage of the production rules for the system is as follows,

(1) It has an affinity for human thinking activity.
(2) It can be treated fragmentarily, and maintained easily.

This system has a total of 450 production rules. The knowledge base is divided into knowledge sources (KS), which have 5 to 20 production rules each. Figure 1.6 shows the knowledge base divided into KSs. The KS is

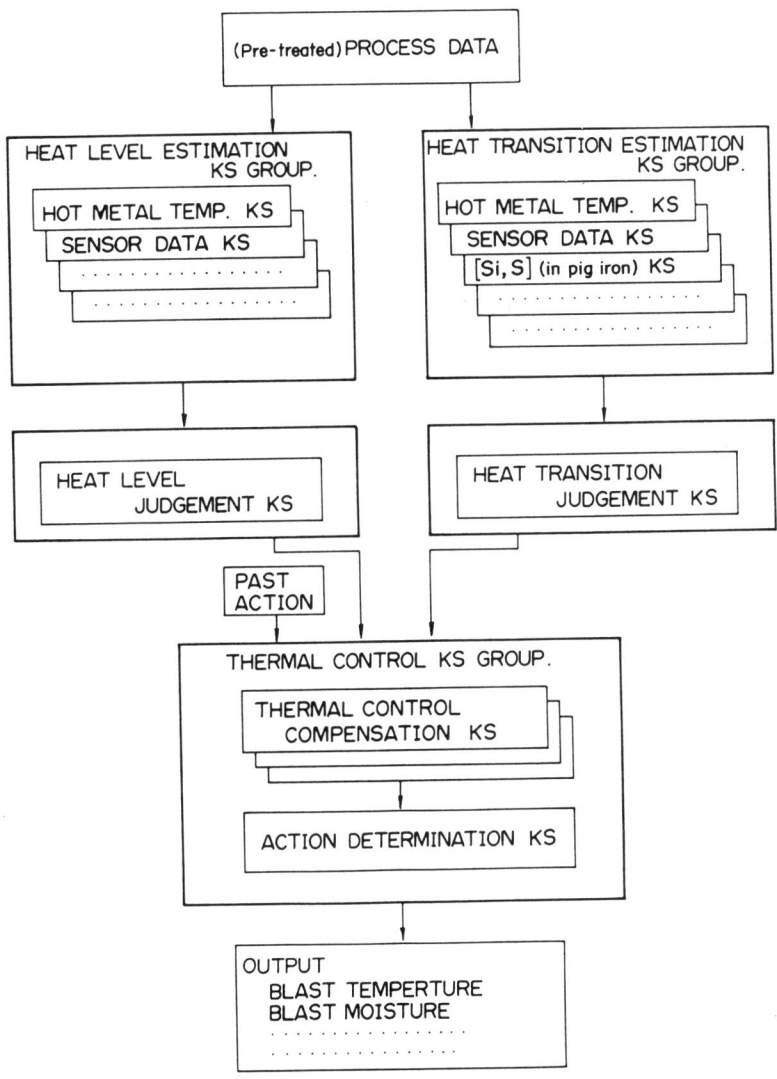

FIGURE 1.6. Structure of the knowledge base.

a unit of reasoning. This way has the following advantage:
(1) The reasoning time increases as the number of the rule increases. If the whole rule base is divided into several units and only the necessary units are referred, reasoning can be efficient.
(2) What kinds of rules should be adopted is also the function of the knowledge rule. Such kinds of rules can be described as the form of KS choice.

In the frames, wherein the total amount is about 300, fact-type knowledge such as the operational constant is stored. Therefore, in case of the change of the operational condition only the frames should be changed, if possible. In the LISP functions, wherein the total amount is about 200, the procedural knowledge such as the formula for calculating the certainty factor is stored.

4.3.2. Example of the Knowledge. An example of the knowledge source is shown in Figure 1.7. It is described in a form of production rule. It has the condition "REMAINED PIG IRON IS *NOT* MUCH" in "*IF*" part. And it has the conclusion "CALCULATE. . . . WITH THE TUYERE NOSE TEMPERATURE. . . ." in "*THEN*" part. (Further, the terms of "certainty factor" (CF) and "membership function" are mentioned later.)

The tuyere nose temperature is one of the indexes of thermal condition. This rule is intended to estimate the thermal condition with the tuyere nose temperature. But in certain conditions, it cannot be suitable for the representative. For example, when much more than the ordinal molten pig iron is remaining in the furnace, the tuyere nose temperature tends to rise regardless of the thermal condition. Therefore, the rule execution should be controlled by the IF–THEN rule with proper conditions. Even a conventional system can control such rule selection. But some of the rules have a lot of complicated conditions, and some conditions have some fuzziness (having the concept of CF value). The rule-based system can easily realize the rule execution control, and it is more acceptable to the users, who have an affinity to them.

5. REPRESENTING FUZZINESS

5.1. Concept of Certainty Factor in the System

In this system, fuzziness including information should be treated in various stages in every sub-system. This system adopts the concept of certainty factor and membership

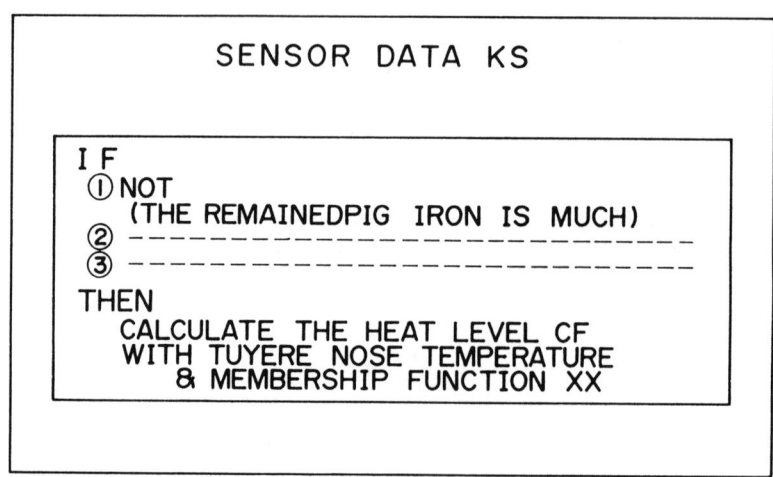

FIGURE 1.7. Example of the knowledge source.

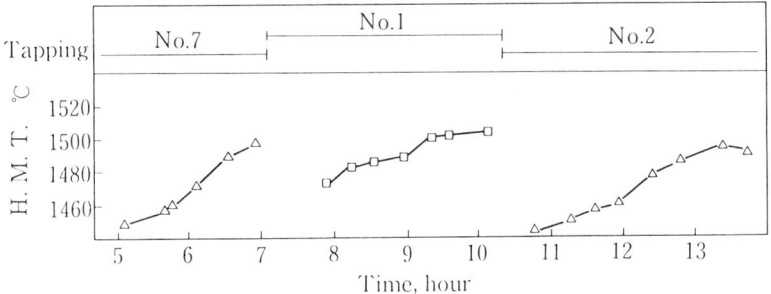

FIGURE 1.8. Typical tendency of the hot metal temperature.

function for handling fuzzy information. Almost all of the fact data are handled with the CF value. One of the characteristic examples is as follows.

The hot metal temperature is the best representative of the thermal condition. But it is the indirectly observed result, not the direct measurement. Even if the thermal condition is completely stable, the hot metal temperature fluctuates depending on the passing time since the start of tapping (one period of pig iron discharging operation, lasting for 2–6 hours). It also includes the fuzziness characteristic of the process. As shown in Figure 1.8, the hot metal temperature gradually rises as time passes in the tap. The saturated and the highest temperature at the end of the tap, as the result, is regarded as a good index of the thermal condition.

When the measurement data is used for the real time control operation, passing time from the start of tapping and inclusion of the characteristic fuzziness should be taken into consideration. The operators can consider such conditions based on their heuristic knowledge. But in systematization, treating such fuzziness is the big problem.

5.2. Three Dimensional Membership Function

Three-dimensional membership function is adopted for handling the fuzziness. An example of the function is shown in Figure 1.9 (right side). The X-axis represents the measured hot metal temperature, and the Y-axis represents heat level, while the Z-axis represents the certainty factor. Once the temperature is measured, the Y-Z cross section of the mountain-shaped function at the measured temperature in the X-coordinate represents the relationship between the estimated heat level and the CF value. The membership function is used to determine the relationship between the heat level and its certainty factor. Several kinds of membership functions are

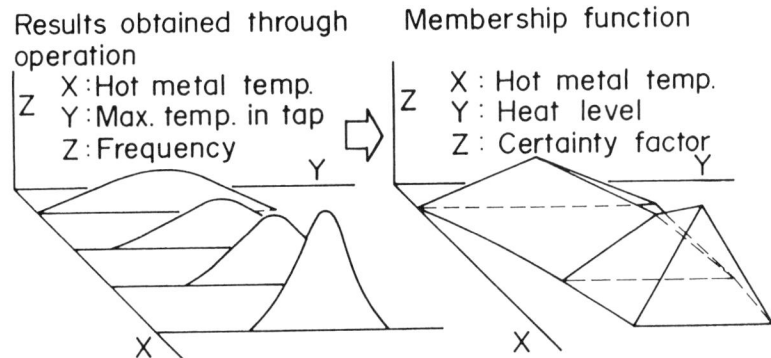

FIGURE 1.9. Three-dimensional membership function and its formation.

prepared so that the right function can be used for the right condition.

It also contributes to the reduction of the rules. Without the function, many similar rules for divided range of the sensor data would be necessary.

The membership function method is also used for determining the thermal condition tendency judging from the various sensors, not only from the hot metal temperature. For each kind of sensor, each kind of function is prepared, and the characteristics of each sensor are considered.

The judgement and CF value determined with each sensor by each function are summarized and final judgment of the thermal condition tendency is determined. In this summarizing, the production rules control what kind of rules and sensors should be adopted or not, highly treated or not.

5.3. Self-learning Function

In order to keep control accuracy following the change in operating condition, the system has a self-learning function. The three-dimensional function mentioned before is re-constructed, at the time of the user's request, using the operational result by the following method.

The highest hot metal temperature in tap best represents the object, as mentioned before. Thus, the self-learning is based on the idea of handling the highest temperature as the true value of the object. In the left graph in Figure 1.9, the X-axis represents the pre-treated sensor data. The Y-axis represents the corresponded highest hot metal temperature in tap. The Z-axis represents the occurrence frequency. Collecting the operational result, a mountain-shaped distribution map is drawn, as shown in Figure 1.9. Since the saturated and the highest hot metal temperature at the end of the tap is the good index of the thermal condition, the Y-axis represents the thermal level. Interpolating the map, the three-dimensional function is made up as shown in the Figure 1.9.

6. THE RESULT OF THE APPLICATION

By the introduction of the system, the blast furnace is stably operated even without the

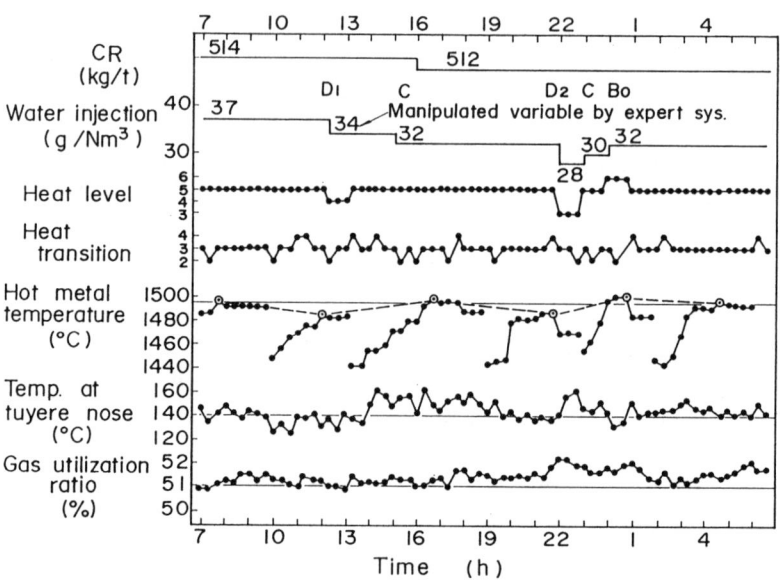

FIGURE 1.10. Example of automatic control by the expert system.

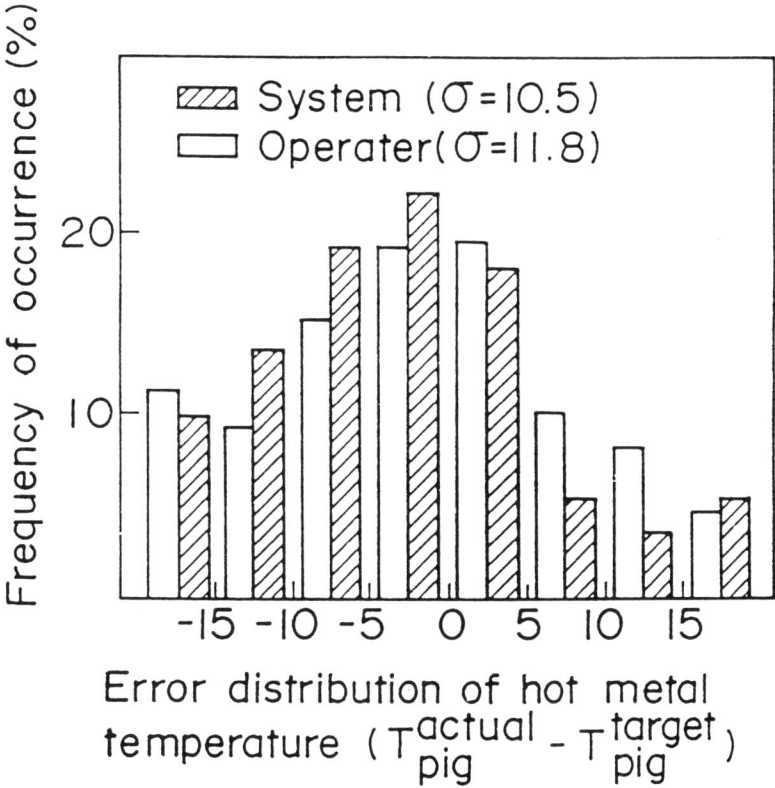

FIGURE 1.11. Comparison between manual and automatic control of variation of hot metal temperature.

most skilled operator. Or, the operator can pay attention to another important thing, instead of paying the most attention to the abnormal condition predicting, thermal condition, and burden distribution.

Among the three sub-systems, the application result of the thermal condition control is shown as follows. Figure 1.10 shows an example of the thermal condition control to the actual operation. Every plotting dot in Figure 1.10 means the result of one reasoning. The water injection was changed from 37 g/Nm^3 to 34 g/Nm^3 at 12:00 hours. The system recognized that the heat level went down at that time, mainly because of the low hot metal temperature. At 16:00 hours, the coke ratio was reduced at the tuyere level, which is manipulated about six hours before at charging. The system recognized the change and compensates the thermal condition by changing the water injection from 34 g/Nm^3 to 32 g/Nm^3. With those actions, the highest hot metal temperature in tap was almost constant at around 1495 degrees, which shows that the thermal condition was kept stable. Figure 1.11 shows the comparison of the hot metal temperature before and after the application of the system, which shows that the system can control the thermal condition as well as the best operator does.

7. CONCLUSION

Many expert systems have been developed and applied as the interactive system. However, this system has been applied as the non-interactive on-line system. The characteristic method for the realization of the on-line system is as follows:

1. All of the fact data are prepared at the start of the reasoning. No interactive operation for fact data inquiry is necessary.
2. Time series process data treatment is carried out by a conventional system engineering method.
3. The knowledge base is divided into knowledge sources (KS) for the effective reasoning.
4. Using the concept of CF value and characteristic function, the number of the rules is reduced.

The system is realized with the combined technology of the conventional system engineering method and newly developing system engineering method, AI technology and so on. NKK is now trying to expand the application field of the combined technology in various process operations.

An Expert System for Large Scale Fault Diagnosis in Steel Manufacturing

TATSURO HIRATA AND ETSURO MINAMI

Equipment Division, Oita Works, Nippon Steel Corporation;
Computer Systems Laboratory, Electronics R&D Laboratories, Nippon Steel Corporation

1. INTRODUCTION

EFFICIENT FAULT DIAGNOSIS in steel manufacturing is essential. Once the production stops accidentally, large amounts of energy are wasted in terminating operations and subsequently resuming them. Moreover, if some production lines pause for a long period of time, material and product flows of the entire steel works are disturbed, necessitating a rescheduling of production plans. Since steelmaking is essentially a continuous process, it is important that any malfunction be repaired as rapidly as possible. Traditionally, human experts are responsible for timely diagnosis of failures, working around the clock in three eight-hour shifts.

Around one hundred expert systems have been developed using a variety of development tools/shells at Nippon Steel, and many of them are actually used in operations. Process diagnosis systems constitute the majority of these systems. Figure 2.1 illustrates the breakdown of these systems by purpose as of 1988. If the first three categories are clustered together, it may be observed that diagnostic systems account for 70% of all expert systems developed at Nippon Steel.

ESTO (Minami et al., 1990) is an expert system shell developed at Electronics R&D Laboratories of Nippon Steel Corporation and was designed and implemented specifically for the development of diagnostic expert systems which operate in fan-in situations. ESTO is based on experience gleaned from earlier experiments with diagnostic expert systems already deployed in the field. The following criteria were deemed essential for the development of ESTO:

- *Development without the need for knowledge engineers.*
  Development and maintenance of earlier systems were heavily dependent on engineers who were experienced in expert system techniques and environments. Knowledge engineers typically spent large amounts of time interviewing domain experts, and compiling their domain knowledge into production rules.

- *Flexible and Opportunistic Reasoning.*
  More often than not, information provided for diagnosis is uncertain or ambiguous. Further, answers to some questions may not be readily available, and the user may choose to guess an answer using empirical knowledge. In other cases, the user may leave some questions unanswered rather than taking the risk of entering erroneous information. During diagnosis, information may be added, modified, or even retracted. Therefore, information available to a diagnostic expert system may not be temporally sound and correct at any time. Such information pollution is an inherent feature of real world situations, and one cannot safely assume that such pollution would not occur in a given application domain. Therefore, diagnostic expert systems should be impervious to reasonable amounts of bogus or fragmented information, and to occasional modification or retraction of previously entered information.

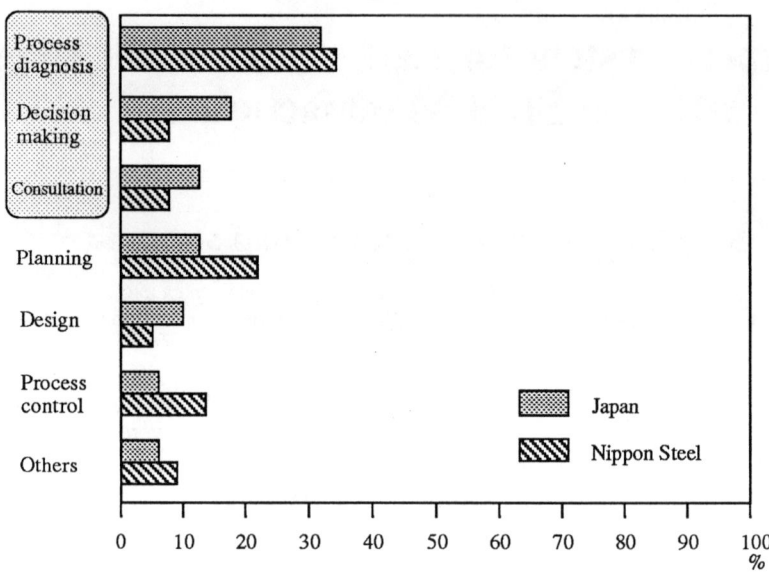

FIGURE 2.1. Breakdown of Expert Systems by purpose. (Source: "AI Vision," ICOT, Nikkei Inc., 1987)

- *Prompt Response.*
  When represented in a rule-based format, diagnostic knowledge in an industrial domain may easily lead to several thousands of production rules. In order to sustain an interactive dialog with the user, the knowledge base should be scanned and executed within a few seconds. Since prompt response has proven essential for user acceptance of interference engines, ESTO is developed in C language in order to achieve high computational performance. An expert system developed in ESTO usually takes less than two seconds to process an answer and to respond with the next inquiry.
- *Rule-free Environment.*
  Frequently, blue collar domain experts perceive the IF-THEN notation of production rules to be somewhat analogous to that of conventional programming languages. Consequently, they tend to express their domain knowledge as a sequentially structured rule set, which is not the way production systems work. Because of such misconceptions, domain experts are often confused and hesitant when they are told to express their knowledge in a production rule format. Therefore, it was deemed important that ESTO be designed as a rule-free expert system development environment.

In an attempt to alleviate the knowledge acquisition problem, ESTO does not require users to describe their knowledge in the form of production rules. In ESTO, users are required to represent their knowledge in classification hierarchies, links, and questions. This approach not only encourages domain experts to work by themselves, but also facilitates the merging of locally developed knowledge bases into a single, coherent knowledge base.

The expert system described in this chapter is designed to automate the diagnostic process by aggregating logical and empirical knowledge of teams of human experts. Most of the domain experts are experienced blue collar foremen with very little experience with computers. Due to the user-friendly nature of the ESTO shell, however, they are not only able to build their own diagnostic systems, but are also able to maintain the knowledge bases by themselves.

2. THE PROBLEM DOMAIN

2.1. Selecting a Problem Domain

A wide variety of techniques have been proposed for maintaining continuous operation of steel works. Preventive maintenance is an effective technique to identify and correct potential problems before they are allowed to occur. However, preventive maintenance is not enough by itself, and maintenance personnel have to be on duty for the maintenance of breakdowns on a 24-hour basis. Furthermore, prompt maintenance is essential in order to minimize losses caused by a breakdown.

Figure 2.2 depicts the breakdown of maintenance tasks by percentage of time spent. Among the tasks a maintenance team is responsible for, fault diagnosis and maintenance takes the lion's share, accounting for over half of available operator time. Unlike other relatively simpler tasks, fault diagnosis requires expertise and empirical knowledge for prompt recovery from adverse conditions. Such expertise is typically scarce, and therefore costly to obtain and maintain.

For the reasons stated above, industrial fault diagnosis is a favorable problem domain for expert system applications. Robust methodologies already exist for diagnosis using expert systems. Moreover, the knowledge bases for industrial diagnosis are well structured, lending themselves easily to efficient symbolic representation.

2.2. Partitioning Problems

Fault diagnosis in steel works includes the following subtasks:
- gathering information;
- pruning information;
- diagnosing the problem to identify faulty equipment, and deciding whether a plant shutdown is required;
- planning and executing "first aid;" and
- planning and executing actual repair work.

Detailed empirical knowledge is required for the second, third, and the fifth subtasks. The second and third subtasks exhibit diagnostic behavior. On the other hand, the fifth subtask is essentially one of planning.

The expert system described in this chapter is still in its first stage of fault diagnosis automation, covering only the first four subtasks. Planning and execution of repair work will be the subject of future enhancements.

The specific constraints imposed upon ESTO by the diagnosis subtasks are as follows:

1. *Gathering information:* Sensors and signal processing elements are already available. The expert system project should address the problem of installing an inter-factory network for information management.

2. *Pruning information and diagnosis:* Knowledge must be acquired from multiple domain experts. ESTO should offer easy and reliable methods for knowledge acquisition and verification, as well as for integration of knowledge from different sources.

3. *Planning and executing first aid:* Written manuals describing contingency plans are available. ESTO should support hypermedia to provide these manuals on-line.

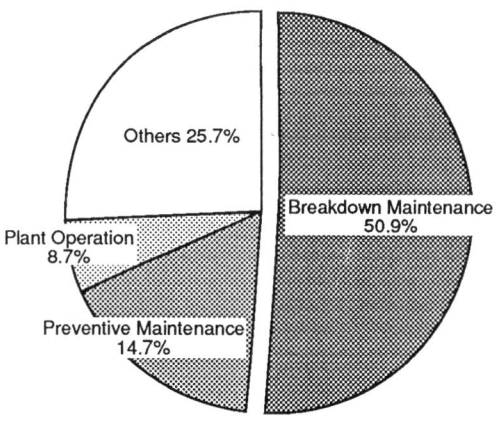

FIGURE 1.2. Breakdown of tasks for maintenance personnel.

2.3. Approaching the Problem

The final product of the research described herein is a large diagnostic expert system that covers three factories at Oita Works of Nippon Steel.

The system is developed in accordance with the following policies:
1. Knowledge acquisition and compilation should be carried out only by blue collar domain experts with diagnostic knowledge.
2. The knowledge bases should be updated and maintained by domain experts who use the expert system.
3. The expert system should efficiently cover wide areas of geographical and inferential breadth.

The last policy requires a distributed hierarchical system architecture. Details of the architecture will be presented in Section 4.

On the bottom layer of the system hierarchy lie the sensors and process computers. A distinction must be made between process controllers and process computers. A process controller is a device with limited interpretive capability, such as an intelligent actuator. On the other hand, a process computer is a device which supervises several process controllers to optimize plant performance. Raw data from the plant is received by the data processing layer, which processes available data into *evaluation indices*. These evaluation indices may either be numerical or symbolic, such as "Pressure is abnormally low." Evaluation indices are in turn consumed by the expert system layer, which constitutes the topmost layer of the hierarchy.

The expert system is distributed over a wide geographical area, networking three factories and numerous buildings. Since it is essential that the expert system is available to users on-site, most of its functionalities, including knowledge base maintenance and diagnosis, are accessible from any terminal connected to the network. Each terminal has access to ESTO which resides on a server workstation. The centralization of the kernel and the knowledge base facilitates version control. Modifications to the kernel and to the resident knowledge base may only be made by users who are authorized to do so.

The first and second policies naturally required the project to start with the development of an inference engine shell. Existing expert system shells typically provide many sophisticated functions and features, which may easily alienate blue collar domain experts who do not feel comfortable with using computers as work tools, or with using formal logic or production rules as representational schemata. Since ESTO was built with such users in mind, an intuitive knowledge representation and a friendly, robust graphical user interface were identified as minimum requirements.

Another hurdle for ESTO was that diagnostic scenarios could not be provided at all times for industrial diagnosis tasks. In cases where the scope is narrow and well-trained knowledge engineers are available, diagnostic scripts may be written with ease. However, a system that executes diagnosis according to predefined scripts requires that a knowledge engineer be available at all times to maintain and update the expert system. For large scale industrial expert systems, this may not be the case. Since knowledge engineers have been diverting their attention to other challenging problems such as planning and design, they regard diagnostic expert systems as being relatively plain and uninteresting. As a result, domain experts are being forced to take care of their own diagnostic systems. However, experts who are not trained in formal logic and production rule technology cannot provide diagnostic scripts with ease. To alleviate the problem, ESTO is provided with the ability to dynamically develop diagnostic scenarios using the knowledge base and the current situation, aggregating fragments of knowledge into executable diagnostic scripts.

The following sections describe the anatomy of ESTO, and the implementation of a large-scale diagnostic expert system on the ESTO shell.

3. DEVELOPMENT OF THE INFERENCE ENGINE

3.1. Knowledge Representation

When a domain expert performs fault diagnosis, he often initiates a question and answer session, either by himself or in collaboration with other experts. The structure of the diagnostic session often parallels the structure of the plant itself, covering aspects of the plant from general information to the more specific. The knowledge representation of the inference engine was designed to be analogous to the diagnosis by classification process in the real world.

The knowledge representation in ESTO has three major components, as illustrated in Figure 2.3. *Questions* and *links* represent the knowledge used in diagnostic reasoning, and *hierarchical classification* (HC) represents the structure of the diagnosed process.

Diagnosis in ESTO is essentially performed by iterating over a loop of questions and subsequent information acquisition. The question-and-answer style is typical of diagnosis by classification, and a similar paradigm is adopted for knowledge representation in ESTO. In ESTO, HC nodes represent the faults that are the focus of diagnosis. Each question constitutes a fragment of diagnostic information which is connected to HC nodes through links. Links are qualified with *influence values* which indicate their relative importance. Since control over the usage of questions is maintained by ESTO's reasoning mechanism, the domain expert does not have to be cautious about the interrelation of questions. This is an important difference from ordinary rule syntax. In a production system, the user has to be careful about answers to questions, since the sequence of rule firing may easily affect the outcome. In ESTO, the reasoning process is controlled by adjusting initial certainty factor values of HC nodes. ESTO then sets the direction of search towards the most favorable goal or subgoal at that stage, as opposed to searching for rules to fire.

3.1.1. Linking Questions to HC Nodes. The hierarchical classification represents the structure of the diagnosed process. Such a hierarchy is usually in the form of a tree. However, ESTO's inference mechanism does not depend on a tree structure. The classification may consist of a set of independent nodes, a tree, a set of trees, or even a combination of

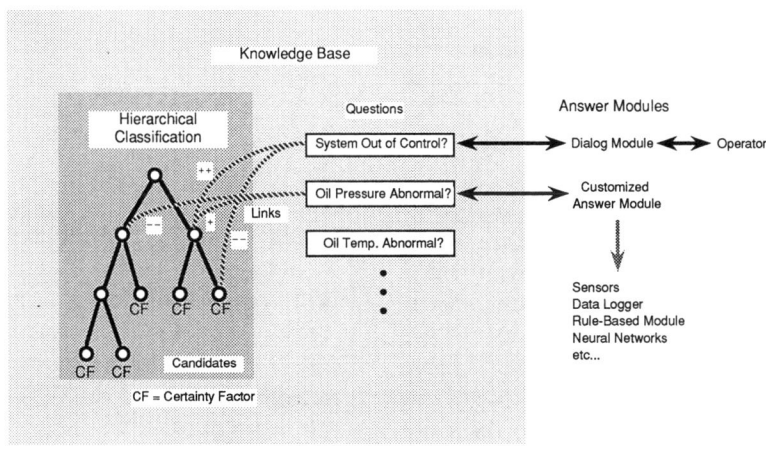

FIGURE 2.3. Knowledge Representation.

independent nodes and trees. The flexibility in representation is what sets ESTO apart from similar expert system shells with rigid classification schemes.

Leaves or terminal nodes of the classification hierarchy represent final diagnoses, whereas intermediate nodes stand for intermediate hypotheses. Questions and their links to HC nodes represent diagnostic knowledge. A link from a question **Q** to an HC node **N** defines the influence of **Q** on **N**. Every HC node is linked to one or more questions. Every link is qualified by an *influence value* which indicates the influence of the question on the belief status of the related HC node. When a question is answered, certainty values of all linked HC nodes are updated. The range of influence values are as follows:

+++	**Increase, Very Strong**
++	**Increase, Strong**
+	**Increase, Weak**
0	**No Effect**
−	**Decrease, Weak**
−−	**Decrease, Strong**
−−−	**Decrease, Very Strong**

Let us assume that a question **Q** is linked to an HC node **N** through a link with an influence value of **Increase, Strong**. When the answer to the question is affirmative, the certainty status of the node **N** is updated with the value **Increase, Strong**. However, a negative answer should not necessarily be evaluated as a strong decrease in the certainty of node **N**. Therefore, each link may define different influence values for affirmative and negative answers.

A descendent node is a more specialized case of its parent node from which it inherits a whole set of questions and links. Automated inheritance precludes the need for tedious copying when a new HC node is defined below an existing node. It also facilitates reliable and structured modification of questions and links. If a descendent is linked to the same question as one of its antecedents, influence values defined in the descendent supersede the values inherited from its parents. This way, behavior specific to the descendent node may be specified without extensive modifications.

3.1.2. Questions and their Destinations. As stated earlier, questions and their links to HC nodes represent diagnostic knowledge. A question consists of a string and an *output module*. The *output module* from which an answer is retrieved may differ from question to question. The *user module* displays question strings on the user interface, and requests answers from the user. In contrast, the *process module* reads raw signals, processes and filters them, and produces numerical answers. The process module may even spawn sophisticated signal interpretation processes to obtain more refined information.

3.2. Reasoning Mechanism

In order to achieve flexible and robust reasoning, it is essential that the reasoning be independent of the HC structure. In ESTO, reasoning does not strictly follow the tree structure of the hierarchical classification. Following a tree structure is essentially equivalent to performing heuristic search, and a heuristic search in this case may cause serious problems in backtracking. Since it is very likely that incomplete and incorrect information be obtained during diagnosis, frequent changes in the direction of reasoning are inevitable. If diagnosis is performed as a tree search, backtracking will be necessary whenever a wrong answer is detected, or a previous answer is modified. Such intensive backtracking will nullify the benefits of hierarchical guidance of search. In a strictly hierarchical approach, it may even be impossible to reason at all if initial questions are left unanswered. Unlike reasoning mechanisms dependent on tree structures (Bylander & Mittal, 1986; Hara et al., 1988) ESTO may accommodate a reasonable amount of inconsistency or nonmonotonicity in its reasoning.

3.2.1. Reasoning Behavior. ESTO parses all nodes in the classification hierarchy, evaluating each question for its cost and efficiency at the time of parsing. The most informative and cost-effective question is selected and evaluated. In most cases, the algorithm is guaranteed to complete diagnosis using a minimum number of questions. Benefits for the domain experts/users are twofold: Firstly, they are relieved from the duty of providing knowledge for explicit control of reasoning (scripts), and thus they may focus their attention on building and maintaining the knowledge base instead. Secondly, they will only be asked the most important questions at runtime, and they will not be annoyed by irrelevant queries.

3.2.2. Updating Certainty Factors. When a question is selected for evaluation, it is sent to the appropriate output module. When the output module is the user interface, the user may respond by selecting one of the following values:

Plausible Strong	[YES]
Plausible Weak	[yes]
Unknown	[unk]
Implausible Weak	[no]
Implausible Strong	[NO]

All HC nodes which are linked to a particular question are subject to belief revision when the question is answered. If the answer is affirmative, the influence value for positive answers is modulated by the strength of the affirmation, and the corresponding certainty factor is updated. A similar procedure is followed for negative answers.

In many cases, none of the terminal diagnoses may be confirmed with full certainty, especially in earlier stages of the diagnostic process. To provide the user with an accurate picture of the current belief status, ESTO ranks and displays plausible hypotheses by their relative predominance among all candidates. Unless a conclusion is reached with absolute certainty, ESTO always gives the user an option to continue diagnosis by asking further questions, or to select the most plausible hypothesis as the final diagnosis.

3.2.3. The Certainty Space. In ESTO, certainty factors of HC nodes are recorded in a global database called the *certainty space.* The certainty space is implemented as a blackboard which may be accessed by other modules in order to post information (Engelmore & Morgan, 1988). Throughout the diagnosis process, the question selection engine allows answer modules to respond asynchronously by passing messages under a *message exchange* protocol. The message exchange protocol supports one-on-one inter-module communications using DARPA Internet Protocols (TCP/IP). Three major benefits of asynchronous inter-module communications are observed: Firstly, specialized modules may be developed independently, and subsequently integrated into the system with relative ease. Secondly, such modular systems are easy to maintain and modify. And thirdly, asynchronous communications facilitate the implementation of the expert system on a distributed environment, where answer modules run on different machines and results are communicated via the blackboard.

3.2.4. Selecting Questions. ESTO propagates all questions linked to a node to all descendents of that node. Similarly, an answer to a question updates the belief status in all HC nodes that the question is linked to. ESTO selects the best question to ask using a combination of criteria. The selection criteria are: 1) informativeness of the question in terms of the diagnosis of a single terminal node, and 2) cost. The definition of "best" question depends on the diagnostic context. At the earlier stages of diagnosis when most of the candidates have more or less the same certainty, the question which may eliminate the largest group of candidates from consideration will be the most informative question. During the final stages when only a few of candidates remain, the question that has the strongest influence value for a candidate in focus is selected on the basis of conclusiveness. ESTO computes an effectiveness index (EQ) for each question at each stage, and the question with the highest EQ index is selected. The effectiveness index is computed as follows:

$$EQ_j = \frac{f(CF_1, CF_2, \ldots, CF_N, I_1, I_2, \ldots, I_N)}{Cost_j}$$

where:

EQ_j Effectiveness of the question j
$Cost_j$ Cost of the question j
CF_i Current certainty factor of the candidate node i
I_i Influence value of the link from the question j to the candidate node i
N Total number of candidate nodes
$f(\ )$ The function evaluating the entropy of a question

3.2.5. Redundancy in the Knowledge Base. Redundancy in questions and links is actually beneficial for robustness in reasoning. When an answer is incorrect, other questions which are linked to the same node could help recover from the error situation. Redundancy is also a safeguard against hazardous effects of inconsistency in knowledge bases, since it leaves a safety margin within which some amount of inconsistency is acceptable.

4. STRUCTURE OF THE EXPERT SYSTEM

Traditionally, when a malfunction occurs in the steel works, operators call on maintenance personnel for diagnosis and repair, as shown in Figure 2.4. However, with the installation of the expert system in Oita Steel Works, plant operators no longer entirely depend on maintenance personnel in cases of malfunction. The expert system is capable of gathering information from sensors on its own, informing plant operators about imminent problems, and diagnosing malfunctions. As an immediate result, the number of maintenance personnel on duty in each of the three shifts may be reduced.

Figure 2.5 shows the architecture of the expert system. The figure only illustrates the

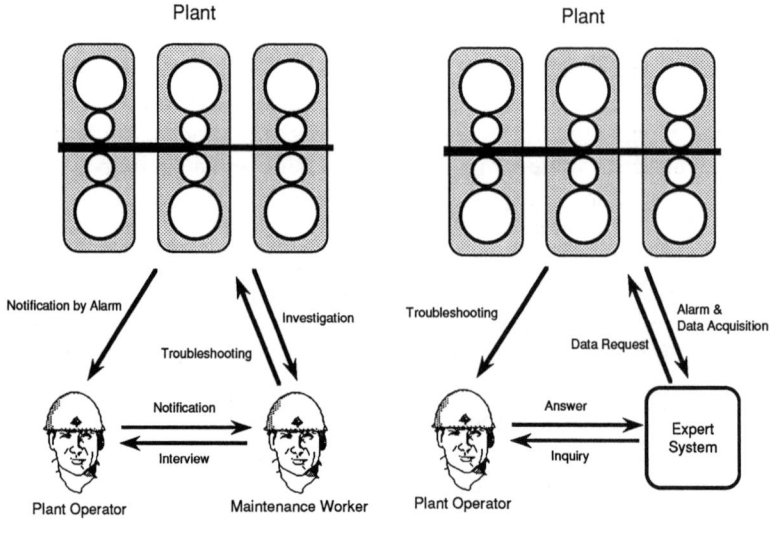

FIGURE 2.4. Diagram of troubleshooting at plants.

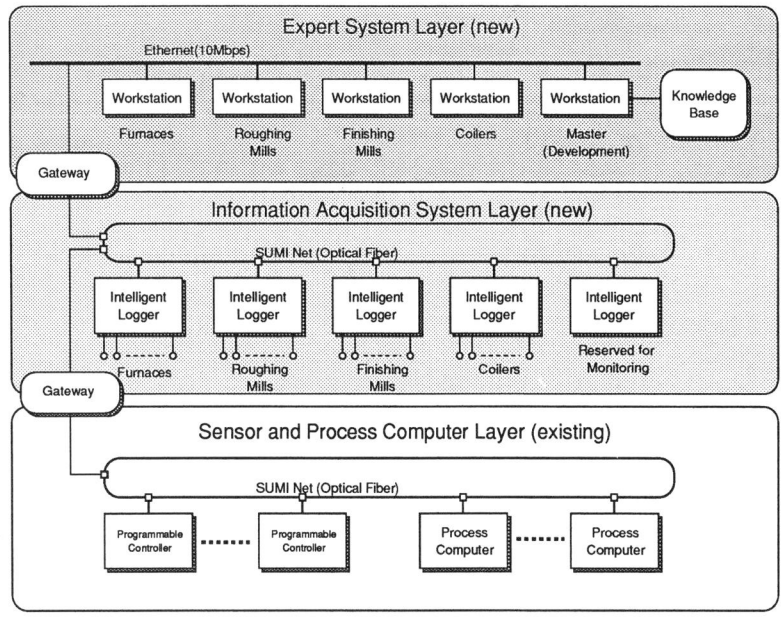

FIGURE 2.5. Architecture of the fault diagnosis Expert System for HOT STRIP MILL in Oita Works at Nippon Steel.

Hot Strip Mill subsystem, which is one of the three factories covered along with the Plate Mill and the Sizing Mill. Data processing in the expert system is both data driven and demand driven. When new numerical information is available at the sensor and process computer layer, it is dispatched to the information acquisition layer. In the information acquisition layer, the information is processed and translated into a format which the expert system may use (data driven). On the other hand, when a request for information is issued by the expert system layer, the request may be handled by specific data processing facilities at the information acquisition layer (demand driven). Users interact with the expert system using networked *Sun Microsystems' workstations*.

4.1. The Information Acquisition System Layer

The information acquisition system layer consists of a network of data processing computers called *intelligent loggers*. A block diagram is shown in Figure 2.6. Each intelligent logger consists of two NEC personal computers working in parallel. The redundancy is aimed at minimizing information loss due to computer hardware malfunction. A single intelligent logger may receive up to 192 analog channels, and 960 digital channels. The highest sampling frequency is 100 Hz, and the computer is capable of storing acquired data for up to 120 minutes. Currently, a total of 13,000 analog and digital signals are sampled and processed by the system using several intelligent loggers.

4.2. The Expert System Layer

The expert system layer consists of several networked SUN workstations. The system is written in C language on the SunView windowing system with Japanese Language Environment (JLE). The system interacts with the user at this level through the ESTO user interface. Figure 2.7 illustrates the architecture of ESTO.

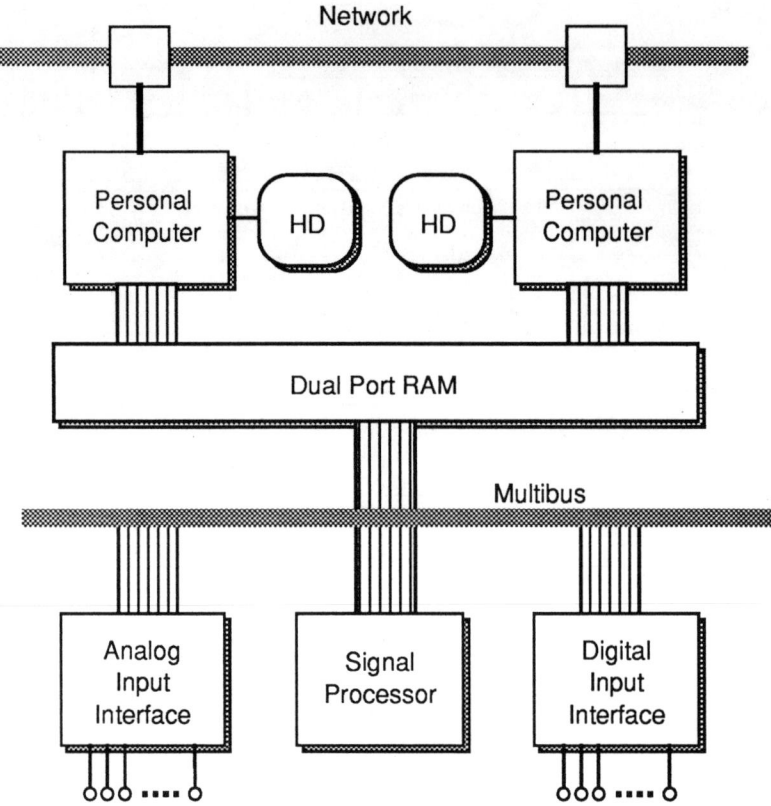

FIGURE 2.6. Block diagram of intelligent logger.

Since most end users of the system have little or no computer training, the ESTO user interface was designed and implemented with naive users in mind. The knowledge editor merely requires the user to be able to select operations from a menu, and to be able to input questions and their influences by typing sentences and clicking the mouse button on desired values. During runtime, the user is shown a record of previous questions and answers, and a list of candidate hypotheses. Users answer questions by clicking the mouse button on one of the answers displayed on the screen. The user may also retract a previous answer by selecting one of the questions already answered. When such nonmonotonicities occur, ESTO automatically updates certainty factors on all affected nodes.

An on-line manual is also available at this layer, providing hypermedia access to plant information in Japanese.

4.3. The Knowledge Editor

ESTO's knowledge editor consists of a set of windows. Figure 2.8 illustrates the main editor. Two major windows are the Node-Tree Display for browsing the classification hierarchy (upper left), and the Question-and-Influence Display (lower left). The Node-Tree Display shows the hierarchical representation of expert knowledge. It displays three levels of nodes at a time, and a user can browse the whole hierarchy by scrolling up and down the existing branches. Further information on a desired HC node, such as creation date and

Fault Diagnosis in Steel Manufacturing

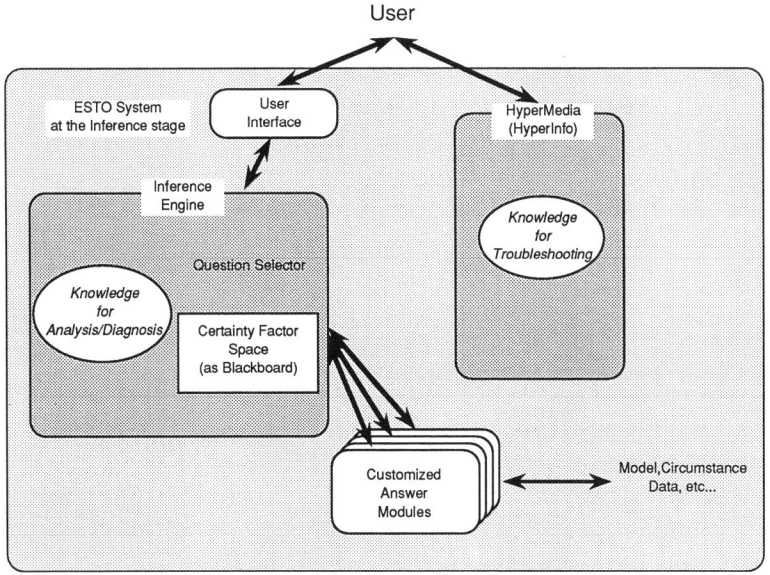

FIGURE 2.7. Architecture of ESTO.

modification history, is available by clicking the mouse button on the node.

4.3.1. Building Knowledge Bases. ESTO knowledge bases are built interactively. The process may roughly be divided into three steps:

1. Defining the classification hierarchy
2. Defining questions
3. Linking questions to HC nodes

The third step is illustrated in Figure 2.8. In this example, a question is displayed in the right middle window. The user is responsible for selecting an HC node, and setting influ-

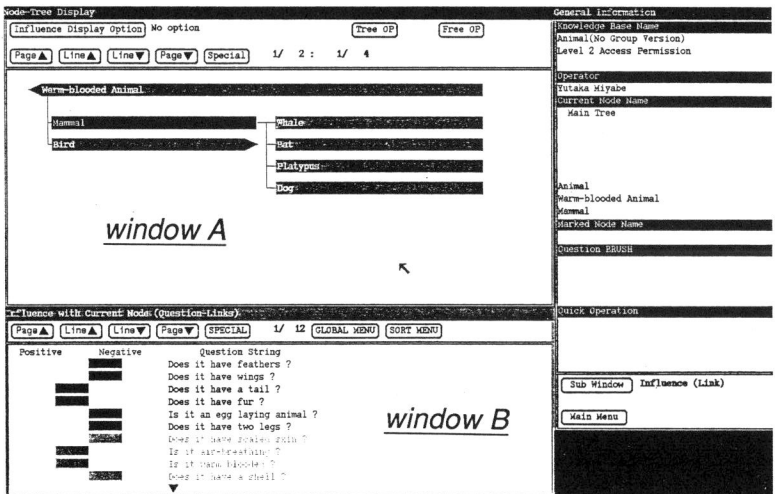

FIGURE 2.8. The Main Editor.

ence values between the displayed question and the selected node.

Modifying a knowledge base is similar to building one. The user can add, delete, and copy nodes using a mouse-driven interface. These operations may be performed either on single nodes, or on groups of nodes. The user can also modify influence values which link a question to HC nodes.

4.3.2. Reviewing and Optimizing Knowledge Bases. Like other shells, ESTO cannot confirm or guarantee the consistency and completeness of its knowledge base. However, a set of tools is implemented to assist the user in reviewing an existing knowledge base for the purpose of optimization.

In ESTO, HC nodes can be compared to each other using the HC node comparison facility. When this option is active, the user selects two nodes (or sets of nodes) to be compared. The Question-and-Influence Display then highlights the differences between the two nodes (or clusters). The difference is shown as a comparison of the questions linked to either HC node, and the related influence values. If there is little or no difference between the two nodes, it may be concluded that there is not enough information to distinguish them.

A similar facility is structural checking, which is performed by the *disassembly and clustering* function. In this case, the user selects the whole or part of the classification hierarchy for structural analysis. Typically, the user first disassembles the structure to produce a set of independent nodes. Then, ESTO is asked to cluster these independent nodes into a classification hierarchy. If ESTO cannot distinguish two nodes on the basis of supporting questions and influence values, it aggregates them into a single node. This feature is useful in getting rid of intermediate nodes which cannot be easily distinguished, where a distinction is irrelevant.

When the structural consistency checking is complete, the links can be optimized. In most cases, optimization is performed by minimizing the number of links. For example, if all descendents of a particular node have a link to the same question, and if all influence values are identical, the question may be linked to the parent node instead, and all individual links to the descendents may be removed. In the case where a few of the descendents are connected to the same question with different influence values, it may still be more economical to link the question to the parent node, and to declare explicit links to the exceptions.

4.4. The Runtime Browser

4.4.1. Executing Fault Diagnosis. During fault diagnosis, the user is first asked to choose the scope of diagnosis by selecting factories and equipment. Figure 2.9 depicts the user interface for diagnosis. The upper window displays the most plausible diagnostic hypotheses at that instant. Since hypotheses are ordered by relative differences and not by absolute values of certainty factors, no numerical values are displayed. As expected, the order of plausible hypotheses changes dynamically as reasoning progresses.

The middle window shows previous questions and answers. The most plausible hypothesis is referred to as *the focused node,* and the contribution of each answer to the belief in that node is shown at the rightmost column of this window.

When a leaf node (end hypothesis) is confirmed during diagnosis, the decision is displayed in the lower window. At this stage, the user may either terminate the diagnostic process, or continue further if more questions are available.

In order to analyze the reasoning, the user may focus on one of the nodes displayed in the hypothesis list. In this case, ESTO displays a trace of the reasoning steps, and the effect of each step on the focused node. Focusing on a specific node is especially useful during debugging or maintaining knowledge bases.

Either during diagnosis or after a conclusion is reached, the user is allowed to retract

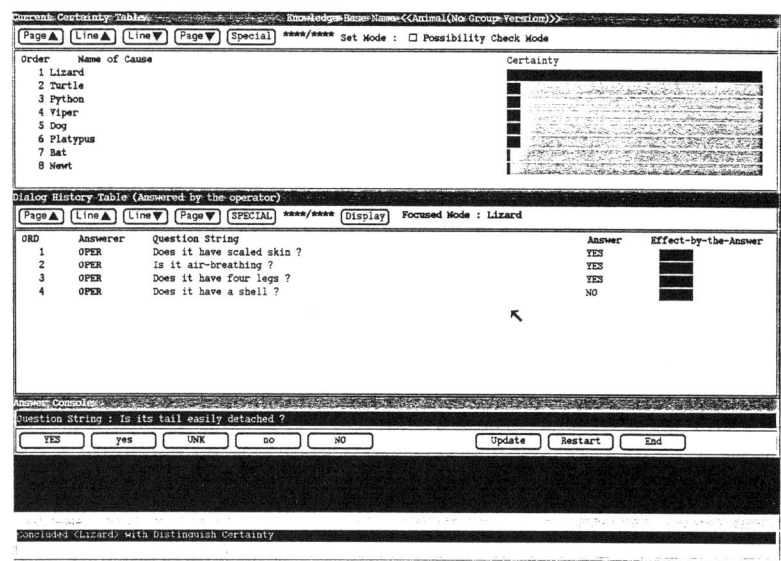

FIGURE 2.9. The Runtime Browser.

answers to previous questions. ESTO immediately updates certainty values of all affected nodes after such an adjustment.

4.4.2. Directing First Aid. When a piece of equipment is diagnosed as faulty, ESTO may provide troubleshooting and maintenance information upon request. The help facility is called HyperInfo, and it is based on the hypermedia paradigm (Parsaye et al., 1989). The information may consist of text, pictures, and illustrations which the user can traverse using a mouse-driven interface. The user is first shown a brief explanation of desired repair procedures. If detailed information is necessary, the user may explore the hypermedia knowledge base freely, bound only by the extent of information available on-line.

The use of hypermedia as a knowledge retrieval tool brings about the familiar problems of entry and navigation in hypertexts (Parsaye et al., 1989). The entry problem is to determine where to start. In general, the user may access the hypermedia knowledge base at any point. It is, however, neither very practical nor very useful to present the knowledge base in its entirety. Fortunately, the diagnosis tool guides and bounds hypermedia access by focusing on the faulty equipment. Therefore, the entry problem is avoided.

The navigation problem is the problem of knowing which parts of the knowledge are already traversed, and how to get from one point to another. In hypertext and hypermedia, a major problem is getting lost after pursuing a number of trivial links. In this case, the user has very little to do, apart from quitting the hypermedia environment and starting afresh. To alleviate the problem, HyperInfo provides a simple navigation utility. HyperInfo displays the recent path through the knowledge base as a list of traversed nodes. When the user is lost, he can return to the point where he sidestepped by selecting a familiar location on the path. A more robust solution is the development of a graphical network browsing facility, which has not yet been implemented on HyperInfo.

5. DEPLOYMENT OF THE EXPERT SYSTEM

The expert system currently handles faults in 500 pieces of electrical and mechanical equipment spread over three factories. The classification hierarchy has a total of 580 sub-trees, 25,000 leaf nodes (equipment parts and components), 40,000 questions, and 110,000 links from questions to nodes. The knowledge base has been developed by six domain experts working full time on the project, along with forty blue collar foremen who provided additional assistance.

The primary purpose of the expert system is to reduce the amount and extent of troubleshooting services performed by maintenance personnel. However, precautions must be taken in order to avoid increasing the workload of plant operators by increasing their responsibility for diagnosis and repair while reducing the workload of maintenance workers. The domain is extremely complex: each of the factories in which the expert system is deployed has product lines of 1 to 2 kms. long. Plant operators are distributed among several operation rooms. Each factory has one to two hundred pieces of equipment which may be the subject of fault diagnosis. Moreover, the mills run very fast, thus high speed (up to several hundred samples per second) data acquisition systems and large mass storage units are necessary. As a result, an automated mechanism to acquire and process data is required to reduce operator workload, and to summarize low-level information for use by the expert system. A series of intelligent loggers have been deployed for that purpose.

5.1. The Hardware Architecture

As discussed before, the architecture of the system may be examined in three layers (see Figure 2.5). The sensor and process computer layer has been operational for some time. However, the expert system layer and the information acquisition layer were built during the course of the project. The expert system layer consists of workstations in each operation room which are connected to each other via ethernet. These workstations run the ESTO interface for the expert system. The information acquisition system layer consists of a number of intelligent loggers which are implemented on PCs. These systems are designed to process vast amounts of data at a low cost, and they are networked using a wide bandwidth fiber optic network (Figure 2.6).

5.2. The Architecture of Customized Answer Modules

Answer modules are activated by related questions, and they typically query the information acquisition layers for answers. However, some answer modules only interact with the user. Since ESTO's inference engine accepts only five types of answers ("YES", "yes", "unk", "no", and "NO"), any numerical answer must be translated to one of these forms. The answer modules are designed to satisfy the following requirements:
1. To specify the appropriate information acquisition methods for the required data.
2. To issue requests to intelligent loggers.
3. To translate the derived data into a form suitable for the inference engine.
4. To send the answer to the inference engine.

Naturally, answer modules are deeply related to the diagnostic knowledge. An analysis of the knowledge elicited from domain experts shows that three types of answer modules are sufficient to represent a wide variety of signal processing situations:
- *Batch Data Answer Module.* This module is used to process batches of data samples, as requested by the inference engine.
- *Continuous Data Answer Module.* This module is used to provide continuous readings of important parameters, such as the average current during the past minute.
- *Long-Term Trend Monitoring Answer Module.* This module handles long-term trends, such as degradation of performance.

5.3. Implementation and Technology Transfer

System engineers and domain experts cooperated extensively during implementation. Once the rough features of the system were identified, four main tasks were pursued simultaneously. These tasks were the implementation of the expert system shell, development of the knowledge base, development of customized modules, and the development of intelligent loggers. The knowledge base was entirely developed by domain experts, taking advantage of the user-friendly nature of ESTO. The domain experts also helped train plant operators on the use of the expert system for diagnosis. The average manpower use was around 25 people, and it took around three years to complete the system. During the most intensive period, the project team consisted of 40 full-time personnel and an additional 6 part-time personnel. As expected, the implementation of the information acquisition system layer required more manpower than the expert system layer did.

The rough features of the system were decided upon after extensive analysis of the diagnostic knowledge elicited from a domain expert by four system engineers. Once the features were identified, a prototype was made. Domain experts were asked to develop a knowledge base using the prototype, and to assess whether they would be able to develop knowledge bases by themselves. The domain expert who initially contributed his expertise to the project has become the leader of the team which developed the final knowledge base.

Once the basic functions of ESTO such as the knowledge editor and the inference engine were ready, the leader trained other domain experts, who would consequently lead the project teams in each of the three factories. The training lasted one week. Subsequently, the factory team leaders started developing diagnostic knowledge bases of their individual factories. The few hundred individual equipment in each factory were classified into twenty categories, and the knowledge for these major categories were acquired first. Next, all domain experts joined efforts in an attempt to consolidate these separate knowledge bases into one functional knowledge base. The verification and refinement of the knowledge base was also handled by the domain experts themselves. Some off-line tests were undertaken to fine-tune the knowledge base, and to assess with precision the relation between some questions and faulty components.

At the final stage, answer modules were built. According to the ESTO protocol, the domain experts were allowed to select appropriate signal processing methods for required data. Although the signal processing modules were developed as regular software products, the domain experts had a say on the functionality and performance of these modules.

When the system was completed, the domain experts started training 170 plant operators for using the expert system for diagnosis. Due to the intuitive user interface of ESTO, training sessions lasted a mere three hours per operator.

5.4. Knowledge Base Maintenance

The maintenance of the knowledge base is performed mainly by domain experts. The number of domain experts who worked full-time for the development of the knowledge base is six, two from each factory. These domain experts ultimately returned to their original duties as maintenance personnel, but they are still responsible for performing occasional maintenance on the knowledge base. Furthermore, some plant operators voluntarily started developing and maintaining knowledge bases about the regular operations of their plants. Plans for future extension include an expansion of the current system to accommodate process diagnosis. Process diagnosis is aimed at monitoring the regular operation of production lines.

6. DISCUSSION

Since such a large scale diagnostic problem cannot be handled entirely by user interaction, information acquisition is performed largely by a network of dedicated signal processing computers called intelligent loggers. Intelligent loggers are not only used by the expert system, but also by field engineers to provide insight into plant operations. Intelligent loggers also warn maintenance personnel about impending failures during preventive maintenance. Prediction of faults is currently a separate feature, but it may be integrated into the expert system in the future.

In this project, the knowledge representation is designed to focus on diagnosis problems. Moreover, the steps of knowledge acquisition and compilation are simplified in order to eliminate the dependence on knowledge engineers to extract and transform domain knowledge. As a result, domain experts with little or no computer expertise can develop and maintain their own diagnostic expert systems.

The reasoning mechanism is robust enough to withstand reasonable amounts of incorrect or inconsistent information, or retraction of previously supplied information. The reasoning process is kept independent of the hierarchical knowledge representation. By not implementing hierarchical classification as a reasoning paradigm, the need for complicated intelligent backtracking algorithms is eliminated. Further, the computations on different nodes of the hierarchy are independent, and ESTO may easily benefit from a parallel implementation in the future.

The modular implementation and adherence to a strict message passing protocol has facilitated the development of a distributed architecture where separate modules run on different workstations and communicate via a blackboard.

The authors argue that a diagnostic system which reasons along a built-in scenario cannot be classified as an "intelligent system." In contrast, an intelligent system is one that can mimic the flexible and dynamic nature of human reasoning. ESTO, by virtue of its distributed, nonmonotonic and dynamic reasoning capabilities, satisfies the requirements of intelligent behavior.

7. CONCLUSION

In this paper, a large scale industrial expert system for fault diagnosis is described. The system is currently being used at the Oita Works of Nippon Steel Corporation, and is expected to reduce the number of maintenance personnel on all three shifts by 35, resulting in a total savings of 2.5 Million U.S.$ per year in cost equivalence.

ACKNOWLEDGEMENTS

The authors would like to thank Mr. Yutaka Miyabe of the Computer Science Laboratory of Nippon Steel Corporation and Dr. Serdar Uckun of the Center for Intelligent Systems of Vanderbilt University for their assistance in all stages of the production of this manuscript.

REFERENCES

Bylander, T., & Mittal, S. (1986). CSRL: A language for classificatory problem solving and uncertainty handling, *AI Magazine,* August.

Engelmore, E.A., & Morgan, T. (1988). *Blackboard Systems.* Reading, MA: Addison Wesley.

Hara, H., Yoshida, H., & Matsumoto, H. (1988). Decision lattice: A formalization of diagnosis problems, (In Japanese). *Knowledge Engineering and Artificial Intelligence,* 59(8), 65–73.

Minami, E., Miyabe, Y., & Dairiki, O. (1990). ESTO: A practical environment for industrial diagnostic systems. *Proceedings of the 3rd. International Conference on Industrial & Engineering Applications of Artificial Intelligence & Expert Systems,* Vol. 2, pp. 684–691, Charleston, SC, U.S.A.

Parsaye, K., Chignell, M., Khoshafian, S., & Wong, H. (1989). *Intelligent databases: Object-oriented, deductive hypermedia technologies.* New York: John Wiley and Sons.

APPENDIX: A SAMPLE SESSION WITH THE EXPERT SYSTEM

Since the deployed expert system runs under the Japanese Language Environment, screen dumps will be of little guidance to readers who cannot read Japanese. Therefore, a simple example in English is chosen to illustrate a session with the expert system. The real expert system works in a similar fashion, albeit on a much larger knowledge base.

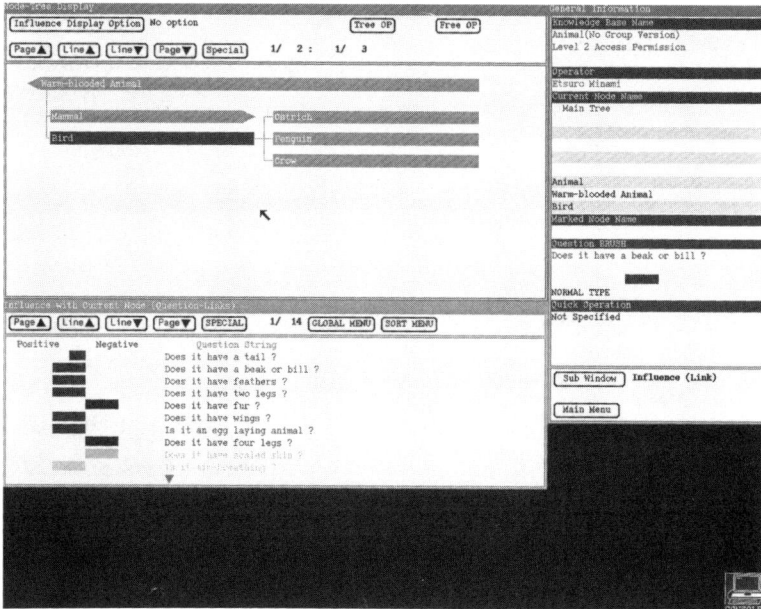

A2. Main Editor a).

a) The upper left window shows part of the classification hierarchy. The window below contains information about links.

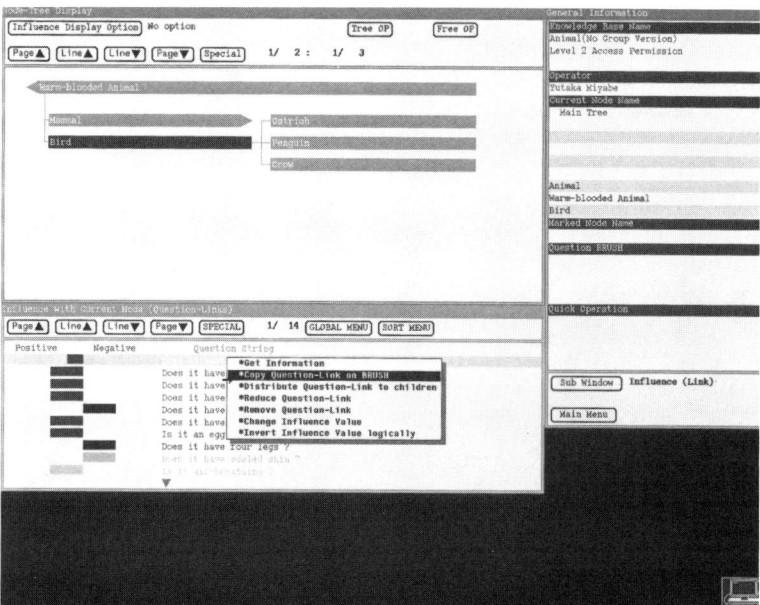

A2. Main Editor b)

b) A link is made between the node "Bird" and the question "Does it have a beak or bill?" with an influence value of "++".

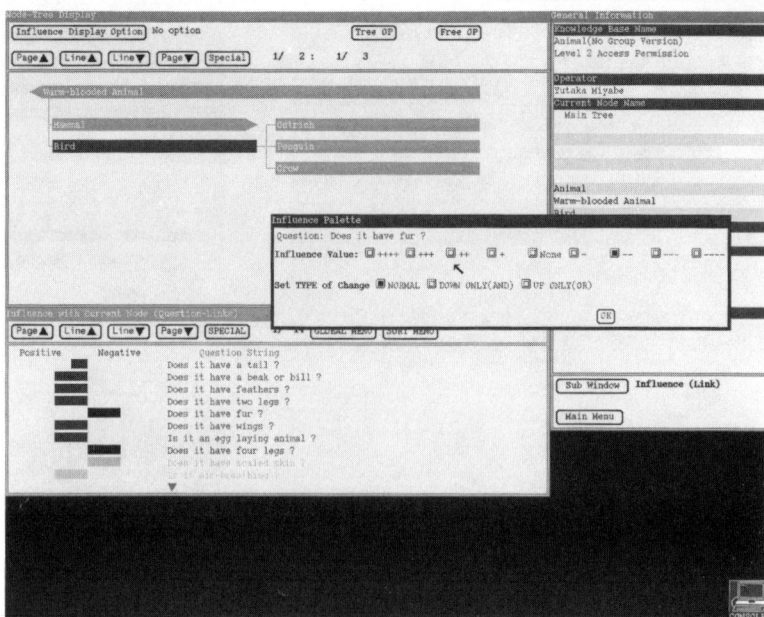

A3. Main Editor c)

c) Modifying an existing influence value.

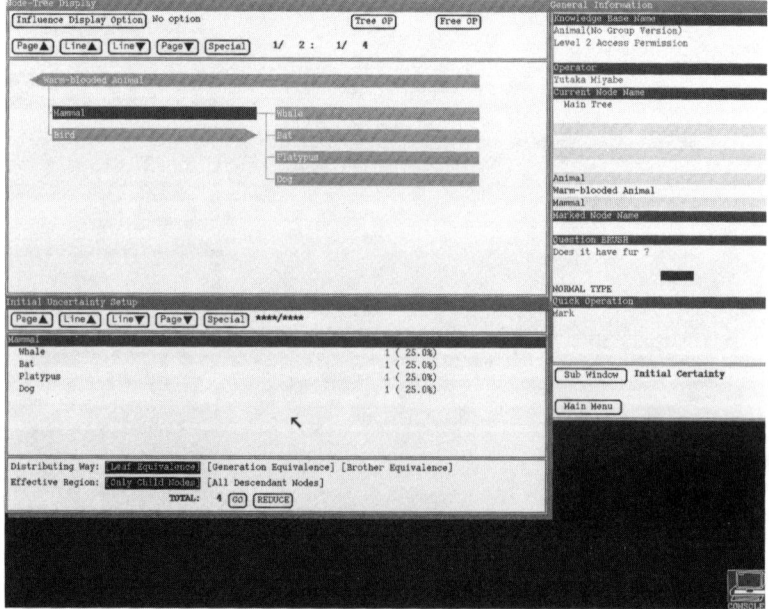

A3. Main Editor d)

d) Setting initial certainty. In this example, each mammal has the same initial certainty.

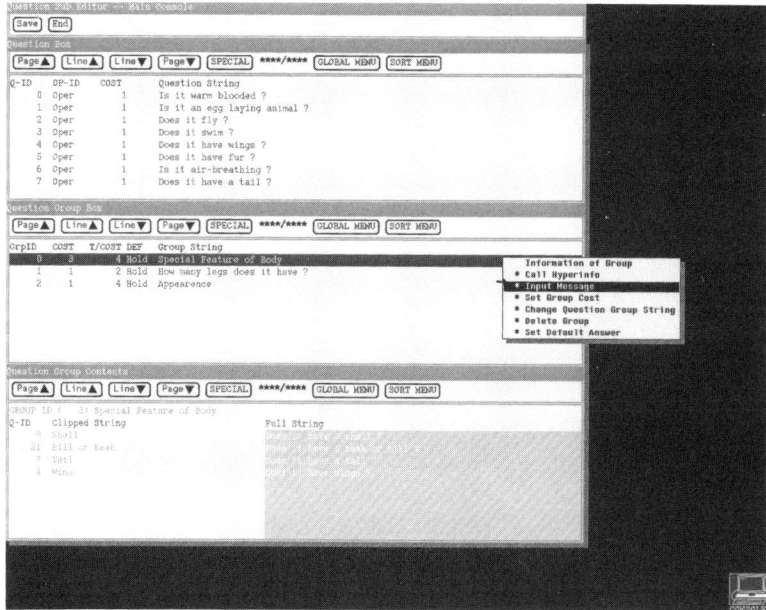

A4. Question Sub Editor

This editor is used to group questions and to specify an appropriate answer module.

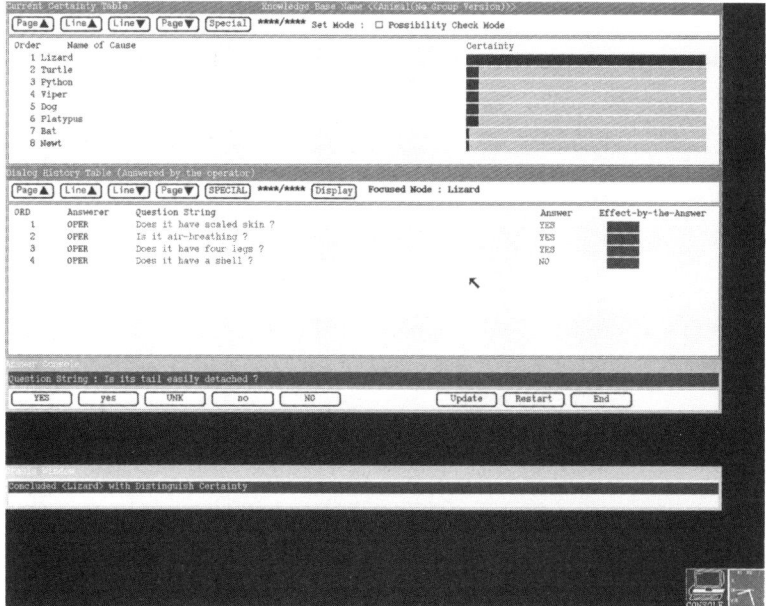

A5. Runtime Browser. a)

a) The upper window lists candidate hypotheses ordered by their certainty factors. The middle window shows the history, i.e. previous questions, answer modules, answers, and whether a certain answer supports the specified candidate or not. The range of answers is a strong affirmation ("YES"), a weak affirmation ("yes"), unknown ("unk"), weak negation ("no"), and strong negation ("NO"). Past answers may be modified at any time.

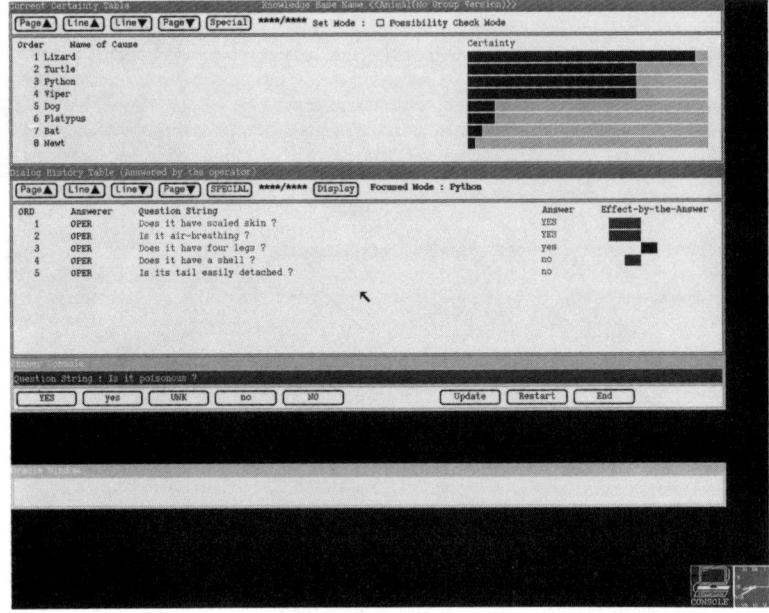

A5. Runtime Browser b)

b) An example of the behavior in case of a wrong answer. In this case, the correct answer is "Python," but the conclusion was "Lizard." Now, the user wants to know the reason for this contradiction reached, and sets the focused node to "Python." The "Effect-by-the-Answer" column indicates that python does not have four legs, but the answer "yes" did not support that statement. This means either the answer is wrong, or the knowledge base is incorrect.

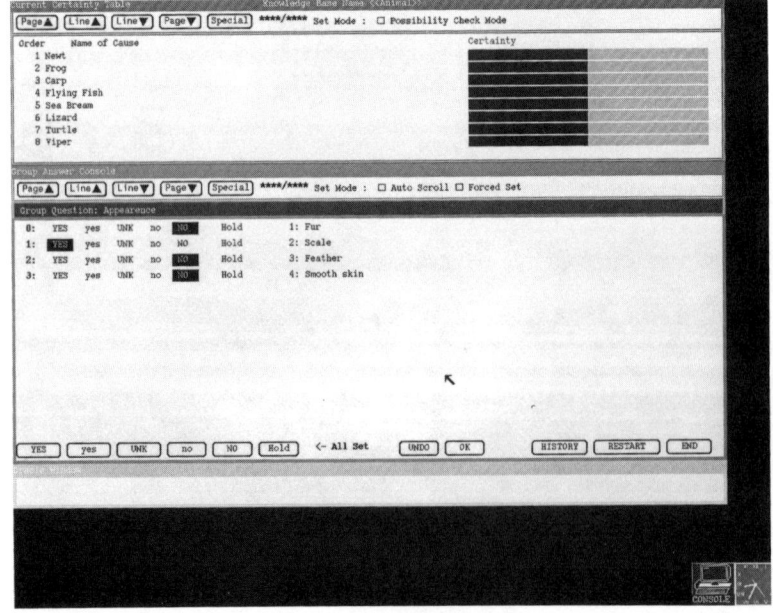

A5. Runtime Browser c)

c) Group questions. A group of questions may be bundled and answered together at the same time. By updating certainty factors only once after all answers are entered, this feature saves computation time.

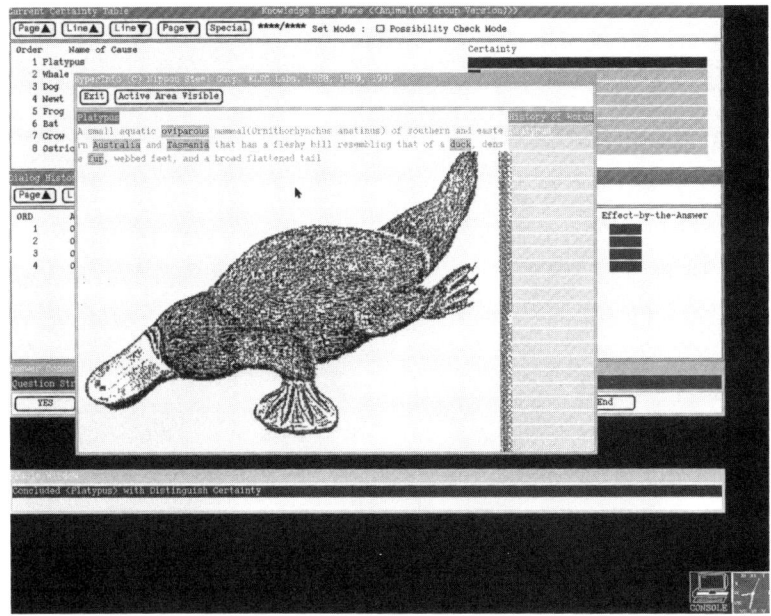

A6. HyperInfo d)

d) HyperInfo. Troubleshooting knowledge is represented as hypermedia.

(A new kind of animal "Human" is being added to the knowledge base)

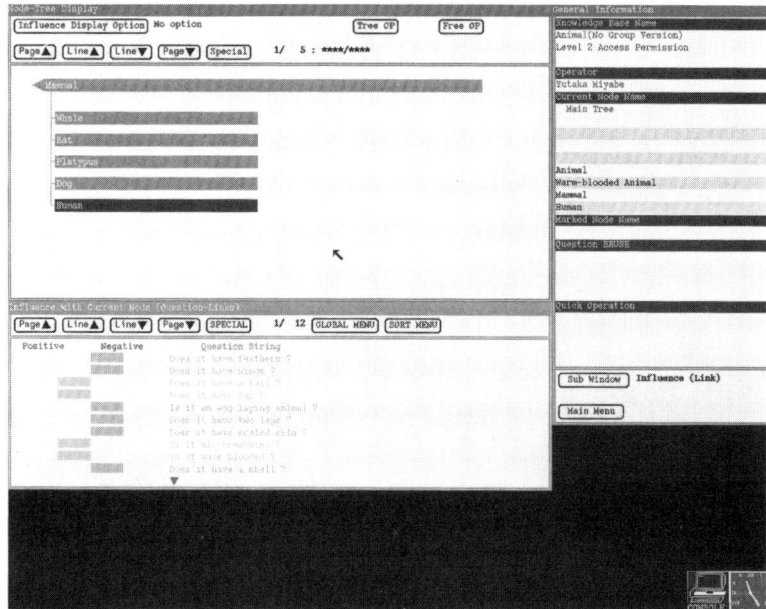

A7. Main Editor Maintenance. a).

a) A new node "Human" is created. By default, all links pertaining to mammals are inherited to "Human." So, "Human" inherits forelocks and a tail.

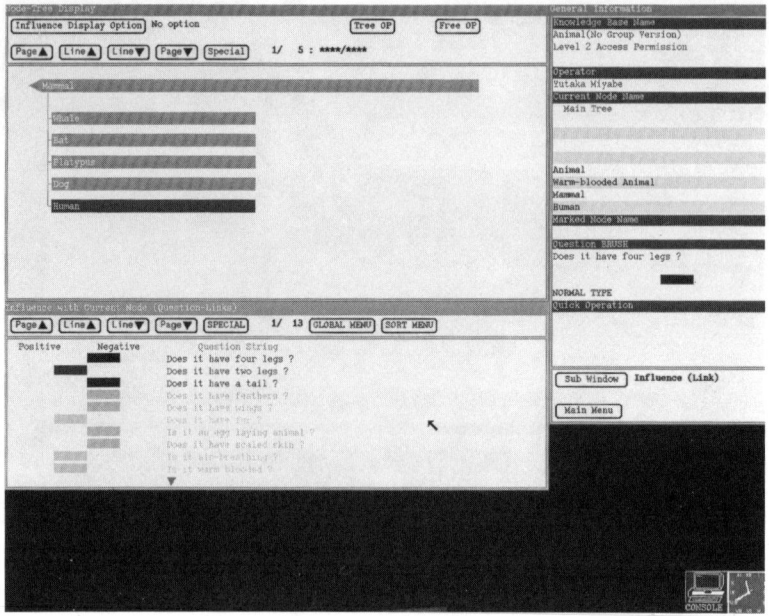

A7. Main Editor b)

b) Modifying the knowledge base. Now "Human" has two legs and no tail.

SCREEN DUMPS FROM THE ORIGINAL EXPERT SYSTEM DEPLOYED AT OITA WORKS

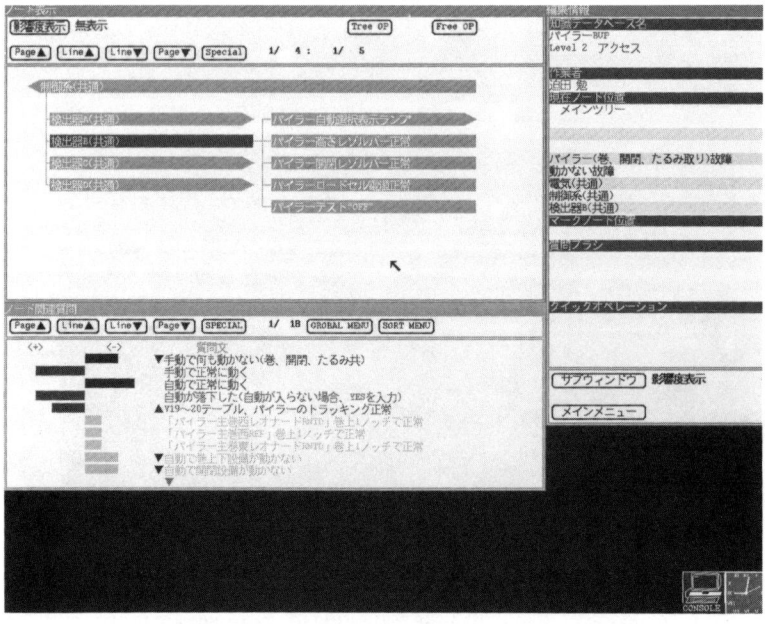

A8. Screen Dumps . . . . upper

Fault Diagnosis in Steel Manufacturing

A8. Screen dumps . . . . lower

Prediction of Blast Pressure in Blast Furnace Operations

SANG-HO YI,* YOUNG-SOO HONG,** AND HOO-KEUN LEE***

*Department of Ironmaking, Senior Researcher, RIST, Pohang, Korea;
**S/W R&D Team, Associate Researcher, R&D Center, POSDATA, Seoul, Korea;
***Department of Ironmaking, Section Manager, POSCO, Pohang, Korea.

1. INTRODUCTION

AS A MEANS to stabilize blast furnace operations. AI (Artificial Intelligence) technology has emerged with the potential for human flexibility (Weiss & Kulikowski, 1984). Up to now, numerical analysis technology and computer aided models for predicting in-furnace conditions have been developed and implemented in the normal operations of blast furnace (Ho et al., 1988). AI technology, especially expert systems (or problem solving technology), highlighted by its supreme feature to overcome the ambiguity of numerical systems, yielded results, and then succeeded in a specific domain on a laboratory and a practical scale (Albaxana & Argyropoulous, 1988; Tsunosaki & Tokekoshi, 1985; Yui, 1987). Research on the applications of this system on the abnormal condition of blast furnace operations has been initiated by Japanese iron and steel works since 1984. From the first product announced by Fukuyuyama #5BF of NKK in 1986, many knowledge based systems have been reported by the five major iron and steel companies of Japan. To apply this newly emerged technology on the blast furnaces, research focused on the implementation of expert systems. At first, we decided to develop a prototype system for short term prediction of the abnormal in-furnace state prior to integration of a real system. As to the role of expert systems, it is only for compensating the defects inevitable in the numerical systems. We studied a selection of proper development tools to suit the problem by comparing several commercially available expert systems building tools in view of their several applications and supporting fascilities, we chose the S.1 developed by Teknowledge Inc. of U.S.A. for the prototype system, and EIXAX II made by Fuji. Inc. of Japan for the actual application. We then developed an expert system prototype to predict blast pressure in furnace operations in off-line base by using S.1.

The system describes in about 10 minutes whether blast pressure will increase or not. Following the satisfactory results from the prototype system, we implemented the system into the on-line based system of actual blast furnace operations using EIXAX II. In this chapter, we present the procedure of extracting the knowledge from human experts and applying it to intermediate (prototype) and final (actual) systems.

2. CONVENTIONAL APPROACH TO THE COMPUTERIZATION OF BLAST FURNACE OPERATIONS IN POSCO

An operational control system has already been designed to estimate and guide blast furnace operating conditions. The system con-

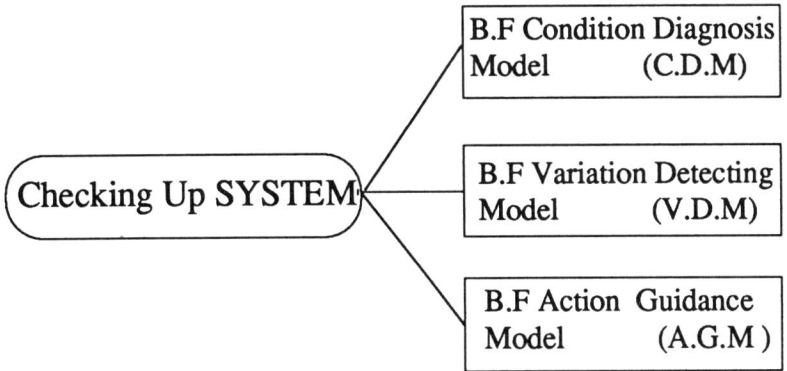

FIGURE 3.1. Conventional computerization of blast furnace operations in POSCO.

sists of Condition Diagnosis Model (CDM) and Variation Detecting Model (VDM). According to the system, blast furnace conditions are expressed in terms of score, that is, Good Caution or Bad in time series. The variables of CDM and VDM are chosen, and threshold values and weights are fixed by statistical treatment of past operational results. The CDM consists of 14 operational indices and evaluates the variation of blast furnace conditions every hour. The VDM consists of 5 operational indices and evaluates the variation of blast furnace conditions such as blast pressure, charging speed every minute. The Action Guidance Model (AGM) estimates the quality of burden materials, puts together the results of CDM and VDM, and makes action guidance messages to the operators. In addition, an estimation model of hot metal temperature, optimization of fuel ratio, evaluation of burden distributions and profiles of cohesive zone have been developed. Figure 3.1 summarizes the conventionally computerized scheme of blast furnace operations in POSCO (1987).

3. OVERVIEW OF BLAST PRESSURE CHANGE

In normal blast furnace operations, some changes can be seen in burden materials by hot reducing gas originating from the furnace bottom, resulting in pressure drop through passing the in-furnace. Figure 3.2 shows the general description of blast furnace.

The degree of pressure drop is determined by the configuration of cohesive zone formed in inside the furnace as well as ore/coke condition. This brings about an imbalance of gas flow at the inner furnace and may be a decisive factor for predicting abnormal burden descending, channeling and overheat load to the furnace wall, which can directly cause depreciation of productivity and an increase of coke ratio. In all, change of blast pressure can be generally considered as a primary operational index for detecting pressure drop in the furnace.

Its theoretical considerations are as follows: despite friction between each burden material and the lifting power by ascending gas flow, burden materials descend by self weighting. Pressure gradually drops as growing gas velocity until the equilibrium is reached between floating-up power and burden load. Mathematically, the pressure drop is identical to the weight per unit area of filling-up layer at the critical point (Nippon Steel Co. Ltd., 1982):

$$\frac{\Delta P}{H} = \alpha \cdot (1 - \epsilon_c) \cdot (\delta s - \delta g) \cdot G \quad (1)$$

Where,
ΔP : Pressure Drop
δs : average density of solid
δg : density of gas

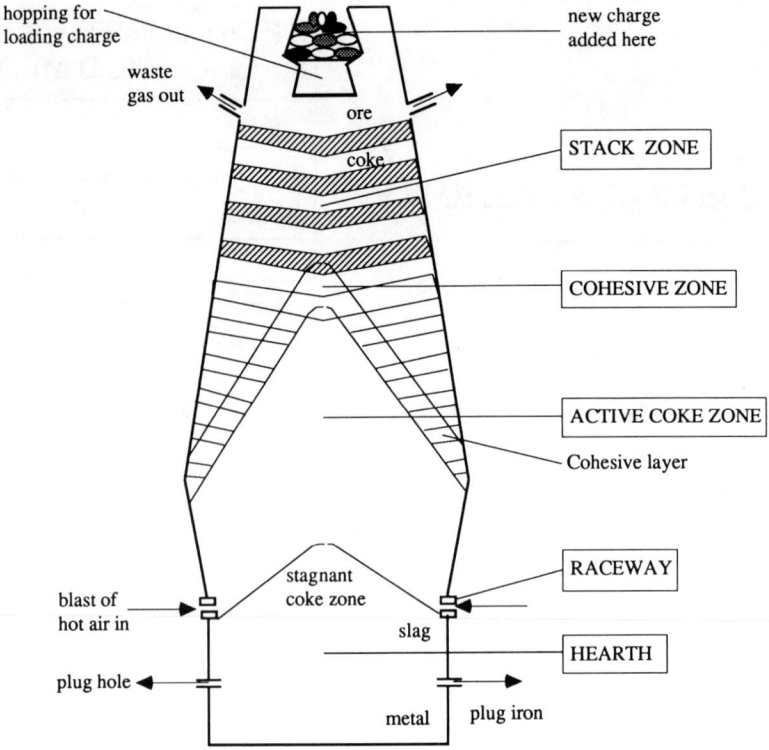

FIGURE 3.2. General view of blast furnace.

G : gravity
ϵ_c : vacancy ratio at the critical point
α : proportional constant
H : height

And blast pressure relatively increases as vacancies decrease as described in equation (2),

$$(\Delta P_2/H)/(\Delta P_1/H) = \frac{(1-\epsilon_2)/\epsilon_2^3}{(1-\epsilon_1)/\epsilon_1^3} \quad (2)$$

where,

ΔP_1 : Pressure Drop at state 1
ΔP_2 : Pressure Drop at state 2
ϵ_1 : vacancy ratio at the critical point
ϵ_2 : vacancy ratio at the critical point

Equations (1) and (2) mean the blast pressure change results from vacancy ratio change. In other words, optimum operations maintain a sound condition by reducing gas velocity and preventing a sudden descent of burden materials caused by the accumulation and fluidization of solids at shaft levels. When gas flow becomes unstable, the following phenomena can be found;
- higher top gas temperature
- abnormal heat balance
- higher CO/CO_2 ratio in top gas
- unstable pig iron content

It can be schematized as Figure 3.3.

The major applicable operational variable related to the increase of blast pressure can be summarized more specifically as follows:

1. Temperatures of furnace top and wall. A change of top gas temperature represents the variations of reducing gas profile and heat level, which is the result of various reduction reactions and heat exchanges through the whole period in furnace. As for blast pressure change, most of the reasons in charge of top gas temperature have to do with the delayed

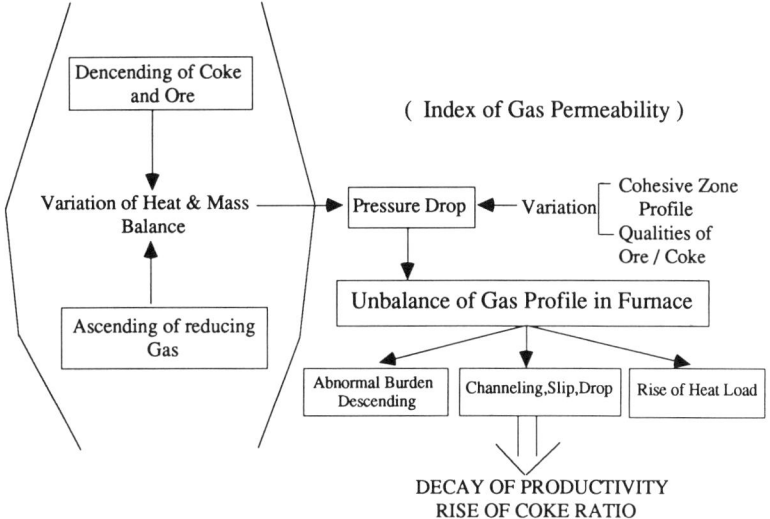

FIGURE 3.3. Schematic diagram for cause and effect of blast pressure change in blast furnace.

descent of burden. According to the operational results, slip, drop and blast pressure change have a great relation to top gas temperature variation. As for blast pressure change, most of the reasons in change of top gas temperature have to do with the delayed descent of burden. The temperature of the lower section of the furnace, for instance those of belly and bosh sections, represent gas permeability, especially in all coke based operations, which causes unstable gas flow combined with changes of heat balance. For this reason, most operators make efforts to lower the temperatures of bosh and belly. But excessive lowering of these temperatures may incur an inactive zone at the furnace bottom, so they should be controlled by proper limits. A change of shaft level #3 temperature has a great relation to blast pressure increase, shaft pressure and change of top gas temperature. Most changes in the shaft level mean unstable gas flows in the lower zone of the furnace, which is guaranteed by the results of linear regression analysis in actual operations of POSCO.

2. Burden descent speeds. Burden descent speed makes a great contribution to predicting the change of blast pressure among other operational indices. When burden descent speed increase, insufficient heat sources can be expected, and vice versa. For this reason, operators should know the frequency of burdening.

Delayed burden descent speed can be visually drawn by wider traces in stock level panels with a velocity of 12–13 min/charge for relatively larger furnace cases. On the contrary, it takes about 10 minutes under normal operational conditions, whereas values usually vary according to specific operations like the uneven burdening process. Lowering the burdening speed implies that burden materials suffer some resistance accompanying the unsmooth burden down. In actual process burden velocity (or sounding speed) is measured by 4 horizontal spots of different values. In this case, slip and drop phenomena can occur with local increase of blast pressure. Burden descent speed depends on the operational speed set up by production schedule, namely the change of ore base.

A sudden change of burden descent speed may cause a blast pressure change. Burden descent speed also affects the change of blast pressure combined with other operational value, such as top gas temperature, shaft pressures and temperatures. In this system burden descent speed is directly connected to diagnosing the change of blast pressure.

3. Pressures of furnace wall. While shaft temperature represents the in-furnace gas flow and contributes to the decision of in-furnace conditions, shaft pressure values can be used for inferring gas flow profile through the pressure of reducing gas, that is, the change of transferred power from inner furnace conditions. A diagnosing system for understanding the in-furnace conditions usually uses the shaft pressure as a principal factor because it stands for the gas permeabilities of each zone of the furnace.

4. Delayed tapping. Tapping is routine in the daily operations of the blast furnace. Most blast furnaces with a relatively large volume have to be tapped incessantly, and delays of tapping can cause a pressure load to the lower zone of furnace. This case however is so unusual and unsystematic that numerical model systems can not adopt this information in spite of its strong correlation with increase of blast pressure. The data for this variable was introduced to the system by using the tapping files in the daily operations. The degree of tapping delay is determined by the difference between latest taps so that it is regarded as a normal state. The set value of tapping delay will be decided by the operator and result from actual operations.

4. BUILDING-UP THE KNOWLEDGE BASE

The knowledge base was integrated to predict blast pressure change in abnormal operations on a short term period referred to by operational manuals and experts experiences. To acquire the relevant knowledge in this domain, we interviewed leading operators who had taken part in monitoring the in-furnace condition and set up the boundary conditions used to determine the state of incoming operational data referring to the statistical evaluation of a year.

Operators who are currently engaged in maintaining a proper furnace conditions usually watch the panel to check the blast pressure change and the state of the in-furnace. Figure 3.4 shows the configuration of the panel used to observe the #1, 2, 3, 4

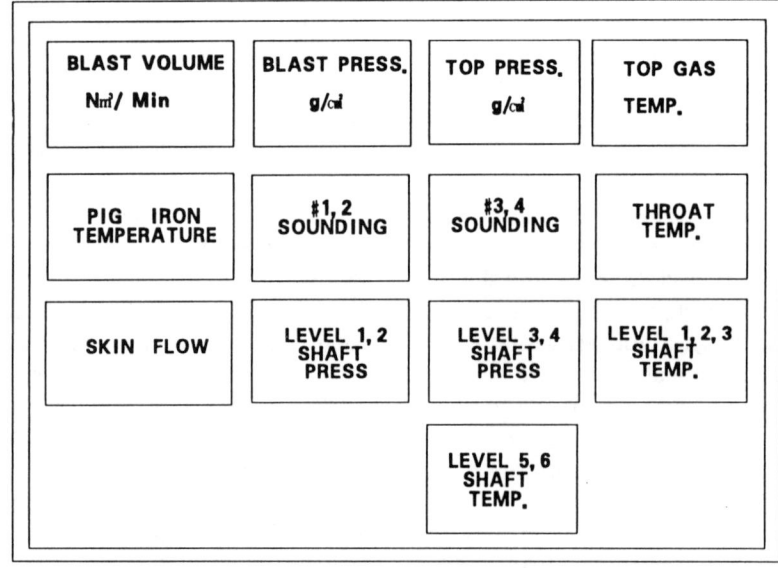

FIGURE 3.4. Operational panel for furnace proper.

Prediction of Blast Pressure

stock level gauges and blast pressure gauge simultaneously.

According to the circumstances, change of stock level gauges precede that of the blast pressure gauge, and the opposite case can also be found. In this knowledge base, available factors used for predicting blast pressure in advance were selected and used, which could be depicted as in Figure 3.5.

After having received primary operational data, intermediate decisions (balance in Figure 3.5) are made, and then a final diagnosis about the change of the blast pressure can be drawn.

Because the decisions of the blast pressure change mainly refer to "changed" cases, we can constrain the excessive certainty factors of the 'changed' cases by generating the 'unchanged' rules at the same time. The resultant diagnosis is arrived at by propagating the accumulated two values. On the other hand, most data dedicated for the prediction system get the form of digit-type values, converting programs in need to easily manipulate each rule in the knowledge base, which is meaningful for the seperation between inference engine and knowledge base as well as consideration of modification in boundary conditions over a year.

A well structured C program for this purpose was made by linking the S.1 system with an EXTERNAL.CONTROL.BLOCK in the prototype system. The knowledge base can be divided into 3 moduli: CLASS, ATTRIBUTE and RULE moduli to represent the knowledge with S.1 tool.

On the other hand, actual systems have three kinds of rule modules concerning the definition of the data class, determination of intermediate levels and decision of the final

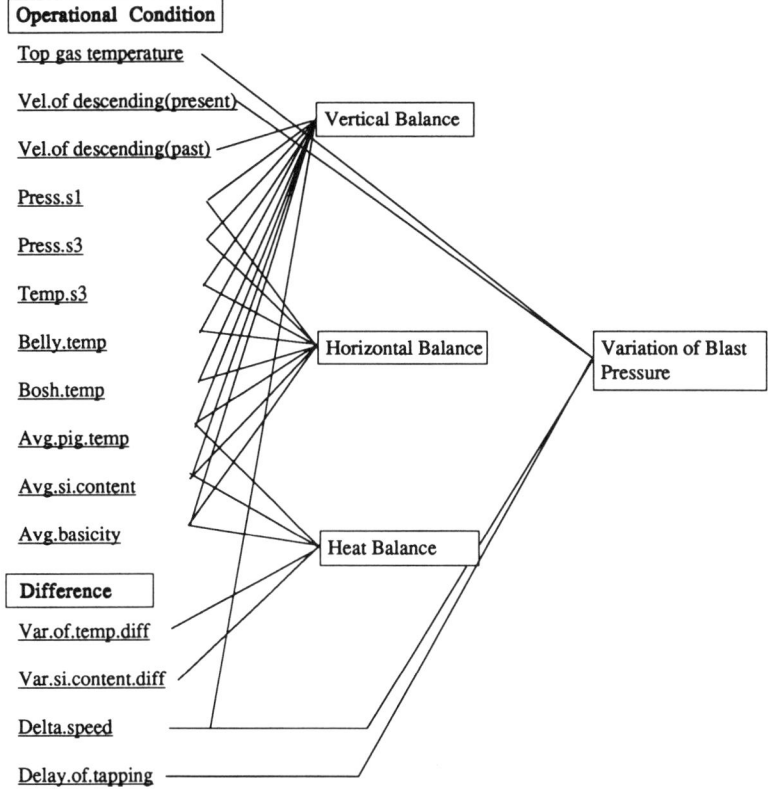

FIGURE 3.5. Hierarchical images of blast pressure prediction.

results, respectively. Because the expert system shells used in the prototype and actual system are different in structuring and representing the knowledge base, some modifications are needed in the implementation of the actual system.

5. SIMULATION TEST AND ACTUAL APPLICATIONS

5.1 Simulation Test

The 'Predictor' developed using the S.1 on the SUN workstation was evaluated to predict the change of blast pressure with actual operational data. The data used for the simulation test was subject to the case that the amount of changed blast pressure is greater than the average value by 0.2 Kg/cm^2. The results achieved from simulation tests were compared to those of actual cases for 1 hour. Operational data available were collected by 10 minute intervals, because available data from process computers in the operation were that frequency and charging speed and descent speed was about 10 minutes during the normal operations. We put simulation tests into practice for No. 4 Blast Furnace of POSCO in an off-line base system. In this trial, there were operational indices disturbing enough to affect the prediction for initial 30 minutes. After this, the system gave the 'changed' blast pressure because of variation of burden descent and a sudden rise of pig iron temperature at that time, in which a CF value of 0.89 was obtained, so the change of blast pressure was apparent in predictive diagnosis (Figure 3.6). All the inference results were displayed on the consultation window with some relevant explanations in S.1 window frame. (Figure 3.7.) The 'Predictor' directed a sudden rise of blast pressure in advance, which was, however, a predictive system simulated with the actual data from past operations, so that we could not be sure of the prediction capability in another situations. But in all test simulations on the off-line based system, we achieved remarkable results that could be applied to an actual system.

5.2 Actual System Applications

The prototype system has been ported and operated in actual operational system. The period of each inference for the prediction of the actual system is 10 minutes, like that of the prototype system. The system is composed of a main control rule module and a rule module for converting digit data to text, and a rule module for deciding intermediate and final conclusions. To produce a predictive decision for blast pressure change, we first

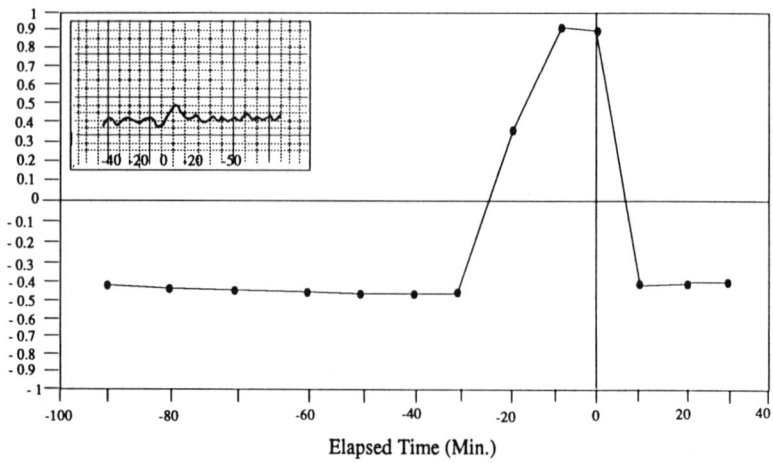

FIGURE 3.6. Simulation test result (smaller rectangular graph stands for actual result).

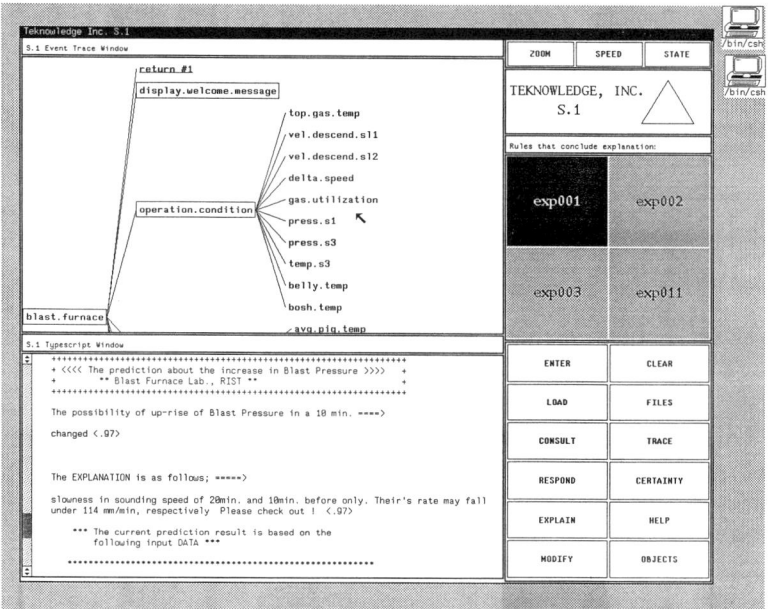

FIGURE 3.7. S.1 window frame under reasoning of blast pressure prediction.

used operational data, and then drew final results from a intermediate conclusion. The intermediate conclusions have two kinds of results, such as 'changed', and 'unchanged,' which mean maintenance and break-down of internal balances in view of some presumed aspects.

The final results can also be obtained as 'changed' and 'unchanged' blast pressure with accumulative values of certainty factors val-

Item \ Time [Min.]		- 50	-40	-30	-20	-10	0	Prediction
Certainty for Blast pressure increase	1 -1							
Actual Blast Pressure $(g/cm^2 \times 10^{-3})$	4.0 3.7 3.4							- STND DATA - CURR DATA
Sounding Speed (mm/Min.)	230 180 130							- STND DATA - CURR DATA
S P 1 $(g/cm^2 \times 10^{-3})$	3.4 2.9 2.0							- STND DATA - CURR DATA
S P 3 $(g/cm^2 \times 10^{-3})$	3.3 2.8 2.3							- STND DATA - CURR DATA
Top Gas Temp. (℃)	206 156 106							- STND DATA - CURR DATA

FIGURE 3.8. Blast pressure prediction image of actual system in POSCO No. 3 BF.

ues. Two values about blast pressure in 10 minutes should compete with each other to give a final prediction. As the knowledge base of the system is mainly composed of the 'changed' blast pressure, the meaning of 'changed' blast pressure is greater than that of 'unchanged.' The total prediction results can be determined by manipulating the certainty factor values of 'changed' and 'unchanged.' The results of each prediction can be plotted with certainty factors to represent the degree of increase of blast pressure in 10 minutes, on which actually measured blast pressure is recorded on a diagnosing interface. (Figure 3.8)

Major concerned factors on the blast pressure change are shown on the same screen for easy reference. This system has been operational since April, 1990 and is a subset of a total prediction system for abnormal conditions in blast furnace operations.

6. CONCLUSION

The expert system to predict blast pressure in blast furnace operations has been developed by starting from an off-line based prototype to an on-line based system. The system gathers information concerning the prediction of blast pressure during daily operations, selects various abnormal cases using information from both operation manuals and expert advice as a knowledge base, and then informs users of its predictions. Through its development and application, we obtained reasonable results both from prototype and actual systems. The system is successfully running at the No. 3 Blast Furnace of POSCO since April of 1990. It is expected that the experiences described herein will be much help in building other systems for blast furnace operations which is also to be the object of our next study.

REFERENCES

1. Albaxana, O.T. & Argyropoulos, S.A. (1988). Journal of Metals, Oct., 6.
2. Ho, Y.S., Ock, L.I., Young, L.J. & Soo, H.Y. (1988). Korean information Science Review, Vol. 6: 2, 19.
3. POSCO (1987): Final report for decision of blast furnace conditions.
4. Nippon Steel Company Ltd. (1982). Handbook of Ironmaking.
5. Tsunosaki, Y. & Tokekoshi, A. Nippon Kokan Technical Report. Overses 5.
6. Weiss, S.M. & Kulikowski, C.A. (1984). A practical guide to designing expert systems. Roman & Allanheld Publishers.
7. Yui, K. (1987). AI 87 Japan, ABSTRACT 417.

An Expert System for Elevator Design

HIROKAZU TAKI, TSUNEYOSHI KATSUYAMA, HIDEKAZU TSUJI,[1]
AKIHIKO NAITO,[2] MOTONORI YOSHIDA AND KIHATIROU OHNISHI[3]

Mitsubishi Electric Corporation, [1]Information Systems and Electronics Development Laboratory,
[2]Head Office, [3]Inazawa Works

1. INTRODUCTION

IN DESIGNING manufactured goods, an estimation process constitutes an important step in checking whether design requirements are satisfied or not. We have applied this process to the design of elevators and have developed an elevator design expert system. In this chapter, we introduce our system, its development process and its problem solving model.

Generally, expert systems are classified as being of either of two types: the analytical type or the synthetic type. A diagnosis expert system is a typical example of the analytical type, while a design system is an example of the synthetic type. Synthetic type systems must treat bigger solution spaces than the analytical type systems. Most currently available expert systems are of the analytical type. Their solution spaces are not big and their problem solving processes are not so complex. However, design problem systems have to handle a huge number of combinations of parts, and thus a huge number of candidate solutions. Most of the knowledge in a design problem can be represented in the form of constraints which express relationships among objects (Marcus, 1987). Since we chose to develop a design expert system on an expert system shell which has a deductive inference engine using production rules, we had to convert the constraints into rules. Therefore, we initially analyze the design process and determine the main tasks involved in the design process. These tasks consist of a generate process, a test process and a modify process, in order to layout part positions according to the constraints. We define certain operators to build these tasks based on previous research outlined in EXPERT MODEL (Taki, 1987). We describe these knowledge representations in the later sections of this chapter.

2. ELEVATOR DESIGN SYSTEM DEVELOPMENT PROCESS

In this section, we explain our design system development process and the system overview. Testing and evaluation of the system was carried out in our factory and is explained in section 3.1.

2.1. The Elevator Design Problem

Design problems can be separated into three classes as follows (Chandrasekaran, 1986):
1. Class-1 design: design components and design methods are unknown.
2. Class-2 design: design components are known, but design methods are not known.
3. Class-3 design: design components and design methods are known.

Mitsubishi Electric Corporation manufactures many kinds of products. The design process for these products covers all three classes. In order to develop design expert systems, it is necessary to extract layout knowledge and parts selection knowledge. However, such knowledge is not available for class-1 and class-2 problems in real design situations. Therefore, we confined our research to class-3 routine design problems and selected elevator design as an appropriate application.

Mitsubishi Electric Inazawa Works have been producing elevators for sixty years. Therefore, it was clear to us that the design knowledge was available and would not be difficult to acquire for the system development.

There are two main kinds of orders for elevators. One is the mass production type elevator whose design is fixed and complete before its order. The other is a custom design which must be specially designed for each order. In this research we focus on the custom design of elevators.

2.2. Parts of Elevator

We now explain a typical traction elevator. This type of elevator lifts a car by cables which are controlled with a counterweight and a traction machine. Figure 4.1 shows the main components of the elevator. These consist of the car, counterweights, the traction machine, a governor which controls the car speed, a machine beam, rails, buffer, etc. The combination of parts and the scale of each part are selected in accordance with design requirements. For example, the car is designed according to maximum weight capacity derived from the number of passengers. The power of the traction machine is selected according to the total weight of the car, counterweight, cables, etc. Since each piece of equipment must be arranged in the narrow space of a building, the spatial constraints make the layout design hard. Therefore, the designer spends much time in designing.

2.3. Knowledge Acquisition and Knowledge Types

The knowledge acquisition process to extract the design knowledge from an expert was done through interviewing. A knowledge engineer from our laboratory stayed at Inazawa Works for one month. He firstly studied the

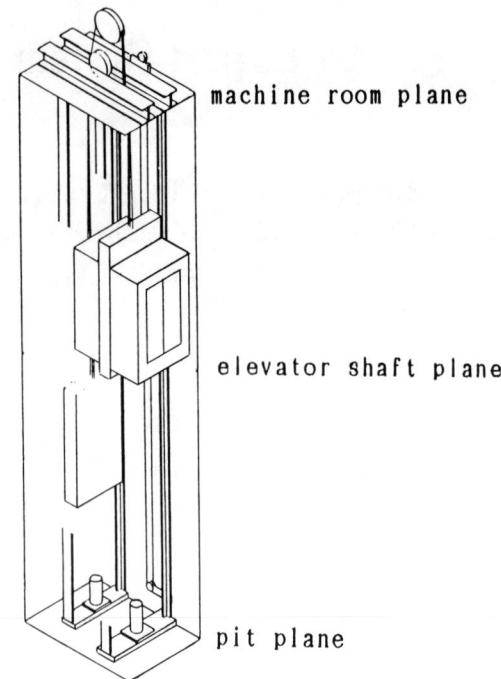

FIGURE 4.1. An elevator configuration.

concepts and basic functions of elevator parts, after which he interviewed the experts about the design process. He extracted relations of parts, partial design processes, parts selection processes and other criteria, and set out the whole design process. We now explain the design process and the extracted fragments of knowledge, as follows:

2.3.1. The Overall Design Process. First, a designer selects the necessary equipment for the elevator according to the requirements of design specifications. He then lays out this equipment under satisfactory conditions in the space of a building.

2.3.2. Knowledge of Layout of Three Dimensional Space. The elevator equipment is laid out in the three dimensional space of the building, and thus its layout is very complex. However, the designer can decompose three dimensional space into three planes. These are the machine room, the elevator shaft and the pit (an underground room). The machine room contains a traction motor, a governor, and machine beams; the elevator shaft contains a car, a counterweight, etc.; and the pit contains a buffer and other equipment.

2.3.3. Equipment Selection Knowledge. Before the equipment layout process begins, the designer selects equipment from parts catalogues according to design requirements. If the subsequent layout process fails, he selects another equipment set. This knowledge can be represented in production rules. In the simple case, the premise part of a production rule is a design specification and the action part is the required equipment. Normally, a few initial specifications lead to a more detailed specification, which in turn leads to equipment selection.

2.3.4. Relations of Equipment. There are two types of relations between pieces of equipment:

1. One type of relation is based on the implementation of a partial function of the elevator. A piece of equipment will not work if it does not have certain relations with another piece of equipment. If the relation is not satisfied, a particular function of the elevator will not be realized.

2. The other type of relation is a spatial relation based on physical constraints. For example, two objects cannot be located in the same place. The knowledge engineer extracted these relations and made maps of object relations. Figure 4.2 shows certain of the equipment relations.

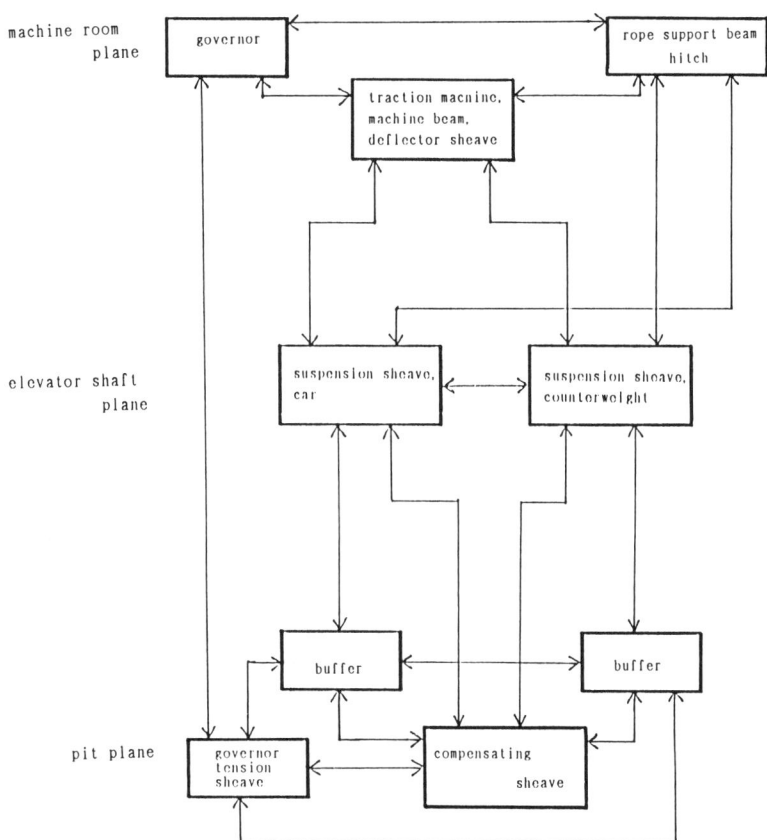

FIGURE 4.2. Equipment relations.

2.3.5. Partial Design Processes. The designer possesses efficient partial design process knowledge through his experience. This knowledge consists of short procedures for design problem solving, and is useful in deciding the total detailed design process. It is also useful in deciding how to use constraints and translate them into rules.

2.4. Knowledge Representation

In this section, we explain the problem solving model and its operators. We also introduce design objects which in this case are pieces of equipment. We will discuss how extracted knowledge is translated into appropriate knowledge representations.

2.4.1. Problem Solving Model. We discuss the layout problem solving model in this subsection. We select a generate-test-modify model for our layout problem, and define detailed representation forms of this model. Operators used in this model are explained in the next subsection.

1. *Role of generators.* They produce candidates consisting of parts, part combinations and part positions.

2. *Role of testers.* They check whether parts and their relations satisfy constraints or not.

3. *Roles of modifiers.* They modify some parameters of a part (for example, a part location) which do not satisfy some constraints.

To make an efficient problem solving system using a generate and test model, we must consider constraints and make efficient generators which do not result in many candidates being rejected by testers, and we must implement an intelligent backtracking mechanism. Fortunately, elevator design experts have efficient generator knowledge, so that the candidate rejection rate is low. For the case where rejection does occur, we have implemented a modification mechanism as a part of the intelligent backtracking mechanism.

2.4.2. Problem Solving Primitives (Operators). Several researchers propose problem solving primitives. Generic tasks (Chandrasekaran, 1986) are a type of primitive which are derived from the experience of developing several expert systems. Other kinds of primitives are used in heuristic classification research (Clancy, 1985). The role-limiting method (or half weak method) (McDermott, 1988) proposes domain-independent tasks. In this research, we use operators in the generate-test-modify model in order to arrange knowledge and derive rules from constraints. Our operators are based on those proposed in EXPERT MODEL (Taki, 1987), and consist of eight types of operations: selection, classification, combination, translation, ordering, input, output and generation. The translation operation consists of three suboperations: calculation operation, value replacement operation and element decomposition operation. Before explaining relations between operators and the generate-test-modify model used in this system, we list the operators as follows:

generator:
(1) equipment selection from a set of equipment
(2) location selection from a set of locations
(3) calculation of values (e.g. size, length) using mathematical functions
(4) replacement of values (e.g. data abstraction)
(5) equipment combination

tester:
(6) value checking
(7) relation checking

modifier:
(8) value increment or decrement

(1), (2), (6) and (7) correspond to a selection operator in EXPERT MODEL, (3) to a calculation operator, (4) to a value replacement operator, (5) to a combination operator, and (8) corresponds to a generate operator. The generate operator in this model is used both for generation and modification. The EXPERT MODEL system provided us with enough knowledge to build the operators, which we then used to accommodate the layout constraints.

2.5. Knowledge Encoding

In this section, we explain the relations between extracted knowledge, represented as fragments of knowledge of parts and their attributes, and operators. We also introduce knowledge representation in ESP (Mitsubishi, 1988), an object-oriented Prolog-like language developed by ICOT (Institute for New Generation Computer Technology) for PSI machines.

2.5.1. Relations Between Constraints and Operators. Extracted knowledge is encoded in the following translation flow diagram:

Extract Knowledge (Problem Solving) →
  Generate, Test and Modify Model →
    Operators → Code of Implementation Representation

Extract Knowledge (Attributes of Objects) →
  Frame Representation   → Code

Knowledge for design problem solving is translated into operators using a generate-test-modify task model. These operators are then translated into implementation codes expressed in the ESP language. Knowledge of design components and their attributes is treated as data for operators and is arranged in frame format. It is subsequently encoded as variables and values in the ESP language. We initially explain relations between problem solving knowledge of elevator design and the generate-test-modify model. We explain how to make location generators from extracted constraints.

Knowledge of layout is what decides the two-dimensional location of an object. In the equipment layout problem, there are three types of location generators.

1. The first operator for location generation sets the object in a given area without other constraints. This operator is constructed from three types of information: the two extreme limits for the location, and possible intermediate locations which are generated between limits. The initial location is at one of the limits. These items of information are derived from an area constraint and a quantizing constraint which determines a numerical location from analogue expressions of the area constraint.

2. The second operator calculates a location for the object using location data of other objects. We must translate relations of objects (mostly physical relations) into mathematical equations. In order to make this operator, we must analyze these equations to fix their input and output values.

3. The third operator selects a location from a location candidate set. We must prepare the location candidate set. We must extract these location candidate from the expert, and make them into the location set.

2.5.2. Sample of Implementation Representation. We introduce an implementation representation sample, written in the ESP language. The following description shows a selection operator which determines door equipment.

```
class door-selection has
:select (Class,Door,Doortype,Doorspec):-
door (Door,Doortype,Doorspec);

local
door (door1,type1,Doorspec):- Doorspec <=800, Doorspec => 1400;
door (door2,type1,Doorspec):- Doorspec <=750, Doorspec => 1500;
door (door3,type2,Doorspec):- Doorspec <=700, Doorspec => 1100;
door (door4,type2,Doorspec):- Doorspec <=1100, Doorspec => 1500;

end.

(caution)
door1,door2,--are doornames and returnvalues.
type1,type2,--are doortypes and returnvalues.
```

This expression contains door specifications, and this knowledge selects doors according to door-specification and door-type requirements.

2.6. Design System Overview

The proposed system consists of two sub-systems: an equipment selection system and an equipment layout system, as shown in Figure 4.3.

2.6.1. Equipment Selection Sub-System. The equipment selection sub-system selects equipment according to design requirements, and has been implemented on our special expert system shell, Acekit (Mitsubishi, 1987). This shell is a kind of intelligent spread sheet. Equipment selection knowledge is represented in rule form. A working memory corresponds to tables or spread sheets. This inference engine checks whether table contents and the premises (if-part) of rules are matched or not. If a match succeeds, a rule is fired and it rewrites one or more items in the table. This change may cause another rule to fire, and the inference continues in this way. A sample design session using this sub-system is shown in the appendix.

2.6.2. Equipment Layout Sub-System. The equipment layout sub-system determines equipment layouts according to design specifications, a selected set of equipment, and design knowledge. The problem solving model used in this system is a generate-test-modify model as we explained in section 2.4. The system designs three planes: the machine room, the elevator shaft, and the pit, and uses equipment determined by the equipment selection sub-system. However, if the layout process fails, the equipment selection system has to select another set of equipment by backtracking. The result of the layout is shown in three windows. After the system lays out all equipment which satisfies design constraint specifications, it asks the user whether the result is satisfactory or not. If the user rejects it, the system searches for another solution. When the user accepts it, the system calculates more detailed information (e.g., data for manufacturing). Samples of layout

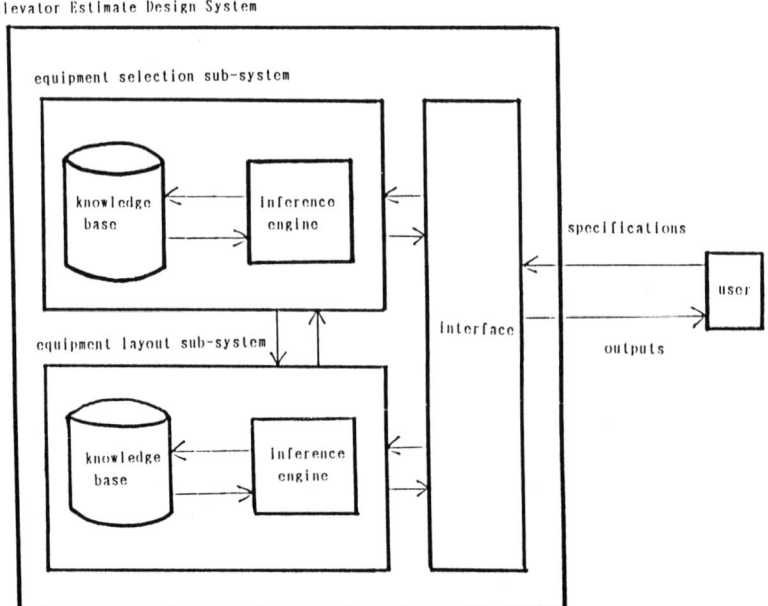

FIGURE 4.3. System configuration.

results are shown in the appendix. The complete system can generate a result ten times faster than a human expert, and therefore save a great deal of the expert's design time.

3. IMPLEMENTATION PROCESS

3.1. Deployment Strategies

The layout system generates results which satisfy design requirements. However, since elevators carry humans, designers must guarantee safety. Therefore, the system is set up in the factory, and the expert designer carries out practical tests as an aid to the design process. Currently, the results of system-designed elevators are being compared with those of a human expert.

3.2. Technology Transfer Strategies

Our laboratory has two kinds of technology transfer programs. One of them teaches the methodology of expert system building, and is called SOLOMON (Ichikawa, 1990). The other teaches how to carry out maintenance in a prototype system and how to add new rules into the knowledge base.

We believe that the most important function of technology transfer is that of educating new knowledge engineers in the organization.

3.3. Maintenance Strategies

Elevator usage requirements are very varied. For example, there is a variety of speeds, load capacities and floor sizes. In our system, maintenance of currently stored knowledge is constantly being carried out in order to facilitate the addition of new knowledge. A knowledge engineer in the factory is eliciting new knowledge from many designers, and a maintenance engineer arranges and encodes the knowledge in the system.

4. SUMMARY

We have introduced our elevator design system and its development process. The system consists of an equipment selection sub-system and an equipment layout sub-system. We adopted a generate-test-modify model as the problem solving strategy. The proposed system enables the human designer to speed up the problem solving process considerably.

We have also established a knowledge extraction process using a particular knowledge representation consisting of operators. We are planning to use this method to build design expert systems in other fields.

REFERENCES

Chandrasekaran, B. (1986). Generic tasks in knowledge-based reasoning: High-level building blocks for expert system design, *IEEE Expert.* Fall, 23–30.

Clancy, W.J. (1985). Heuristic classification. *Artificial Intelligence.* 27(3), 289–350.

Ichikawa, T. (1990). A problem solving oriented system development methodology: SOLOMON. Japan Information Processing Society, Proc. of Tutorial of Information System Planning and Design, 241–257 (in Japanese).

Marcus, S., Stout, J. and McDermott, J. (1987). VT: An expert elevator designer that uses knowledge-based backtracking. *AI Magazine.* Winter 1987, 41–58.

McDermott, J. (1988). Preliminary steps toward a taxonomy of problem-solving methods. In S. Marcus ed., Automating knowledge acquisition for expert systems (p 225–256,) Boston: Kluwer Academic Publishers.

Mitsubishi Electric Corp (1987). MELCOM PSI-2 Intelligent spread sheet development tool ⟨Acekit⟩ Manual. (in Japanese).

Mitsubishi Electric Corp. (1988). MELCOM PSI-2 programming and operation total manual (in Japanese).

Taki, H., Tsubaki, K. and Iwashita, Y. (1987). Expert model for knowledge acquisition. *Proc. of IEEE 3rd Annual Expert Systems in Government Conference,* 117–124.

DESIGN PROCESS AND INTERACTION OF THE SYSTEM

We have proposed a system for the design of elevators. The system consists of two sub-systems: the equipment selection sub-system and the equipment layout sub-system. This appendix initially describes functions of the equipment selection sub-system. Figure A1 shows a multiple-window view of the

A Design Process and Interaction of The System

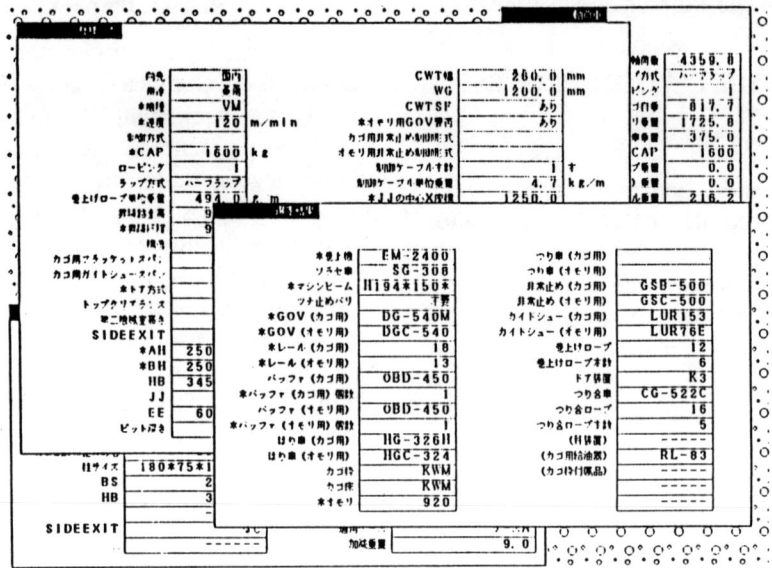

FIGURE A1. The parts selection windows.

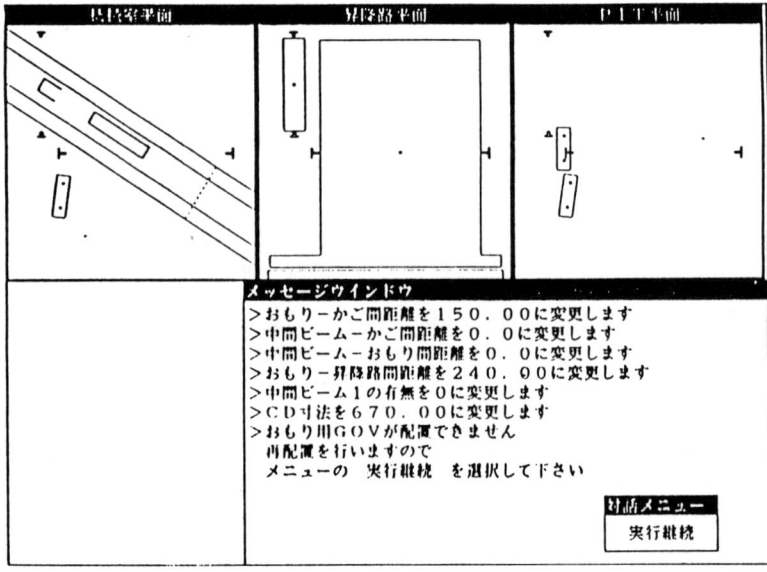

FIGURE A2. The windows of layout design.

Elevator Design

equipment selection sub-system in tabular form, which constitutes the user interface. The user inputs various requirements according to the data columns in the window spread-sheets, e.g., he inputs the speed of the car as 90m/minute in the upper left window. This input data affects many rules, which in turn determine various design items, one by one.

The equipment layout sub-system receives a set of equipment as layout objects from the equipment selection sub-system. Figure A2 shows the design process in five separate windows. The upper left window shows the plane of the machine room, with the governor located in the upper right and the machine beam located between the upper left and the lower right corner of the room.

The upper middle window shows the plane of the elevator shaft. The car is located at the center and a counterweight at the upper left corner of the room.

The upper right window shows the plane of the pit in Figure A2. A tension sheave and a compensating sheave are located in the upper right side and the left side of the room.

The lower right window shows the system messages which include inferencing process messages and interactive questions. The lower left window is designed for showing results of design parameters.

Figure A3 shows a top-view of the machine room plane of the elevator. It contains a machine beam on which a traction machine is located; two governors which keep a safe speed for the elevator; and two T-marks which show the counterweight location and the car location. In the layout process, these parts are located by generation operators and their locations are checked by test operators. If a design constraint is not satisfied, a modify operator alters location-parameters.

Figure A4 shows the elevator shaft plane, with

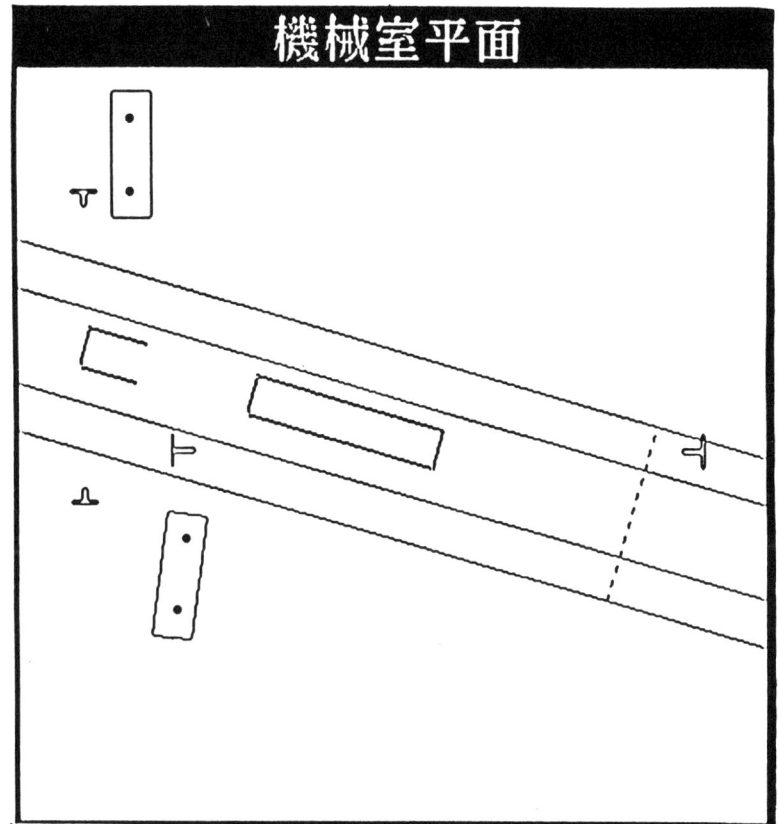

FIGURE A3. A window of a machine room plane.

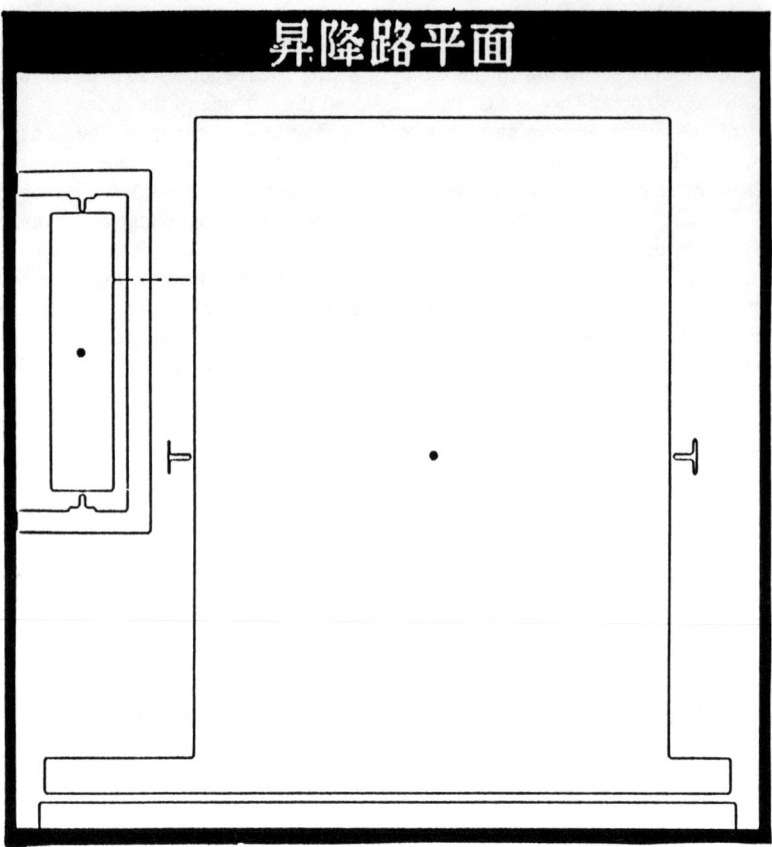

FIGURE A4. A window of an elevator shaft plane.

a top-view of the elevator car and the counterweight. The big box located at the center of the window is the car. At the lower side is the entrance/exit of the car, and at the upper left is the counterweight. As the counterweight is located on the left in this case, the center of the car is shifted to the right. If the counterweight is located in the upper side, the center of the car is shifted to the lower side.

Figure A5 shows the pit plane, with a top-view of buffers and sheaves. The two small circles are buffers which are located in the center and at the left. Two sheaves are located in the upper left and the lower left. The two T-marks show locations of the car and the counterweight.

Figure A6 shows output of the equipment layout sub-system, illustrating the solution layout in seven windows. The upper three windows show locations of the main equipment. However, these windows do not include detailed location information, which is shown as parameter values in the lower three windows. The upper left window shows equipment locations in the machine room; the upper middle window shows the car and counterweight locations of the elevator shaft; and the upper right window shows buffer locations in the pit. The lower left window shows detailed values of equipment locations in the machine room, e.g., coordinate values of part locations and the distance between one part and another.

The second window from the lower left also shows detailed values of equipment locations in the elevator shaft. The third window from the lower left shows detailed values of equipment locations in the pit. The lower right small window shows interaction messages.

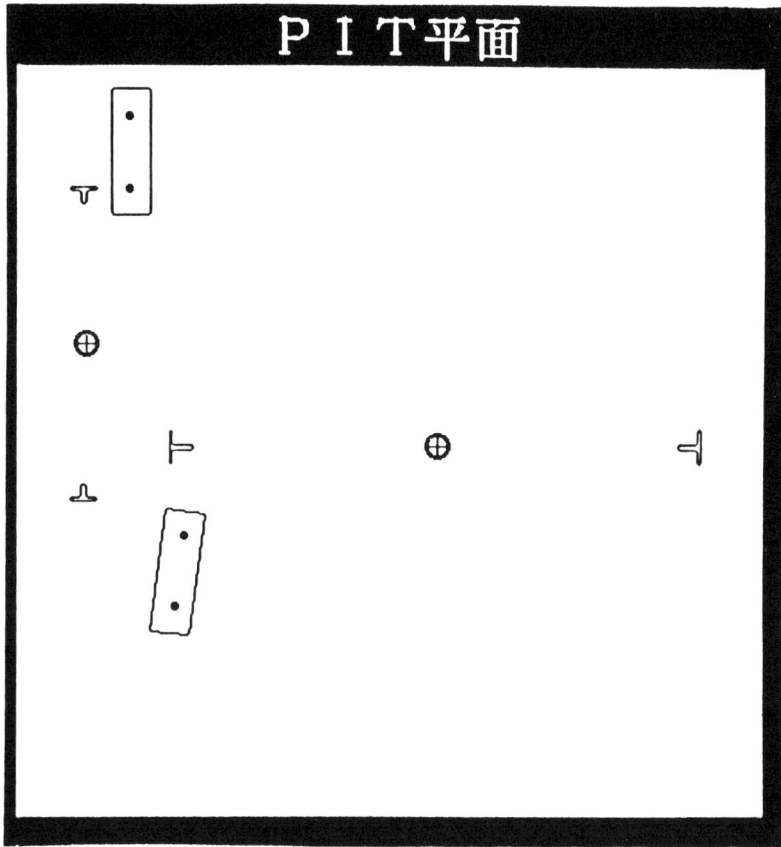

FIGURE A5. A window of a pit plane.

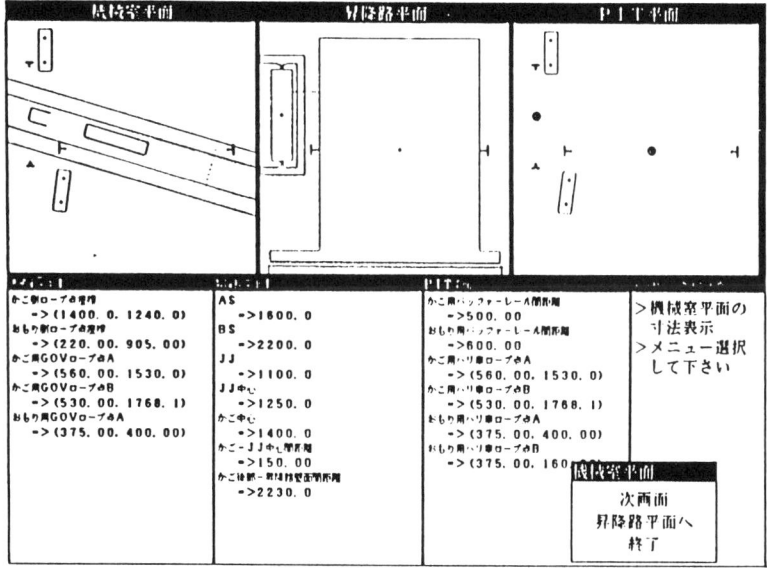

FIGURE A6. Output of the equipment layout sub-system.

Alarm Based Operational Guidance System

SEIICHI TERUNUMA,* HIROSHI TAKATSUTO,* MEGUMU YOSHIDA,**
HIROKI YAMAMOTO**** AND TOMOKO KANEKO***

*Power Reactor and Nuclear Fuel Development Corporation, Ibaraki, Japan;
**TOSHIBA Corporation, Isogo Engineering Center, Yokohama, Japan;
***TOSHIBA Corporation, Fuchu Works, Tokyo, Japan;
****TOSHIBA Corporation, Nuclear Engineering Laboratory, Kawasaki, Japan.

1. INTRODUCTION

AN ALARM based operational guidance system has been developed for safe and stable plant operation and improved reliability.

Development of the system was started in 1984, making use of an experimental fast reactor JOYO which is the first plant in the chain of liquid metal fast reactor development in Japan. Main programs and a part of the knowledge base were constructed in 1985. The knowledge base was extended and the system validation was performed by connecting it to the operator training simulator. As a result, a display of the system was installed in the JOYO central control room and its on-line operation was started by partially linking it to the actual plant in May 1988.

The system uses an artificial intelligence (AI) technology to support the plant operator by presenting a causal alarm, selecting a suitable guidance diagram and monitoring sequence actions in anomaly plant situations. Its main components are a knowledge base and an inference engine. The knowledge base is a collection of valuable operation experience and plant design information.

The inference engine frames alarm sequences by referring to the knowledge base and diagnoses in the plant emergency conditions. The result of the diagnosis is displayed on a cathode ray tube (CRT), and the most appropriate operational diagram which enables plant operators to take the first necessary action is output from a printer.

1.1. The System

It is very important for a large scale complex plant to take proper and quick action under abnormal conditions. In such a plant, many alarms are sometimes induced from a single causal alarm. The operator must identify the cause from among the many alarms, and take proper and quick action. But this is one of the most difficult tasks for operators, because it requires plant knowledge, operation experience and skill. In order to reduce the burden on the operations, the development of the alarm based operational guidance system was initiated. The major objective of this system is to supply operators quickly with information concerning the cause of alarm (first hit alarm) and the sequence abnormality of major equipment interlocks (sequence monitoring), and with guidance indicating proper steps to be taken (first operation) when numerous alarms occurred.

This system has the following three main functions.

1. Identifying the cause of abnormal events (called the causal alarm function): This function looks for the cause of abnormal events and determines, from among many activated alarms, the one which is closest to

the cause of these alarms and outputs the associated information for display.

2. Monitoring the operation of the major plant interlocks (called as the sequence monitoring function): As to the main device sequential operations and alarms which must occur instantaneously or with predetermined delay after an event, an operation prediction is made based on the interlock sequence logic. When a predicted operation fails to occur within the specified time period, it is identified that the sequence proceeded abnormally and the associated information is output for display.

3. Selecting the alarm which must be dealt with first by the operator and also selecting a pertinent manual for the alarm (called as the first operation alarm function): From the abnormal condition and the importance levels of alarms, this function selects an alarm which an operator must first cope with and outputs operation manual information associated with that alarm. Here for simplicity, the alarm, which must be dealt with first by the operator, is called 'the first operation alarm.'

Even when multiple events resulting from different causes occur simultaneously, this system is capable of identifying individual abnormal condition from one another and making diagnosis for each of the abnormal condition.

This paper describes the diagnosis method and the verification test result of this system.

2. DEVELOPMENT SCHEDULE

The development of this system was started in 1984, based on a development schedule which consists of the following steps:
1. Design for system concept.
2. Development of the software.
3. Fabrication of the knowledge base.
4. Verification test using on-site simulator.
5. Application to the actual plant.

The system concept was chosen to check the man-machine interfaces between the plant operators and the system, which includes the system function and the type of knowledge base. The knowledge base was fabricated step by step and its fabrication was completed in March 1990. Total rules of the design knowledge base were reached about 1400 rules as the "if-then" type of production rule. The software and the knowledge base was tested and improved using the on-site full scope simulator to verify the knowledge base and the diagnosis method. Thereafter, full scope actual operation of this system was started in November 1990.

3. SYSTEM CONFIGURATION

The hardware is comprised of a 32-bit mini computer (TOSBAC DS600/40 II), a image information filing device (TOSFILE) and two cathode ray tubes (CRTs). One is utilized for diagnosis results and other is for program management. The hardware configuration is shown in Figure 5.1. Flow of the system processing is shown in Figure 5.2. The main process of the system is classified in the following 3 steps:

1. *Monitor process.* On/off signals of alarms and major equipment status and process states (analog values) are accessed in real time to monitor the operating conditions of the plant.

2. *Diagnosis process.* How the abnormal condition has propagated is determined by using the plant status data and the knowledge base on the plant and performs the identifying the causal alarm, monitoring plant sequence and selecting the first operation.

3. *Output and man-machine process.* Results of the above diagnosis are displayed on a CRT after six seconds and an operation diagram that describes the corrective actions to be taken are automatically output from the TOSFILE after 30 seconds, when the signal that shows the plant abnormality was triggered in the system. In addition to this, on demand from an operator, the following functions of man-machine communication are provided:

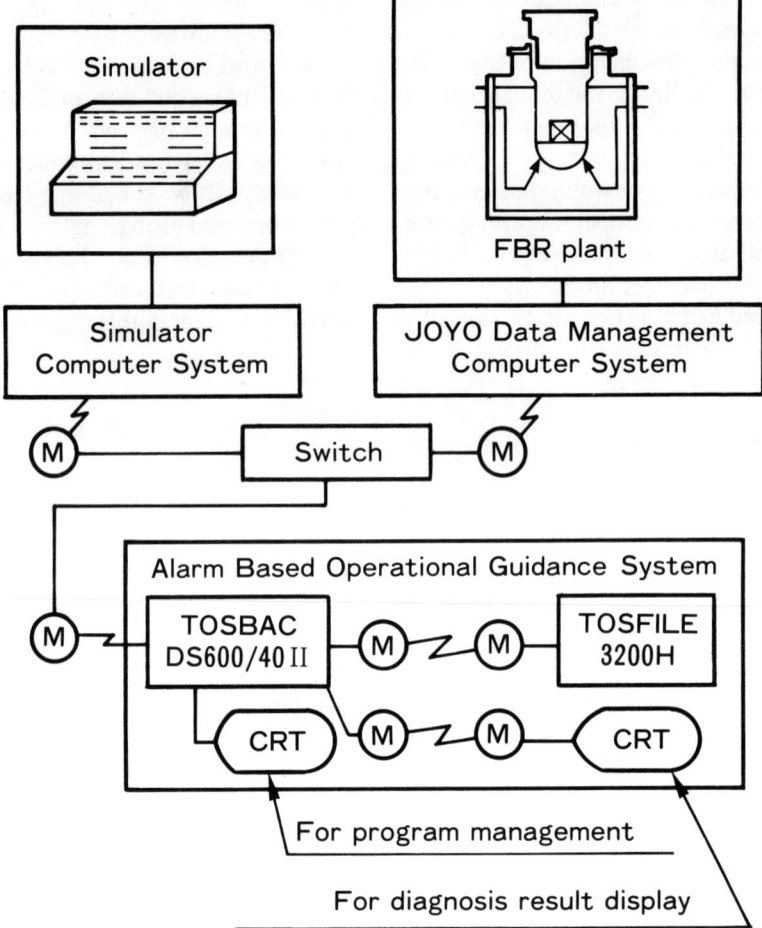

FIGURE 5.1. Hardware configuration.

- Presenting the process of inference.
- Displaying the emergency operation manuals.
- Displaying input signal status.

4. DETAIL OF THE SYSTEM

4.1. Monitor Process

Flow of the monitor and diagnosis processing are shown in Figure 5.3. The monitor process is divided into two smaller processes which are plant data acquisition process and anomaly monitoring process.

Plant Data Acquisition Process. The plant data acquisition process collects plant data from the actual plant, or simulated plant data from the operator training simulator. The actual plant to which this system is applied has a data management computer system, which takes in plant signals to supply operators with various kinds of plant information. For effective utilization of these existing facilities, it was decided to transfer the plant signals from the data management computer system to the computer of this system. As shown in Figure 5.1, the actual plant and the computer

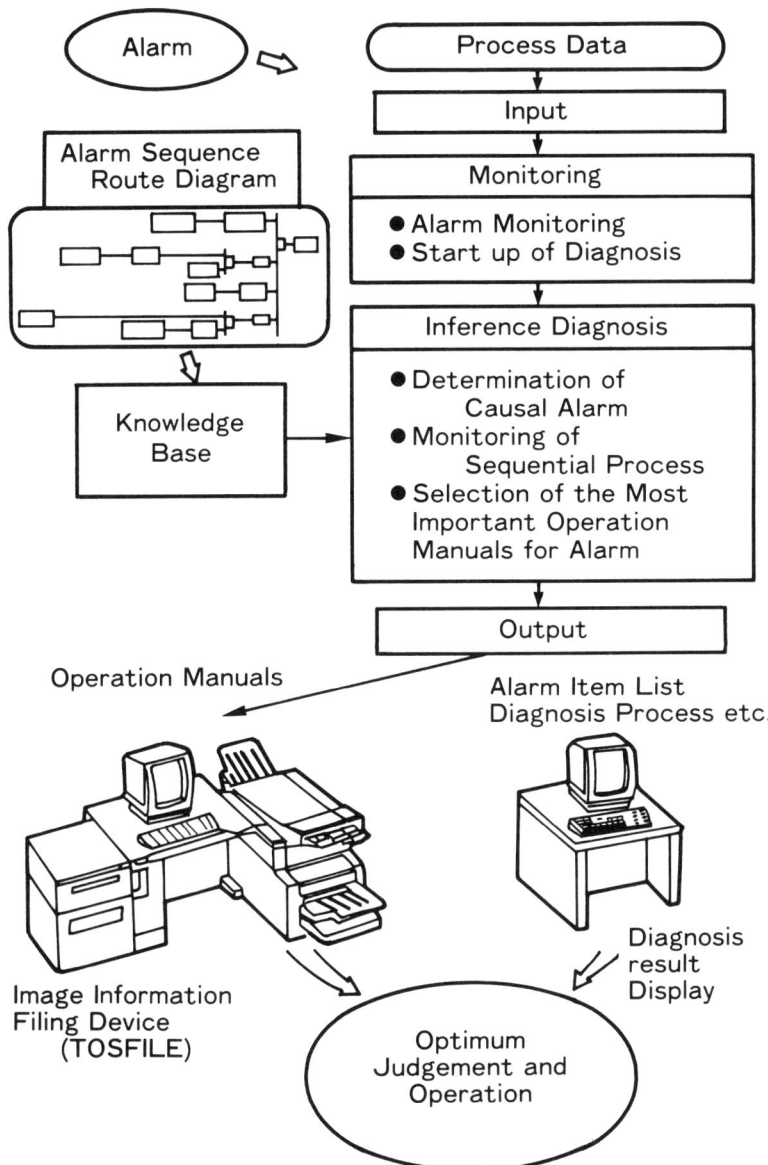

FIGURE 5.2. Flow of the system processing.

of the simulator can be switched over by a selector switch. The same format and procedure are applied to transmission both for the actual plant data and for the simulated plant data to this system.

The data management computer sends such data as plant alarms, on/off status of major equipments (about 700 points) and process states (analog values, about 40 points) to the computer of this system every two seconds. The anomaly monitoring function checks the data which are fed in at 2-seconds intervals.

Based on the data received, the anomaly

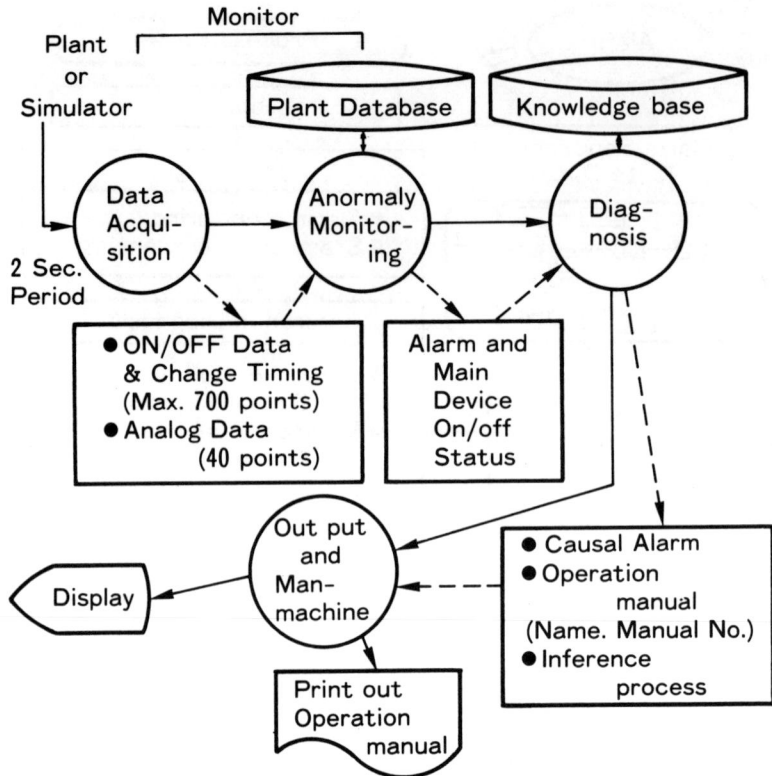

FIGURE 5.3. Flow of the monitor and diagnosis processing.

monitoring process first update the information in this system, such as status change including alarm and major equipment on/off status, status change time and analog value.

Each alarm and major equipment on/off status signal has a particular level of importance or urgency as follows:

1. Level A: Alarm signals which show the failure to start of a backup system which should operate automatically at the occurrence of a scram, an isolation of a containment vessel or a loss of an electric power etc.

2. Level B: Alarm signals which show the occurrence of a scram, an isolation of a containment vessel or a loss of an electric power etc.

3. Level C: Alarm signals which have the possibility of trigger for the occurrence of alarms categorized to level B.

4. Level D: Alarm signals which have the possibility of trigger for the occurrence of alarms categorized to level C.

5. Level E: Alarm signals except alarms categorized to above level A to D.

6. Level F: Major equipment on/off status signals which are necessary to describe the sequence between alarms.

Anomaly Monitoring Process. When an alarm has occurred at an importance level E or higher, the anomaly monitoring function starts the diagnosis process which is periodically activated at the interval of six seconds to make diagnosis on the data collected in three transmission cycles. In addition, the anomaly monitoring process also keeps the history of signal status change which may occur every two seconds.

In commonly known off-line expert systems, the fixed plant conditions which were already determined are entered into the system by some method (for example, by operator's input in the form of interrogation), and then a conclusion is drawn, thus terminating the diagnosis. However, in this system, where we aim at the real-time diagnosis in response to the continually changing conditions of the plant, it is necessary to perform diagnosis at certain intervals.

4.2. Diagnosis Process

The diagnosis part of this system is divided into an inference engine and a knowledge base. Its configuration is the most typical form as an expert systems.

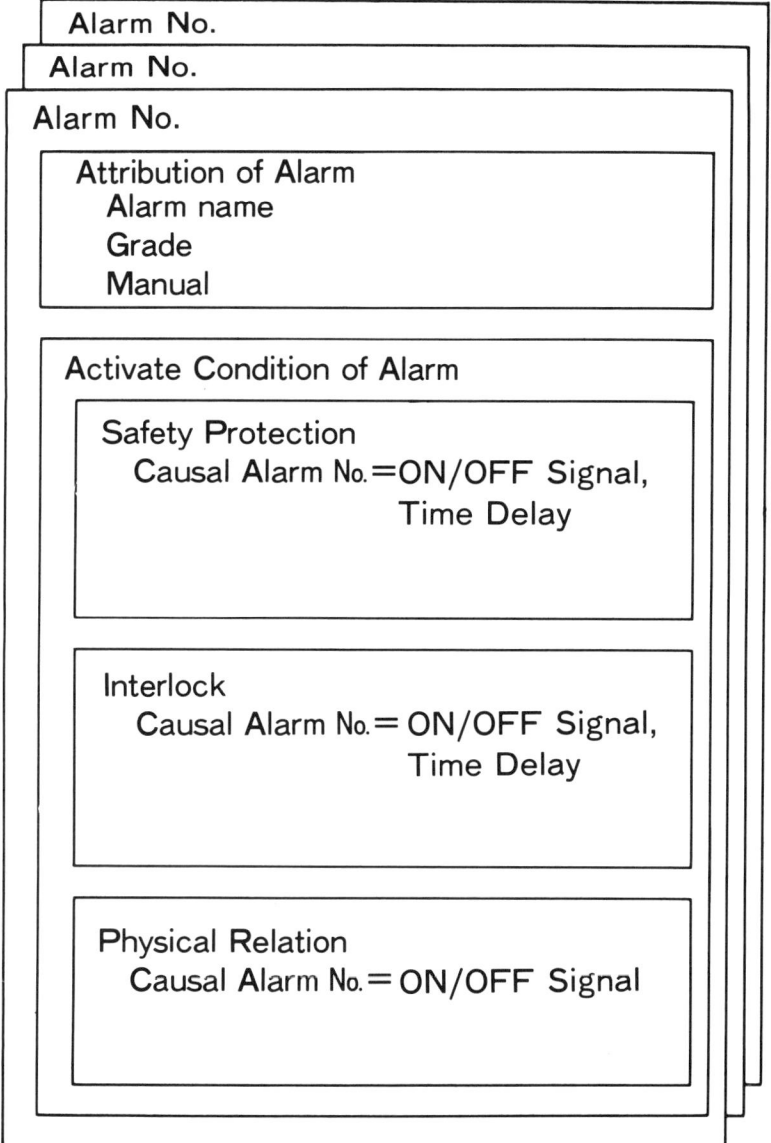

FIGURE 5.4. Constitution of design knowledge base.

Knowledge Base. The knowledge base consists of a design knowledge base and an experience knowledge base.

The design knowledge base contains an attribution and an activate conditions of each alarm in frame form as shown in Figure 5.4. The attribution consists of the importance level and the number of page of the operation manual corresponding to each alarm. The activate conditions contain alarm messages, relationship between alarms and time delays. The relationship is divided into those which propagate by physical causality and those which propagate by the actuation of a plant protection system or a plant interlock.

The experience knowledge base contains the empirical knowledge which is required to improve the accuracy of the inference diagnosis, in rule form as shown in Figure 5.5. The experience knowledge base is used to define the causal alarm or the first operation alarm in case these are not defined by using the design knowledge base.

Inference Engine. The inference engine consists of an alarm handling diagnosis part and a pattern diagnosis part.

In the alarm handling diagnosis part, only the binary signals which contain the alarm signals and major equipment on/off status signals are treated, and the status of each binary signal, which can cause the activated alarm, is checked with the relationship between alarms stored in the design knowledge base. As a result of this processing, the alarm sequence of activated alarms is determined. The alarms which does not have any activated upstream alarms is judged as the causal alarm of events (see Figure 5.6). Several alarms may be identified as the causal alarm, in some cases. If these alarms influence each other, the causal alarm is determined by the occurrence time. If these alarms are not influencing each other, it is assumed that several abnormal events occurred.

The sequence monitoring which is another function of the alarm handling part is carried

- Pattern 1
  - IF(alarm A=ON) AND (alarm B=ON)
  - (alarm C=OFF)
  - THEN"Causal Alarm"=alarm D

- Pattern 2
  - IF(alarm A=ON) AND (alarm E=C.A*)
  - THEN"Causal Alarm"=alarm E

- Pattern 3
  - IF(alarm A=ON)
  - AND (Measurement Value X<Prediction Value Y)
  - THEN"First Operation"=alarm F

(Note)* : Shown that alarm E is identified with one of the Causal Alarm in the alarm handling diagnosis process.

FIGURE 5.5. Constitution of experience knowledge base.

Alarm Based Operational System

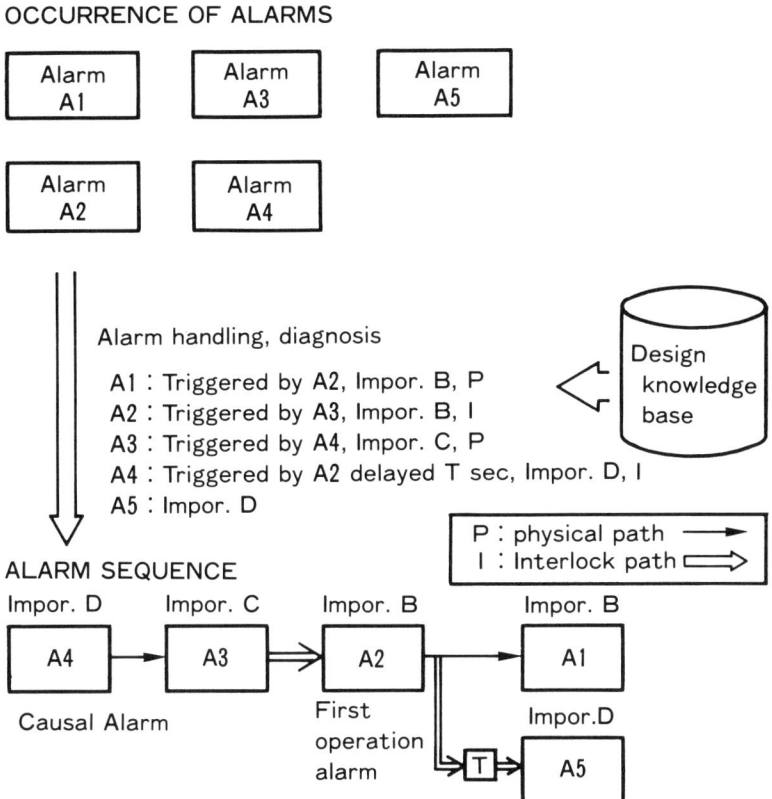

FIGURE 5.6. Fabrication schema of alarm sequence diagram.

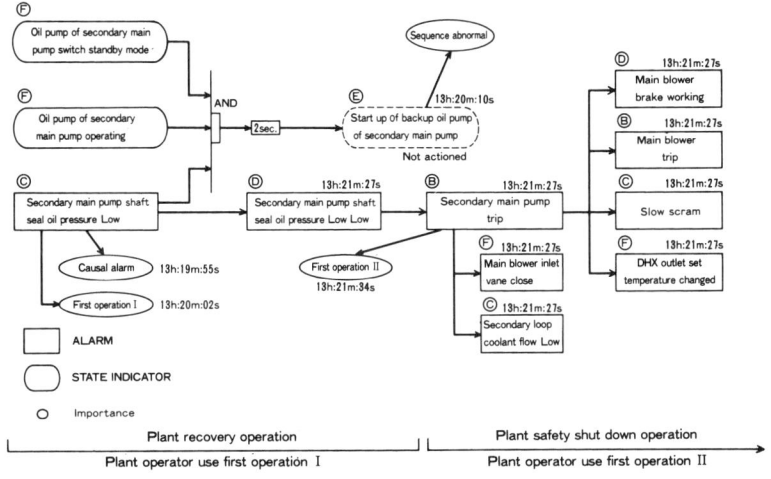

FIGURE 5.7. Alarm sequence diagram.

out. The presence of alarms which are certainly triggered by other alarms in the alarm sequence are checked. If such an alarm is present, it is regarded as a predicted alarm together with the delay time associated with it. If a predicted alarm whose delay time has already run out is present at the next diagnosis period, this system checks whether or not the predicted alarm is actually occurring.

In the pattern diagnosis part, the processing result from the alarm handling diagnosis part is compared with the patterns stored in the experience knowledge base. If the same pattern exists, the processing is carried out to define the causal alarm or the first operation alarm.

The path of these inference diagnosis process is output for display.

4.3. Example of System Function

An example of an alarm sequence which is prepared in the alarm handling diagnosis part is shown in Figure 5.7.

This example is the abnormality which is caused by the occurrence of "secondary main pump shaft seal oil pressure low." After "secondary main pump shaft seal oil pressure low-low" occurs, tripping the secondary main pump, the abnormality expands, because "backup oil pump for secondary main pump start failure" occurs as a consequence. Preparing this alarm sequence in the alarm diagnosis part, "secondary main pump shaft seal oil pressure low" which does not have any activated upstream alarms, is judged as the causal alarm. "Secondary main pump trip" has the highest importance level and the most upstream alarm in the alarm sequence. So, "secondary main pump trip" is judged as the first operation alarm. Also, "backup oil pump for secondary main pump start failure" is judged an anomaly by the sequence monitoring, because a stand-by component did not start in spite of the shut down of the usual component.

The diagnosis result displayed in this example is shown in Figure 5.8.

The screen has three areas: one for a causal alarm, one for a first operation alarm and one for displaying the abnormal sequence.

The causal alarm area shows the name of the alarm which was determined as the first hit alarm, the alarm number on the annunciator panel, and the time of occurrence. In this example, "Secondary main pump shaft seal oil pressure low" is displayed.

The first operation alarm area shows the name of the manual associated with the first operation alarm, and level of importance which is mentioned in the chapter of 4.1 monitor process. In this example, two first operation alarms are displayed. One is the secondary main pump shaft seal pressure low,

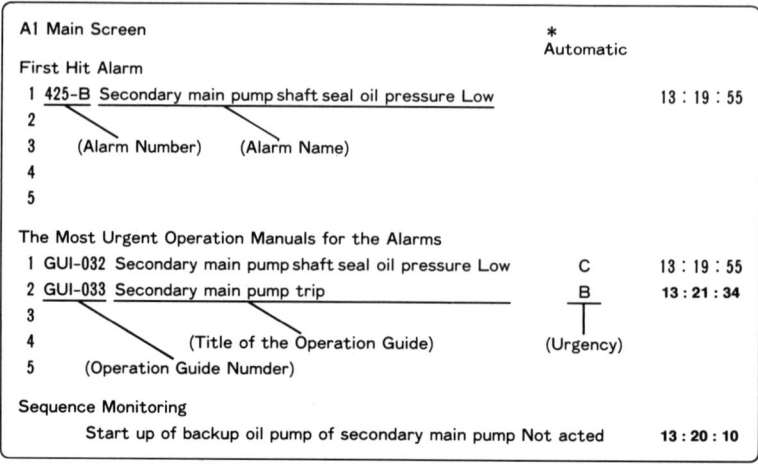

FIGURE 5.8. Example of diagnosis result.

whose purpose is to recover the oil pressure trouble. The other is the secondary main pump trip whose purpose is to shut down the plant safely.

The sequence monitoring area displays the name of the alarm/equipment action that failed to occur at predicted time. In this example, "Back up oil pump start failure for secondary main pump" is displayed.

5. VALIDATION

Validation of this system was carried out using the simulator according to a test procedure. The main purposes of this validation test are as follows:
- Verification of the knowledge base
- Improvement of a diagnosis system including the inference engine

This system was tested with about 500 cases of malfunction. To achieve the main purposes above, the information output from this system was inspected by many plant specialists, and the knowledge base and inference engine were improved. Based on the verification test, the following results are noted.
1. In this system, a frame type expression is used in the design knowledge base. As a result, the design knowledge data is easily enlarged and flexible to use.
2. In order to improve and refine the knowledge base, the application of AI techniques is very important. Advanced diagnosis methods used in plant operation experience will be incorporated into this system. These methods include feed-back from many verification tests.
3. By using the simulator which includes the JOYO dynamic characteristic model, the "know-how" of plant operation experts is added to the knowledge base. The rules of the design knowledge base were reached at about 1400 rules and the experience knowledge base became 45 one.
4. According to the verification test results, we have verified the usefulness of this system for plant operator support. Especially in the occurrence of the multi-caused abnormality, the information from the system is very helpful to the operators.

6. APPLICATION EXPERIENCES

On-line operation with the system partially connected to the actual plant "JOYO" was started in May, 1988, and full scope operation was in November, 1990. Through the on-line operation, signals of minor trouble were input to this system and the following operational experiences are obtained.
1. The diagnosis result and the operation diagram are output in good timing to the operator's actions.
2. The system function was confirmed satisfactory in the operation of the actual plant.

We are going to operate this system continuously and will improve its man-machine and operator supporting functions.

7. CONCLUSION

The system development placed an emphasis on the ability to provide an operator with quick and precise information about the cause of alarms during abnormal conditions in the large complex plant and with guidance for proper corrective actions to be taken, and could improve the operability of the plant.

As the application experience in JOYO increases, further knowledge will be gained to increase the knowledge base to cover the entire plant. The man-machine function will also improve to make it easy and effective to use. We are studying a more sophisticated diagnosis function that can determine the details of a cause for anomaly.

Diagnosis System for a Gas Turbine Air Conditioning Plant

K. P. CHOW, K. CHUI, AND S. S. LO

Department of Computer Science, University of Hong Kong;
Operations Branch, Tsing Yi Power Station, China Light and Power Company, Limited;
Gas Turbine Branch, Tsing Yi Power Station, China Light and Power Company, Limited

1. INTRODUCTION

IN A RECENT RCM pilot project carried out at the Gas Turbine Office, Hok Un Power Station, Hong Kong and China Light Power Company Limited, a vast amount of knowledge was gathered about the BBC Gas Turbine Control Module Air Conditioning System, in order to collect a complete set of possible failure modes that can occur in the system. The objective of the study was to propose a set of tasks that can be scheduled as part of regular maintenance. One side effect of the project was that a set of failure effects were identified. These failure effects were derived from the set of failure modes determined in the study. Traditional data processing techniques can be used to computerize a set of schedule maintenance tasks. On the other hand, information, such as failure effects, cannot be efficiently utilized if traditional techniques are used for implementation. If this knowledge can be organized systematically and retrieved efficiently, it will be very useful. Therefore, another study was commissioned to study the feasibility of computerizing this failure knowledge. The study was carried out with the following goals:

1. To organize the knowledge, failure modes and failure effects, so that a diagnosis engineer/technician may identify the possible failure modes in case there is a problem.
2. To help train an engineer/technician so that he or she can study the possible failures even when the machine is running normally.

2. DEVELOPMENT PROCESS

2.1. Problem Selection and Description

The Air Conditioning System was used in the study as it is the subject of the RCM pilot project. Moreover, the system is also self-contained. The subject is small enough so that a prototype system can be completed in a short period of time. On the other hand, the complexity of the system is large enough so that its structure can represent the complexity of other similar systems.

The primary functions of the Gas Turbine Control Module Air Conditioning System are: to maintain an air temperature below 24°C and relative humidity below 70% in the control module; to maintain a dust free atmosphere in the control module; and to shut down the system and warn the operators in case of failure. It consists of three components, namely Air Recirculation System, Condensing Unit, and Refrigerant Compressors and Control.

The Air Recirculation System is responsible for maintaining adequate air recirculation and a dust free atmosphere in the control module, and maintaining the relative humidity of return air below 70%. Heat is removed from recirculation air to refrigerant via the evaporator. Two air supply fans are running at all times to ensure enough air is delivered.

Refrigerant Compressor and Control comprises two separate and fully automatic refrigerant circuits. The hermetic compressor is responsible for attracting the vapor coolant from the evaporator, and squeezes or compresses it to the correct condensing unit. Provisions are made to avoid spurious tripping and at the same time safeguard the compressor from damage during low load period.

The Condensing Unit is responsible for removing heat from the high pressure coolant and automatic operation of the condenser fans. The liquid refrigerant is then throttled through the thermo expansion valve to the evaporator to complete the refrigeration cycle.

The BBC Gas Turbine Air Conditioning System has two compressors, two air supply fans and two condenser fans. Additional protective devices exist to ensure the system shuts down automatically under abnormal situations. In case of malfunctioning, operators will be notified by a set of alarms which can be summarized as follow:

1. Air Conditioning Disturbance at MCR/UCR.
2. "Control Room Temperature high" at Gas Turbine Office.
3. "Control Room Humidity high" at Gas Turbine Office.
4. Local warning light "Compressor Disturbance," one for each compressor.
5. Local warning light "Condenser Fan Disturbance," one for each condenser fan.
6. Local warning light "Supply Air Fan Disturbance," one for each air supply fan.
7. Local warning light "V-belt switch".
8. Local warning light "Electric heater failure".

For details of the air conditioning system, please refer to text on refrigeration and air conditioning (Althouse et al., 1982). The goal of the diagnosis system is to isolate the possible faults that may occur in the system given the status of the alarms and a set of observable failure effects or symptoms.

2.2 Knowledge Acquisition

The knowledge acquisition process has been carried in the way that the expert sits together with the knowledge engineer to work out the preliminary version of the system. We divide the knowledge acquisition process in several stages and describe them separately in the following sections.

2.2.1. Background Knowledge. The background knowledge of the Air Conditioning System is based on the RCM Information Worksheet carried out by the RCM pilot study. For each component of the subject or the item under study, the following information was collected in the RCM Information Worksheet:

1. Function that is served by the component
2. Functional failure
3. The list of possible failure modes of the functional failure.
4. The failure effects of each failure mode

For example, the Refrigeration System of the Air Conditioning System has the following function, functional failure and failure modes:

Example 1

Function	To be capable of automatic starting of No. 1 compressor when return air temperature rises to 24°C and stopping when temperature drops to 23°C
Function Failure	Fails to start No. 1 compressor on rising air temperature
Failure Mode 1	Control loop for No. 1 compressor on controller B25.1 fails
Failure Mode 2	Controller B25.1 set point adrifted
Failure Mode 3	Control circuit fails

For each failure mode, a list of failure effects were collected. For example, the Failure Mode 1 will render the automatic operation of No. 1 compressor inoperative. If turbine is operating and ambient temperature is high, control room temperature will rise above 28°C and Digit Link will initiate start up of the back up air conditioners and activate the alarm "Control room temperature high" at Gas Turbine Office.

From the background information, a preliminary set of rules were identified. The rules are extracted from the failure modes and the corresponding failure effects. Following are some examples of rules:

Example 2

IF   Control room temperature maintained above 28°C
AND Turbine is operating
OR Ambient temperature is high
THEN Control room temperature is high
AND Control room temperature high alarm activated
AND Three window type air conditioners automatically started

IF   Controller B25.1 set point adrifted
THEN Control room temperature maintained above 24°C

The set of rules collected were forward chaining in nature, i.e. given a certain failure mode, a list of failure effects are identified. Usually the failure effects are observable. On the other hand, if the failure effects is true, a failure mode is just one possible cause of the failure effects. The goal of our diagnosis system is to identify the failure mode subject to a set of observable failure effects. Therefore, the set of rules was transformed so that it can be used for diagnosis purpose. A preliminary version of the diagnostic system was completed and tested. After testing the system for a short period of time, the engineer reported that the questions generated by the system were not consistent with the questions that were asked by a diagnosis engineer in real life. He was not comfortable with the questions proposed by the system. As a result, the preliminary system and the set of rules were thrown away but the following conclusions were made:
1. List of failure modes are the goals of diagnosis.
2. Rule is the appropriate form to represent the diagnosis knowledge.

2.2.2. User Interaction Model. Instead of using the failure modes and failure effects information in the RCM information sheet, we start the implementation again using a different approach. We start by studying how a diagnosis engineer diagnoses the system. The engineer analyses the possible faults of the system by asking a sequence of questions, in a certain order. Based on the answers to the questions, the engineer is able to deduce the possible faults in the system. Moreover, the engineer analyzes the system by considering each component separately. Therefore, the system is divided into separate components. As the Air Conditioning System has three major components, the diagnosis system also has three parts to handle each component. When the system is initiated, the user is required to enter the status of the alarms. If no alarm is activated, the user has the choice to end the consultation or diagnose any other component of the system. The user is allowed to analyze the system even without the alarm because there may be a fault with the alarm circuit. If an alarm exists, the system will start the analysis of the corresponding component automatically. After a particular component is selected, a list of questions will be asked which follow closely with the diagnosis process of the engineer. Example 3 illustrates some questions for the Air Recirculation System.

Example 3

Question 5: What are the operation modes of the No. 1 Compressor?
Answer: Running
         Not running

If the answer to Question 5 is running then ask Question 6.

Question 6: What is the running condition of No. 1 Motor Compressor Set?
Answer: Running with normal noise and vibration
Running noisily
Running and vibrating excessively, knocking and jumping on foundation base

If the answer to Question 6 is running noisily then ask Question 7.

Question 7: What kind of abnormal noise observed?
Answer: Sharp clicking noise
Dull clicking noise
Erratic beats and squeaks
Heavy compressor knocks
Decidedly regular metallic pounding

For each answer to Question 7, different failure modes were identified. They are summarized in the table in Example 4.

get confused, and may be uncomfortable with the behavior of the system.

As the sequence of the user interaction is well defined, the next step is to construct the diagnosis rules from the given set of questions and the expected answers. The construction of rules will be discussed in the next section since additional rules are needed to ensure the flow of questions are asked in a specified given order. From the user interaction model, a preliminary system is implemented and tested again.

2.2.3. Decision Tables. As the size of the system expands, some cases needing to be considered were getting very tedious and complex. In such situations, decision tables are used to help reasoning. Example 5 is a decision table which states the relationship between the control room relative humidity (RH), the Dehumidifier Heater (E1.10) when

Example 4

Answer to Question 7	Failure Mode or Action
Sharp clicking noise	No. 1 Motor Compressor–defective suction valve
	No. 1 Motor Compressor–defective discharge valve
Dull clicking noise	No. 1 Motor Compressor–worn cylinder line, piston ring or piston pin
Erratic beats and squeaks	No. 1 Motor Compressor–worn motor/compressor bearing
Heavy compressor knocks	No. 1 Motor Compressor–internal parts broken End consultation
Decidedly regular metallic pounding	Inadequate lubrication due to defective oil pump/clogged oil strainer
	Defective oil/gas differential pressure switch B17.3 End consultation

From the discussion with the diagnosis engineer, the engineer emphasizes that the ordering of the question is very important. If questions are not asked in the specified order, the diagnosis engineer may misunderstand,

the "Control room humidity high" alarm (RH-ALARM) is activated. There are a total of four possible cases, of which only one is normal.

Some tables are very complicated as there

Example 5

RH	E1.10 in operation	RH-ALARM	Failure Modes
>70%	Yes	Activated	Normal
>70%	No	Activated	Portable dehumidifier–AC power supply failure
			Portable dehumidifier–Control circuit fault
<70%	Yes	Activated	Control room relative humidity indication loop drifted
<70%	No	Activated	Control room relative humidity indication loop drifted

are two sets of motors in each component of the system and we have to consider the possible failure modes under different combinations of motor failures, for example:

No. 1 Compressor	Running
No. 2 Compressor	Not running
No. 1 Condenser Fan	Running at high speed
No. 2 Condenser Fan	Not running

Tables were constructed which are used to construct the diagnosis rules.

2.3. Knowledge Representation

2.3.1. Frames. The Air Conditioning Diagnosis System is organized as a collection of frames (Harmon & King, 1985). Each frame corresponds to a component of the Air Conditioning System. It can be viewed as a collection of information about the component. There are a total of twelve frames in the system. The frames together form a tree. The root frame (root of the tree) corresponds to the whole system, which is instantiated whenever the user starts the system. Immediately under the root frame are three subframes corresponding to the three components of the system: Air Recirculation System, Condensing Unit, and Refrigerant Compressor and Control. Four subframes are attached to the Air Recirculation System corresponding to (1) No alarm is activated; (2) Local warning light "Supply Air Fan Disturbance" is activated; (3) Local warning light "V-belt switch" is activated"; and (4) Local warning light "Control Room Humidity High" is activated. Two subframes are attached to the Condensing Unit corresponding to (1) No alarm is activated; and (2) Local warning light "Condenser Fan Disturbance" is activated. Two subframes are attached to the Refrigerant Compressor and Control corresponding to (1) No alarm is activated; and (2) Local warning light "Compressor Disturbance" is activated.

When the user starts the system, he or she is required to enter the status of all the alarms. If no alarm is activated, the user can decide to analyze each subsystem. If alarms are detected, the system will select the corresponding subsystem to be analyzed based on the alarm information. Analyzing a subsystem corresponds to entering the corresponding subframe. If faults were detected in the other subsystem, the system terminates the current frame and enters the subframe of the corresponding subsystem.

2.3.2. Rules. The basic knowledge representation technique for the diagnosis knowledge is rule. The whole system is basically a backward chaining system. As discussed in the literature (Harmon & King, 1985; Hayes-Roth et al., 1983), diagnosis paradigm is used for problems that require the user to input symptoms or characteristics of a situation in order to determine which of several alternative solutions may be appropriated. Backward chaining is the common approach to tackle these types of diagnosis problems. The Air Conditioning System fault diagnosis problem falls into this category and backward chaining is used as the basic inference strategy.

For each diagnosis rule, the action part usually corresponds to a list of failure modes or some unobservable failure effects. The condition part is usually a combination of observable failure effects and/or alarm statuses. Each rule's condition usually corresponds to answers of several questions. We shall use Example 3 in the previous section to illustrate this idea. The failure modes corresponding to the answer to Question 7 can be written as the rules in Example 6, under the subframe Refrigerant Compressor and Control:

Example 6

IF   No. 1 Motor Compressor Set is running
       AND No. 1 Compressor Set running condition is running noisily
       AND Sharp clicking noise is observed
THEN No. 1 Motor Compressor Set–defective suction valve
       AND No. 1 Motor Compressor Set defective discharge valve

IF   No. 1 Motor Compressor Set is running
       AND No. 1 Compressor Set running condition is running noisily
       AND Dull clicking noise is observed
THEN No. 1 Motor Compressor Set–worn cylinder line, piston ring or piston pin

IF   No. 1 Motor Compressor Set is running
       AND No. 1 Compressor Set running condition is running noisily
       AND Erratic beats and squeaks
THEN No. 1 Motor Compressor Set–worn motor/compressor bearing

Rules corresponding to the decision table can also be generated easily. Each entry in the decision table with failure modes corresponds to one diagnosis rule. In Example 7 are example rules from the decision table in Example 5.

Example 7

IF   Relative Humidity > 70%
       AND Dehumidifier Heater E1.10 is NOT in operation
       AND Alarm Control room humidity high is activated
THEN Portable dehumidifier–AC power supply failure
       AND Portable dehumidifier–Control circuit fault

IF   Relative Humidity < 70%
       AND Alarm Control room humidity high is activated
THEN Control room relative humidity indication loop drifted

In some situations, forward reasoning provides better control of the system, e.g. if the local warning light "Compressor Disturbance" for No. 1 Compressor is active, we should enter the subframe which analyzes the component Refrigerant Compressor and Control. With these cases, forward chaining rules are used. Following is a list of different types of forward chaining rules used by the Air Conditioning Diagnosis System.

1) If the value of one parameter is known, another one can be deduced immediately, e.g.

IF   Discharge pressure is high
THEN Suction pressure is high

IF   Suction pressure is low
THEN Discharge pressure is low

2) Forward chaining rules are also used to control the flow of execution. For example, if no alarm is activated and the user still wants to analyze the Condensing Unit, the following rule is used:

IF   No alarm is activated
       AND user select Condensing Unit
THEN Enter the subframe Condensing Unit

3) Forward chaining rules are also used to set up the list of goals to be handled in a particular session as each subframe is designed to handle the subsystem under different conditions. For example, the Condensing Unit is capable of handling the faults of No. 1 Condenser Fan and/or No. 2 Condenser Fan. On the other hand, the failure mode for the two

fans are different. Therefore, under different situations, a set of different goals will be used. For example,

IF   No. 2 Condenser Fan false alarm signal
THEN Activate the list of goals:
      Condenser Fans V-belt slipping
      Condenser Fans loose fan propeller or fan blade
      Condenser Fans worn or dry fan/motor bearing
      Condenser Fans defective anti-vibration mounting

2.3.3. Parameters. Parameters are used to store individual piece of information associated with the system. The parameters of the system can be divided into the following four types:

1) *Alarm.* The status of an alarm which will be supplied by the user when starting the system.
2) *Failure Modes.* The list of possible faults associated with the system.
3) *User Input.* The list of observable failure effects.
4) *Unobservable Failure Effects.* The list of failure effects that is not observable but can be deduced.
5) *Control Parameters.* The parameters that are used to control the flow of the system.

Example 8 consists of examples of different types of parameters. In Example 8, the heat load condition (FE012) depends on whether the turbine is operating or not and the ambient temperature.

2.4. Knowledge Encoding

2.4.1. Frames. The Air Conditioning Plant diagnosis system is implemented using PCPLUS®. PCPLUS® is an EMYCIN-like program developed by Texas Instruments to run on IBM PC® or compatible. PCPLUS® supports frames which divide a system into smaller components (Texas Instruments, 1988). Each frame contains parameters and rules that address a piece of the overall problem. The components of the diagnosis system can be implemented directly using the frame structure provided by PCPLUS®. The root frame is called BBCACS-BBC Gas Turbine Air Conditioning Plant. The three subframes directly under the root are called ARS-Air Recirculation System, CU-Condensing Unit, and RS-Refrigerant Compressor and Control. The twelve frames together form a tree as follows:

BBCACS
  ARS
    ARSN ; No alarm activated
    ARSA ; "Supply Air Fan Disturbance" activated
    ARSB ; "V-belt switch" activated
    ARSC ; "Control Room Temperature High" activated
  CU
    CUN   ; No alarm activated
    CUA   ; "Condenser Fan Disturbance" activated
  RS
    RSN   ; No alarm activated
    RSA   ; "Compressor Disturbance" activated

Example 8

Parameter Type	Parameter Name	Description
Alarm	ALARM01	Air Conditioning Disturbance at MCR/UCR
	ALARM04	Condenser Fan failure
Failure mode	RS-FM3A5-1	No. 1 Motor Compressor defective suction valve
	RS-FM3A5-2	No. 1 Motor Compressor defective discharge valve
	RS-FM3A6	No. 1 Motor Compressor worn cylinder linear, piston ring or piston pin
User input	COMPRESSOR-OM-1	Operation mode of No. 1 compressor
	USER014	Colour of crankcase oil
Unobservable failure effect	FE012	Heat load condition
Control parameter	NORMAL-COND	The status of the consultation

Analyses of a particular component of the Air Conditioning Plant is by instantiating the corresponding frame using the PCPLUS® function called CONSIDERFRAME. For example, if no alarm is activated and the user wants to analyze the Condensing Unit, the following rule will be fired:

IF subsystem selection = Condensing Unit THEN CONSIDERFRAME CU

2.4.2. Parameters. The Alarms parameters are set up as initial data. Users are prompted to enter the statuses of these parameters when starting the diagnosis system. These statuses will guide the system to enter the appropriate subsystem for analysis. The input of these parameters is organized in a tabular form as shown in the Appendix.

Failure modes are represented by PCPLUS® parameters of boolean type, i.e. the failure mode can either exist or not. A TRANSLATION property is attached to each failure mode. Example 9 shows some failure modes.

Example 9

RS-FM04B03
 TRANSLATION : Condenser Fans V-belt slipping

RS-FM04B05
 TRANSLATION : Condenser Fans loose fan propeller or fan blade

RS-FM04B06
 TRANSLATION : Condenser Fans worn or dry fan/motor bearing

RS-FM04B07
 TRANSLATION : Condenser Fans defective anti-vibration mounting

Uncertainty is not used in the system as the goal of the system is not to identify the most probable failure mode, but instead aims at proposing a list of possible failure modes that may exist in the Air Conditioning System. The task of isolating the fault is the responsibility of the engineer. When the engineer goes through the list of questions asked by the system, he or she may already isolate the fault.

User Input parameters are represented using PCPLUS® parameters. On the other hand, a PROMPT property will be attached to each User Input parameters. When the backward chaining system tracing through the rules requires the value of an User Input parameter, the value of the corresponding PROMPT property will be displayed and the user is then required to enter the answer. As the list of answers to a question can be enumerated, and each engineer may have different wordings for different observations, each question is provided with a list of possible answers and user is asked to select one of them. Default value is also assumed for many parameters. Following are some examples of User Input parameters:

Example 10

COMPRESSOR-OM-1
 TRANSLATION: No. 1 Compressor operation mode
 PROMPT: Operation mode of No. 1 Compressor:
 EXPECT: "running" "not running"

COMPRESSOR-C-1
 TRANSLATION: No. 1 compressor running condition
 PROMPT: What is the running condition of No. 1 motor compressor set?
 EXPECT: "running with normal noise and vibration"
  "running noisily"
  "running and vibrating excessively, knocking and jumping on foundation base"
 DEFAULT: "running with normal noise and vibration"

Unobservable Failure Effects are just PCPLUS® parameters with no particular restriction on its properties except that the PROMPT property must not be defined. Control parameters are also encoded as PCPLUS® parameters which may be observable or unobservable.

2.4.3. Rules. The rules discussed in Section 2.3.2 is represented directly using PCPLUS® rules. Each PCPLUS® rule has a condition part and an action part. The condition part describes the logical relationship among a set of parameters and the action part describes the result that is true if the condition is evaluated to be true. For example, the diagnosis rules given in Example 6 is represented as follows:

Example 11

```
RULE005
    IF      COMPRESSOR-OM-1 = "running"
            AND COMPRESSOR-C-1 = "running nois-
            ily"
            AND COMPRESSOR-N-1 = "sharp clicking
            noise"
    THEN    RS-FM3A5-1 AND RS-FM3A5-2
RULE007
    IF      COMPRESSOR-OM-1 = "running"
            AND COMPRESSOR-C-1 = "running nois-
            ily"
            AND COMPRESSOR-N-1 = "dull clicking
            noise"
    THEN    RS-FM3A6
RULE009
    IF      COMPRESSOR-OM-1 = "running"
            AND COMPRESSOR-C-1 = "running nois-
            ily"
            AND COMPRESSOR-N-1 =Q "erratic beats
            and squeaks"
    THEN    RS-FM3A2
```

For each forward chaining rule, an ANTECEDENT property is attached to it. For example:

Example 12

```
RULE049
    IF          DISCHARGEP-1 = "high"
    THEN        SUCTIONP-1 = "high"
    ANTECEDENT: TRUE
RULE050
    IF          SUCTIONP-1 = "low"
    THEN        DISCHARGEP-1 = "low"
    ANTECEDENT: TRUE
```

A UTILITY property is attached to each goal parameter or failure mode. It is an integer range -100 to 100. The order of the analysis of the list of goal parameters depends on the utility value of the parameter. When the utility value of a goal is -100, it will not be traced, i.e. the failure mode will not be analyzed. The diagnosis system uses the utility to set up different list of goals to be analyzed under different situations. The forward chaining rule which controls the execution order of the system manipulates the utility value of the goal parameters. Following is an example:

Example 13

```
RULE100
    IF      ! ALARM04
    THEN    set-utility RS-FM04B03 0
            set-utility RS-FM04B05 0
            set-utility RS-FM04B06 0
            set-utility RS-FM04B07 0
```

2.5. Knowledge Testing and Evaluation

Prototyping is used as the basic development approach for the construction of the diagnosis system. After the user interaction model approach to tackle the collection of the diagnosis knowledge was finalized, the diagnosis engineer starts writing the list of questions and the corresponding answers. The knowledge engineer encodes the diagnosis knowledge using PCPLUS® parameters and rules.

The first preliminary version of the system was constructed with both the diagnosis engineer and the knowledge engineer (KE) sitting together at a PC and entering the rules and parameters. After each additional piece of knowledge is added to the system, the engineers try out a simulation of a particular fault to determine whether the system is executed as predicted. During the testing process, we find that a single piece of knowledge or a small collection of knowledge is very easy to debug and verify. On the other hand, if the knowledge base has more than 50 rules, we found the debugging process is very complicated. Our approach of making sure every individual piece of knowledge implemented is correct allows us to concentrate on debugging the newly added knowledge whenever a problem appears.

After the completion of the preliminary prototype, the KE has an understanding of how the diagnosis engineer organizes his information in the question/answer format and the requirements needed. The diagnosis engineer also has a basic understanding of the reasoning mechanism of the system. The development process can then be speeded up. At a later stage, the diagnosis engineer can pass the question/answering information on a piece of paper to the KE and the KE can construct the corresponding set of rules and parameters for the system. While the size of the knowledge base is increasing, the time needed to debug the system when an error occurs is also increasing. At this stage, if the question/answer information is well documented on paper and the diagnosis engineer informs the KE on a problem case with the corresponding sequence of answers to the questions, the KE can debug the knowledge base with little input from the diagnosis engineer. Up to this stage, both the KE and the diagnosis engineer has a thorough understanding of each *others'* understanding of the diagnosis system.

For each refined prototype, the diagnosis engineer brought the system back to his office so that other engineers could play with it and report any possible problems. As the knowledge base increases in size, the number of execution paths going through the system increases exponentially. It is impossible for the KE and the diagnosis engineer to find all possible problems by themselves. Feedbacks from testing by other engineers provide another way to evaluate the performance of the system.

Any reported problems will be identified and fixed. An updated version is then released for further testing. As the development and testing were going on at the same time, when the development was completed, we believe that more than 70% of the problems of the system were isolated and fixed.

3. IMPLEMENTATION PROCESS

The system was completed in approximately four months. The completed system has approximately 500 rules and 400 parameters. Out of 500 rules, about 60 rules are used for controlling the execution of the system, about 100 rules are used for reporting and printing the failure modes.

As one of the diagnosis engineers actively participated in the development process, the completed system was delivered without too much user resistance. At the end of the project, we found that the diagnosis engineer was the most appropriate person to deliver the system and to train the users, as he understood the structure of the system very well and also knew how to communicate with the users. As reported in many other studies, sudden impact to current working habit is one of the major reasons for unsuccessful implementation of a software system. In order to make sure the delivery can be performed smoothly, the system is introduced as a tool to help identify possible failure modes of the air conditioning plant instead of as an expert diagnosis system to replace the existing staff.

After delivering the system, both the knowledge engineer and the diagnosis engineer were responsible for maintaining system. The primary job of the knowledge engineer is to support the control flow of the system while the diagnosis knowledge is to make sure the knowledge base is consistent and up to date. It is believed that when the system becomes stable, the knowledge engineer will not be necessary to maintain the system.

4. CONCLUSION

We report here the development process of an expert system for diagnosing a Gas Turbine Air Conditioning Plant. The user interaction model is used in the knowledge acquisition process and prototyping is used in development. We found that incrementally debugging a small knowledge base makes the debugging process easier at later stages of the development.

The completed system has achieved the goals of systematically organizing the diagnosis knowledge, causal relationship between failure modes, and failure effects. The system can also help to identify possible failure modes in case there is a problem; and help to train an engineer to study possible failures. Use of the user interaction model makes the order of the questions generated by the system similar to the questions produced by the diagnosis engineer. The decision table provides a systematic enumeration of cases under different possible failure effects combinations of components in the air conditioning plant.

NOTE

1. Initial training and consulting support in RCM for the Gas Turbine project were provided by Aladon Ltd, a UK-based consulting company.

®PCPLUS is a registered trademark of Texas Instruments.
®IBM PC is a registered trademark of International Business Machines.

REFERENCES

Althouse, A., Turnquist, C., & Bracciano, A. (1982). *Modern refrigeration and air conditioning.* South Holland, Illinois: The Goodheart-Wilcox Company, Inc.

Harmon, P., & King, D. (1985)., *Expert Systems.* New York, John Wiley & Sons.

Hayes-Roth, F., Waterman, D., & Lenat, D. (1983). *Building expert systems.* Reading, Massachusetts: Addison-Wesley.

Texas Instruments. (1988). *PCPLUS Reference Guide,* Texas Instruments Incorporated.

APPENDIX

A sample session from the Air Conditioning System Fault Diagnosis System are given below. The sample session is an analysis of the Refrigerant Compressor and Control subsystem when alarms "Air Conditioning Disturbance at MCR/UCR" and "No. 1 Compressor Disturbance" are activated.

SAMPLE SESSION

```
                    BBC GT AIR CONDITIONING SYSTEM

   ┌ Current objective: ─────────────────────────────────────────┐
   │                                                             │
   │        BBC GT CONTROL MODULE AIR CONDITIONING SYSTEM        │
   │                                                             │
   │           AUTOMATIC FAILURE MODE DIAGNOSIS SYSTEM           │
   │                                                             │
   │                                                             │
   │                                                             │
   │                                                             │
   │                                                             │
   │                                                             │
   │                                                             │
   │                                                             │
   │ ** End - press ENTER to continue.                           │
   └─────────────────────────────────────────────────────────────┘
```

SCREEN 1. Starting the diagnosis system.

System for Air Conditioning Plant

```
                    BBC GT AIR CONDITIONING SYSTEM

┌─────────────────────────────────────────────────────────────────────┐
│ Please enter the following alarm information:                       │
│                                                                     │
│    Air Conditioning Disturb at MCR/UCR                          Y   │
│                                                                     │
│    Control room humidity high at Gas Turbine Office active      N   │
│                                                                     │
│    Control Room Temp High at Gas Turbine Office active          N   │
│                                                                     │
│    Local warning light No.1 Compressor failure active           Y   │
│    Local warning light No.2 Compressor failure active           N   │
│                                                                     │
│    Local warning light No.1 Condenser Fan failure active        N   │
│    Local warning light No.2 Condenser Fan failure active        N   │
│                                                                     │
│    Local warning light No.1 Supply Air Fan failure active       N   │
│    Local warning light No.2 Supply Air Fan failure active       N   │
│                                                                     │
│    Local warning light V-Belt Switch active                     N   │
│                                                                     │
│ Press F10 to continue.                                              │
└─────────────────────────────────────────────────────────────────────┘
```

SCREEN 2. Alarms "Air Conditioning Disturb at MCR/UCR" and "No. 1 Compressor failure" activated.

```
                    BBC GT AIR CONDITIONING SYSTEM

┌─ Current objective: ────────────────────────────────────────────────┐
│                                                                     │
│       Analysing the refrigerant compressor and control              │
│                                                                     │
│                                                                     │
│                                                                     │
│                                                                     │
│                                                                     │
│                                                                     │
│                                                                     │
│                                                                     │
│                                                                     │
│                                                                     │
│ ** End - press ENTER to continue.                                   │
└─────────────────────────────────────────────────────────────────────┘
```

SCREEN 3. Analyzing the refrigerant compressor and control.

BBC GT AIR CONDITIONING SYSTEM

```
What are the operation modes of Compressors?
    Operation mode of No.1 Compressor:
    Operation mode of No.2 Compressor:

    Operation mode of No.1 Compressor:

    running
    not running




1. Use arrow key or first letter of item to position the cursor.
2. press ENTER to continue.

Press F10 to continue.
```

SCREEN 4. No. 1 Compressor "not running" selected.

BBC GT AIR CONDITIONING SYSTEM

```
What are the operation modes of Compressors?
    Operation mode of No.1 Compressor:                    not running
    Operation mode of No.2 Compressor:

    Operation mode of No.2 Compressor:

    running
    not running




1. Use arrow key or first letter of item to position the cursor.
2. press ENTER to continue.

Press F10 to continue.
```

SCREEN 5. No. 2 Compressor "running" selected.

BBC GT AIR CONDITIONING SYSTEM

```
    Is No.1 Compressor selected to "auto"?

YES
NO








1. Use arrow key or first letter of item to position the cursor.
2. press ENTER to continue.
```

SCREEN 6. "YES" selected.

BBC GT AIR CONDITIONING SYSTEM

```
    What compressor protection has operated on No.1 Compressor circuit?
        (default is none)

     Yes
↔    ·   high pressure cutout
↔    ·   low pressure cutout
     ■   low oil/gas differential
↔    ·   motor overload
↔    ·   motor winding thermistor protection
↔    ·   none




1. Use arrow key or first letter of item to position the cursor.
2. Select all applicable responses.
3. After making selections, press ENTER to continue.
```

SCREEN 7. "Low oil/gas differential" selected.

```
             BBC GT AIR CONDITIONING SYSTEM

┌─────────────────────────────────────────────────────────────────┐
│                                                                 │
│  No.1 Compressor is protected against inadequate lubrication by the oil/gas │
│  differential pressure switch B17.3. Possible causes for low oil/gas        │
│  differential are RS-FM3A8, RS-FM3A3, RS-FM14A1, PD-FM4A2                   │
│                                                                 │
│  RS-FM3A3: No.1 Compressor - inadequate lubrication due to insufficient oil │
│  charge in crankcase                                            │
│                                                                 │
│  RS-FM3A8: No.1 Compressor - inadequate lubrication due to defective oil    │
│  pump/clogged oil strainer                                      │
│                                                                 │
│  RS-FM14A1: No.1 Compressor - defective crankcase heater causing too much oil │
│  foaming during start up                                        │
│                                                                 │
│  PD14A2: No.1 Compressor - oil/gas differential pressure switch B17.3 setting │
│  too high                                                       │
│                                                                 │
│  Press F2 and QUIT if you want to quit                          │
│                                                                 │
│  ** End - press ENTER to continue.                              │
│                                                                 │
└─────────────────────────────────────────────────────────────────┘
```

SCREEN 8. Failure modes found.

```
             BBC GT AIR CONDITIONING SYSTEM

┌─ Conclusions: ──────────────────────────────────────────────────┐
│                                                                 │
│  BBCACS Air Conditioning System Disgnosis Consultation Finished │
│                   ┌─ Commands: ──────────┐                      │
│                   │  CONTINUE            │                      │
│                   │  HOW                 │                      │
│                   │  TRACE ON            │                      │
│                   │  PRINT CONCLUSIONS   │                      │
│                   │  REVIEW              │                      │
│                   │  SAVE PLAYBACK FILE  │                      │
│                   │  NEW START           │                      │
│                   │  QUIT                │                      │
│                   └──────────────────────┘                      │
│                                                                 │
│                                                                 │
│                                                                 │
└─────────────────────────────────────────────────────────────────┘
```

SCREEN 9. Consultation finished, "QUIT" selected.

Diagnosing Steel Structures at Hydro Power Stations

Takao Terano,* Shouichi Matsui,** Hideharu Nakamura,**
and Kousuke Yamamoto**

*Graduate School of Systems Management, The University of Tsukuba, Tokyo;
**Central Research Institute of Electric Power Industry (CRIEPI), Tokyo, Japan

1. INTRODUCTION

This chapter describes the result of a seven-year project for developing Hydro Steel Structure Diagnosing System (HSDS). HSDS diagnoses the current conditions of key steel structures at hydro power stations; e.g., dam gates (roller gates and radial gates), penstocks, hydroway bridges, and steel screens. HSDS consists of knowledge-based systems, relational databases, structural analysis programs, and an integrated user interface. HSDS has two knowledge-based systems: Dam Gate Diagnosing Adviser (DGDA) and PenStock Diagnosing Advisor (PSDA).

This paper is mainly concerned with the knowledge-based systems. First, we introduce overview of the target domain, system configuration, and functions of HSDS. Second, the development process of HSDS is discussed focusing on the characteristics of the earlier versions of DGDA and PSDA. Third, the implementation process is investigated from the point of deployment, technology transfer, and maintenance strategies.

HSDS now runs on a FACOM M-380 mainframe computer, and can be used at any site of electric utilities via telephone lines by personal computers (PCs) with a terminal emulation function, a Kanji-character printer and a facsimile.

1.1. Steel Structures

Key steel structures at hydro power stations are dam gates (roller gates and radial gates), penstocks, hydroway bridges and steel screens. These structures usually show no trouble during operations. Their lifespans are over fifty years. However, if abnormal events occur, they could cause severe damage of both the power generating facilities and the environment around the station. Thus, diagnosing such steel structures is a critical task for preventive maintenance in electric power utilities.

The difficulty of diagnosing such public-oriented structures arises from the fact that symptoms of the structures must be interpreted from both structural engineering and empirical knowledge standpoints. The structural engineering knowledge is important because the steel structures are always stressed and corroded by hydro resources. The empirical knowledge is important because delicate symptoms which cannot be measured by any mechanical equipments can be detected by experienced human experts. The task for the diagnoses requires knowledge of (1) structural analyses, (2) interpretation of quantitatively measured data, (3) interpretation of qualitatively surveyed data, and (4) empirical expertise. These prerequisites will fit knowledge engineering approaches to develop computerized diagnosing systems.

At the Central Research Institute of Electric Power Industry (CRIEPI), research and investigation on evaluation of the safety of these steel structures have been conducted for over twenty years. CRIEPI has much expertise on the task. The objectives of this project are to develop a reliable computerized system for diagnosing the steel structures and predicting their life-spans, and to transfer the expertise at CRIEPI to electric power utilities.

This paper describes the result of a seven-year project which has developed an integrated system, HSDS. HSDS consists of knowledge-based systems, relational databases, structural analysis programs, and an integrated user interface. The knowledge-based systems consist of DGDA and PSDA. Both are frame- and rule-based systems. This chapter is mainly concerned with the knowledge systems.

This paper is organized as follows. Section 2 introduces HSDS system overview: the domain, system configuration, and functions. Section 3 discusses the development process of HSDS. First, the task of HSDS is analyzed. The objectives of HSDS have been changing as the project phases proceed. Then, knowledge acquisition and encoding, knowledge representation and reasoning, and knowledge testing and evaluation are described for each prototype. On the other hand, in Section 4, a discussion about the implementation process is focused on the current version of HSDS, actually in operational use. Section 5 gives conclusions and future works. The Appendix provides sample sessions to illustrate the functions of HSDS. The original output reports and display images are all in Japanese; however, the information in the Appendix is translated into English.

2. SYSTEM OVERVIEW

2.1. Domain Description

The overview of a typical hydro power plant and its main steel structures is illustrated in Figure 7.1. The structures and components of a roller gate and a radial gate are shown in Figure 7.2. Main components of a penstock are shown in Figure 7.3. There are over 1000 hydro power plants operated and maintained by electric power utilities in Japan. A typical dam sites has 2 to 16 dam gates, almost of which are either roller gates or radial gate. Penstocks are steel structures which connect a reservoir to a power plant. Hydroway bridges are often used for supporting penstocks. Steel screens are used to prevent dusts from coming into penstocks. These steel structures are inspected monthly, yearly, or whenever the operation conditions are changed. They are thoroughly investigated about ten or fifteen years. These activities are

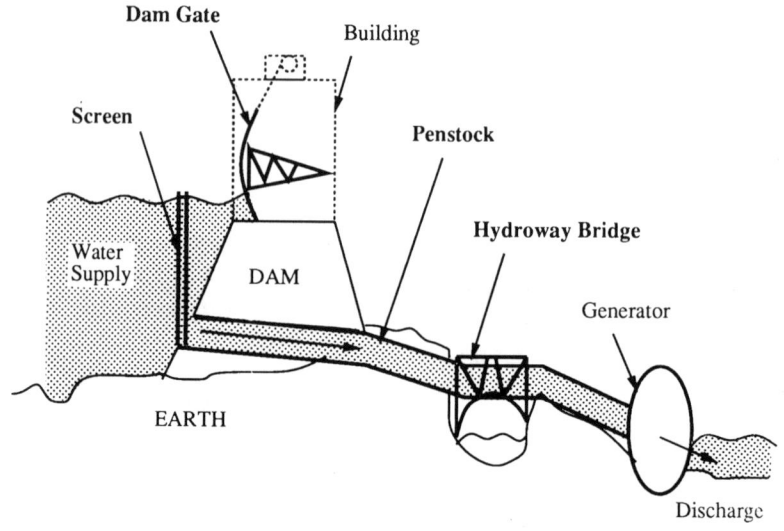

FIGURE 7.1. Overview of hydro power plants and the key steel structures.

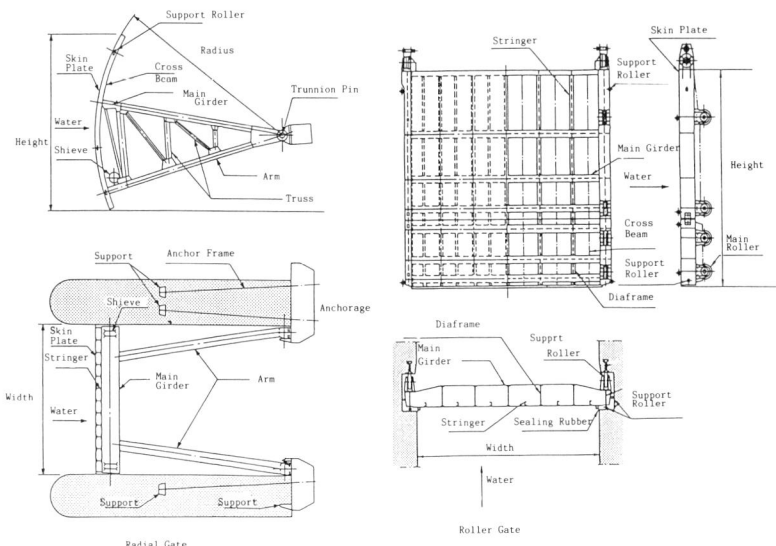

FIGURE 7.2. Structures of dam gates (radial gates and roller gates).

scheduled by the utilities. Each of the investigations costs about $50,000. HSDS will be mainly used to support such intensive investigations.

2.2. System Configuration and Functions

Figure 7.4 shows the system configuration of HSDS. HSDS consists of knowledge-based systems, relational databases, structural analysis programs by finite element method (FEM), and an integrated user interface.

As mentioned earlier, the knowledge-based systems consist of the Dam Gate Diagnosing Adviser (DGDA) and PenStock Diagnosing Advisor (PSDA), and they are represented in frames and rules. The frames keep the information of the structures: components of the structures and their relationships, their design

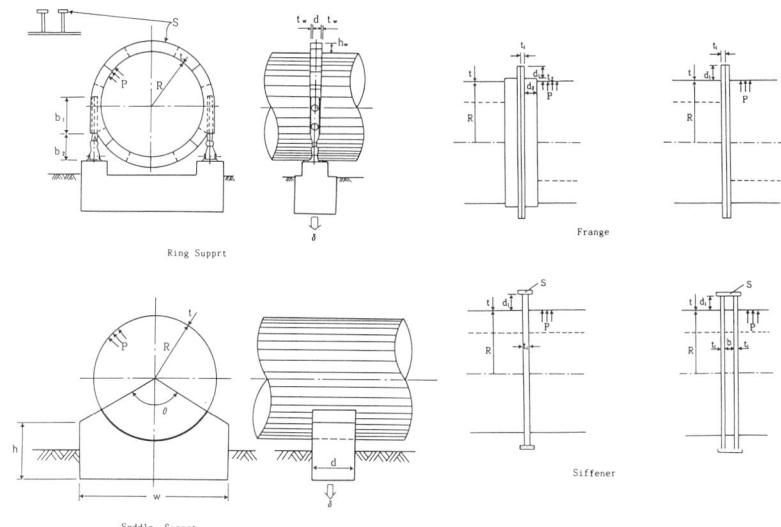

FIGURE 7.3. Main parts of penstocks for structural analysis.

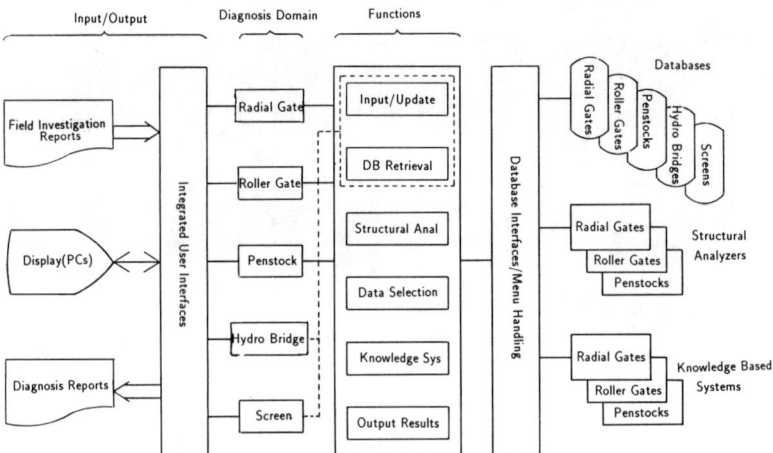

FIGURE 7.4. System configuration of HSDS.

information, measured data, and analytical data. The rules represent empirical knowledge for interpreting the data, diagnosing the structures, and predicting the remaining lifespan. DGDA and PSDA diagnose the structure specified by the users one by one.

The task of the knowledge-based systems are summarized as follows:

1. The systems interpret quantitative items on each part of the structures by comparing both measurement information and structural analysis information. Structural conditions of the structure can be precisely understood in this process.

2. The systems interpret qualitative data items which represent the current condition of the structure. The data items are collected through the field investigation, and are classified into the categories of external appearance, operationality, environments and years of use. These data are interpreted by using empirical decision rules for reasoning and by using the Analytic Hierarchy Process (the AHP; a non-Bayesian decision analysis method; Saaty, 1980), for evaluating the qualitative items.

3. The systems diagnose the current condition of each structure from the above quantitative and qualitative points of view by using a forward reasoning method.

4. The systems predict the remaining life-span of structures by using a simple extrapolation function.

The relational databases contain information of almost all the hydro-station sites in Japan. The databases include:

1. Design information of each structure;
2. Historic maintenance data of each structure;
3. Measured data from field investigation;
4. Numerical results from structural analyses; and
5. Diagnosed results from the knowledge-based systems.

The structural analysis programs are developed for roller gates, radial gates and penstocks. The programs have typical structural models for numerical computation by finite element methods. Small number of the design parameters determine the characteristics of the structural models. The programs are easy-to-use systems with a few parameters. The models can cope with almost all the types of steel structures used in Japan. The results of the computation are shown to users by both numerical tables and graphical drawings.

The user interface is built on a character-based low cost terminal or PC, which is carefully designed for the following purposes:

1. To allow easy input of the qualitative and quantitative data from the field investigation documents;

Diagnosing Steel Structures

TABLE 7.1
Steel Structures and Functions of HSDS

Structures	Database	FEM Program	Expert System
Dan Gate	340 sites	whole structure	empirical diagnosis structural diagnosis life-span prediction
Penstock	1,140 sites	main parts	empirical diagnosis structural diagnosis welded joint diagnosis life-span prediction
Hydro-Bridge	360 sites	—	—
Screen	390 sites	—	—

2. To use each sub-system by the menu driven method; and
3. To give final diagnosis documents with Japanese explanations.

The diagnostic targets and the functions of HSDS are summarized in Table 7.1. HSDS now runs on a FACOM M-380 mainframe computer, and can be used at any site of electric utilities via telephone-lines by PCs with a terminal emulation function, a Kanji-character printer and a facsimile. DGDA and PSDA are implemented in Eshell; a hybrid shell with a blackboard architecture. The databases are implemented in PLANNER; a simple relational database system. The structural analysis programs are implemented in FORTRAN77. The user interfaces are implemented in PFD (the Programming Facility for Display users), which is an SPF (the Screen Programming Facility provided by IBM Corp.) like menu-programming facility. These hardware and software facilities are all provided by Fujitsu, Ltd.

3. DEVELOPMENT PROCESS

The brief history of development of HSDS are shown in Table 7.2. In the succeeding

TABLE 7.2
Time Table of the Development of HSDS

Date	Development
April, 1985	Developing Structural Analysis Systems & Databases for Dam Gates
April, 1985	Making a Decision for Developing Knowledge-Based Systems
May, 1985	First Knowledge Elicitation for Radial Gate Diagnoses
June, 1985	Developing DGDA ver. 1 on a Mainframe (Lisp, Simple Rule-based)
Sept., 1985	Introducing KEE & Symbolics Lisp Machine
Oct., 1985	Knowledge Translation and Structurization for KEE
Oct., 1985	Developing of DGDA ver. 2 on a Symbolics with KEE (for Demonstration)
Nov., 1985	Developing of DGDA ver. 3 on a Symbolics with KEE (for Knowledge Structurizing)
March, 1986	Developing of DGDA ver. 4 on a Mainframe with Eshell
1986–1987	Operational Testing of DGDA
March, 1987	Developing PSDA ver. 1 on a Mainframe with Eshell
1987–1988	Operational Testing of PSDA
March, 1988	Developing PSDA ver. 2 on a Mainframe with Eshell
1988	Operational Testing of DGDA
1988	Operational Testing of PSDA
March, 1989	Developing PSDA ver. 3 on a Mainframe with Eshell
March, 1989	Integrating HSDS ver. 1 on a Mainframe
1989	Operational Testing of HSDS; Training Course; Refining HSDS
March, 1990	Integrating HSDS ver. 2 on a Mainframe
1990	Operational Testing of HSDS; Training Course

TABLE 7.3
Problem Types, Basic Tasks and Problem Solving Functions of ESs

Problem Types	Basic Tasks	Problem Solving Functions
Analysis Problems		
(1) Interpretation	feature extraction incomplete matching to the model identification of system structure estimation of system states processing uncertainty processing incompleteness multiple interpretation	classification by hierarchy model retrieval estimation of sub-structures hierarchical generate & test uncertain reasoning hypothetical reasoning co-operative reasoning
(2) Diagnosis	hierarchical classification of events hierarchical representation of system interpretation tasks selection of measurement points identification of unusual events efficiency by shallow models completeness by deep models	event driven reasoning goal driven reasoning uncertain reasoning hypothetical reasoning co-operative reasoning trade-offs of efficiency and completeness cost/benefit analysis
(3) Control	representation of system structures representation of dynamic behavior diagnosing tasks state estimation by models priority for stable operation priority for energy-saving operation operator guidance	diagnosing system states estimation by simulators prediction by qualitative reasoning multi-objective estimation of rules action guidance analysis of deadlocks avoidance of interlocking
Synthesis Problems		
(4) Planning	hierarchy of planning processes combinatorial searching interaction of constraints estimation of environments intelligent backtracking retrieval & reuse of planning cases multi-objective evaluation of plans	topdown refinement least commitment blind search intelligent search by hypothetical reasoning reuse of cases by analogical reasoning multi-objective evaluation of plans decision making under risks
(5) Designing	representing components and relations hierarchical representation of problems generation of alternatives evaluation of sub-problems intelligent backtracking retrieval & reuse of designing cases parallel problem solving	topdown refinement least commitment optimization functions verification functions intelligent search by hypothetical reasoning reuse of cases by analogical reasoning co-operative reasoning

subsections, we will describe the development process of HSDS.

3.1. Task Analysis of HSDS

HSDS was a demand-pull system. The nature of the problem required a knowledge-based systems approach. Our outcome did not come by seeking good application with the knowledge systems techniques in hand. However, when starting the HSDS project in 1984, there were few experiences in the literature; thus, the development process and the features of HSDS had to be repeatedly evaluated. The results are shown below.

From the knowledge engineering standpoint, engineering expert systems are categorized into two types: analysis-type (interpreting, diagnosing, and controlling) and synthesis-type (designing and planning). The task of analysis-type systems is to reveal the property of the target systems when the system structure and the component properties are given. The task of synthesis-type systems is to determine the system structure and the component properties when the properties of the target problems are given as the design specifications (Terano, 1989).

General features, basic tasks, and problem solving techniques, are identified in each type (see Table 7.3). The concepts of "generic tasks" proposed by Chandrasekaran (1986) are almost equivalent to both concepts of "basic tasks" and "problem solving techniques" in Table 7.3. However, we distinguish the terms in the following way: Basic tasks define the properties of target problems which can be given in the specifications. Problem solving techniques define the way to provide problem solving components which can be directly implemented.

Following the categories, HSDS belongs to both interpretation and diagnosis expert systems. The features of HSDS are summarized in Table 7.4. To implement the problem solving functions, we mainly use usual knowledge representation techniques: rules, frames, forward inferences, and attached procedures. To identify structural conditions, we use conventional programs by FEM in FORTRAN 77.

Furthermore, to diagnose the structures, we must use empirical knowledge for interpreting qualitative investigation data. Because such data and empirical knowledge are subjective, that is, intrinsically uncertain, we de-

TABLE 7.4
Features of HSDS

Basic Tasks	Fit	Problem Solving Functions	Used
(Interpretation System)			
feature extraction	O	classification by hierarchy	X
incomplete matching to the model	X	model retrieval	O
identification of system structure	X	estimation of sub-structures	O
estimation of system states	O	hierarchical generate & test	X
processing uncertainty	O	uncertain reasoning	O
processing incompleteness	X	hypothetical reasoning	X
multiple interpretation	O	co-operative reasoning	X
(Diagnosing System)			
hierarchical classification of events	X	event driven reasoning	O
hierarchical representation of system	O	goal driven reasoning	X
interpretation tasks	O	uncertain reasoning	O
selection of measurement points	X	hypothetical reasoning	X
identification of unusual events	O	co-operative reasoning	X
efficiency by shallow models	O	trade-offs of efficiency and completeness	O
completeness by deep models	O	cost/benefit analysis	X

O: fit or implemented; X: not fit or not implemented.

veloped a new method for handling such uncertainty, which combines the AHP with ordinary frame-/rule-based knowledge representation. The method was useful during the knowledge encoding and knowledge refinement phase.

3.2. Knowledge Acquisition and Encoding

The knowledge of HSDS was basically acquired from both the top-level human experts at CRIEPI and the textual information on structural engineering and hydro power stations. The knowledge-bases were verified by the authors, and were validated by the managers and operators of electric utilities who are the end users of HSDS.

The development phase consists of exploratory prototyping, experimental prototyping, and evolutional prototyping stages. In each stage, there are appropriate knowledge acquisition and encoding activities. In this subsection, these activities are discussed for each version of HSDS.

3.2.1. Development of DGDA. For DGDA, the first and second versions were exploratory prototypes. When developing the first version of DGDA, the basic knowledge for diagnosing radial gates was provided by the third author of this paper. Although the initial knowledge was elicited in hand-written form which was not operational, the knowledge was thereafter translated into rule-forms so that it can run on a simple lisp-based production system. It was a very simple system, however, the feasibility of HSDS was confirmed.

The second version of DGDA was developed in KEE (Fikes, 1985) on Symbolics to reveal the problem solving techniques. KEE was selected because of its high knowledge representation facilities and its excellent user interface. In this version, the knowledge was structured in both rule and frame representations. The knowledge was elicited from the third author, and was encoded by the first author. The second version was also used as a demonstration for beginning users. The effect of the demonstration was remarkable because of the advanced user interface provided by KEE.

The third version of DGDA was an experimental prototype to identify the appropriateness of frame and rule structures. In the third version, the basic techniques and the structures of knowledge bases were fixed using the functions that KEE provides. The physical steel structures was modeled in frames; the diagnosing knowledge was represented in rules; and the technique for using the AHP was introduced. They were commonly used for succeeding versions of HSDS. The first case studies were carried out at this point, and the results are described in the next subsection.

The fourth version of DGDA was an evolutional prototype to be used in operational conditions. In the fourth version, the functions of diagnosing roller gates were implemented for the first time. The knowledge bases were confirmed by the other human experts considering several standards. However, for the fourth version, it was very difficult to integrate conventional systems (databases and structural analyzers) with the knowledge-based systems. The difficulty of deploying of HSDS was also pointed out. Thus, we decided to re-implement the whole system on a mainframe computer. The knowledge-based systems were rewritten in Eshell. Eshell was the only tool that runs on the mainframe computer we had. Considering the systems performance such as inference speed and memory requirement, the structures and contents of the knowledge bases were refined to simpler forms in comparison with the previous versions.

3.2.2. Development of PSDA and Integration. The basic techniques used for PSDA were already identified during the development of DGDA. Thus, the exploratory phase could be omitted. The first and the second versions were experimental prototypes to identify the structures of knowledge bases.

In the first version of PSDA, the upper level diagnosing knowledge was directly converted from the one used in DGDA. However, the results sometimes did not coincide with the judgements of human experts.

In the second version of PSDA, the knowledge base was refined to give proper conclusions. To cope with users' requirements, the initial scope of structural analyses (which aimed at the whole structure) was focused on the main parts of a penstock. The knowledge for interpretation was also changed accordingly. The changes of knowledge base were confirmed in parallel by both the development team and intended users.

The third version was an evolutional one to be used to evaluate systems performance. Using the third version, the field investigation data was tested.

As an integrated system of DGDA and PSDA, HSDS was evolutionally developed. The first version of HSDS was used to evaluate the feasibility of deployment. In the second version, the user interface was improved. In both versions, training courses were open for the members of electric utilities. The evaluation results from the courses were also used to refine the user interfaces.

3.3. Knowledge Representation and Reasoning for Empirical Diagnoses

As described above, the unique feature of HSDS for empirical diagnoses is that HSDS uses AHP with ordinary frame/rule-based knowledge representation. The method is outlined below using the case of DGDA (Terano, 1988). The same method is used for the case of PSDA in which more complex decisions are required.

With DGDA, the qualitative items whose importance should be evaluated can be grouped into a hierarchical structure as shown in Figure 7.5. The structure which is introduced naturally at the initial stage of system design coincides with the frame structure of the dam gate in the knowledge base. Each item, except the number of years used, has a score value of 0, 1, 2, or 3 (going from "good" to "bad"). It stands for the observed condition of components in the field investigation reports of each dam site.

To evaluate the importance of each item, the pairwise comparison of the AHP are carried out by human experts. The resulting weights represent the importance of each component. Table 7.5 shows the weights of each component derived from the AHP.

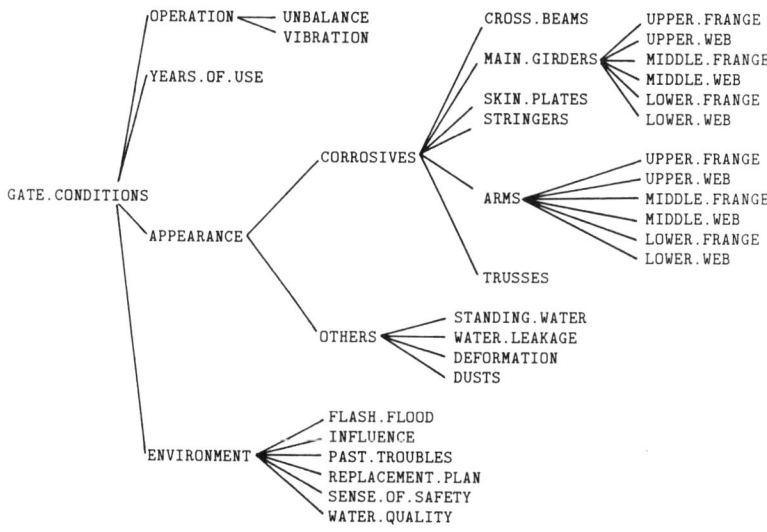

FIGURE 7.5. Qualitative data evaluated by the AHP.

TABLE 7.5
Weights Used for Judging Qualitative Data

Upper Concepts	Items	Score	Weight	Evaluation
External Appearance	(Corrosives)			
	Main Girders	0, 1, 2, 3	0.25	
	Arms	0, 1, 2, 3	0.25	Evaluate
	Skin Plates	0, 1, 2, 3	0.10	Sum of Score * Weight
	Cross Beams	0, 1, 2, 3	0.05	
	Stringers	0, 1, 2, 3	0.05	=0.0–1.0: Good
	Trusses	0, 1, 2, 3	0.05	=1.0–1.5: Fairly__Good
	(Others)			=1.5–2.0: Not__So__Good
	Water Leakage	0, 1, 2, 3	0.10	=2.0–3.0: Bad
	Standing Water	0, 1, 2, 3	0.05	
	Deformation	0, 1, 2, 3	0.05	
	Dusts	0, 1, 2, 3	0.05	
Operation Conditions	Unbalance	0, 1, 2, 3	Max of Unbalance or Vibration	=0: Good
				=1: Fairly__Good
	Vibration	0, 1, 2, 3		=2: Not__So__Good
				=3: Bad
Environmental Conditions	Flash Flood	0, 1, 2, 3	0.083	Evaluate
	Influence	0, 1, 2, 3	0.25	Sum of Score * Weight
	Past Troubles	0, 1, 2, 3	0.083	=0.0–1.0: Good
	Replace Plan	0, 1, 2, 3	0.25	=1.0–1.5: Fairly__Good
	Sense of Safety	0, 1, 2, 3	0.25	=1.5–2.0: Not__So__Good
	Water Quality	0, 1, 2, 3	0.083	=2.0–3.0: Bad
Years of Use	—	0 or 3	—	=0: under 40 years
				=3: over 40 years

The estimated values of higher level components are interpreted by rules to form a final decision. For example, the values in Table 7.5 are used in the following rule:

IF   the Appearance is Good,
       the Operation-Condition is Good,
       the Environmental-Condition is Good,
AND Years-Used is More-Than-40-Years
THEN the Dam Gate is USABLE;

where the meanings of the words 'Appearance', 'Operation-Condition', 'Environmental-Condition' and 'Years-Used' are defined in the frame taxonomy.

3.4. Knowledge Testing and Evaluation

HSDS aims at supporting an important task for *preventive maintenance* of hydro power stations. However, the correctness of diagnosed results from the system cannot be proved in principle, because there have been very few abnormal cases by which the performance of the system can be evaluated. Thus, the system can only be validated in that (1) the knowledge bases are credible for users; (2) the system is matured in its integrity; (3) the performance must be evolutionally refined; and (4) the user interface is adequate for naive users. It took a very long time to evaluate HSDS.

At the end of the experimental prototyping phase of DGDA, the performance of HSDS was first studied using the third version of DGDA with 25 typical cases obtained from the site data. The result was quite satisfying, although the system concludes a little more severely than the judgements of human experts. The validations of succeeding version of HSDS were carried out by the human experts at CRIEPI and the managers at the electric utilities.

Performance of the final version of HSDS was intensively evaluated through the study of over 70 other cases which were collected during the field investigation and maintenance activities. These cases are, of course, carefully selected so that they become representative cases. It took three years to complete the studies. The results were validated by the managers and the maintenance personnels of the electric utilities, who will become the end users of HSDS. The results were also summarized in a manual: *Guideline for Diagnosing Steel Structures at Hydro Power Stations.* The guideline is a prototypical one, and will be refined hereafter at each electric utility according to its proper maintenance strategy.

4. IMPLEMENTATION PROCESS

This section summarizes the strategies of deployment, technology transfer and maintenance of HSDS.

4.1. Deployment Strategies

HSDS heavily uses computer resources for structural analyses, databases, and knowledge-based systems, still requiring to be used at any sites of electric utilities. So, the system must be a centralized system to be used by low cost terminals via telephone lines.

As described in Section 2, the current version of HSDS is installed in a mainframe computer at CRIEPI. The interaction is not so comfortable. However, the deployment strategy is reasonable, because most users use HSDS only several times per year.

4.2. Technology Transfer Strategies

By developing HSDS, the expertise for diagnosing steel structures at hydro power stations has become explicit. The basic idea of the knowledge bases is also provided in document forms. The standardization of investigation activities has also been attained by the prototype manual: *Guideline for Diagnosing Steel Structures at Hydro Power Stations.* The current manual defines the details of activities.

The usage of HSDS is transferred to the personnel of electric utilities after a two-day training course. Henceforth, the course will be held twice a year.

4.3. Maintenance Strategies

As the life span of steel structures is very long, HSDS must also be maintained for many years. To do so, the knowledge bases must be maintained in CRIEPI, and should never be directly modified by the end users. The contents of databases are kept as long as HSDS is used, and are never deleted, because the past records would be of use when unusual event happens. The users can only access the contents of databases on the structures of their own utilities to keep security of the system.

5. CONCLUDING REMARKS

This chapter has described the development of HSDS. There are many deployed expert systems in the world (Schorr, 1989); however, we could not find any similar systems in the literature. The use of structural analyzers and databases makes HSDS unique and usable to provide reliable diagnoses in the domain.

The future work to be done seems to be the following:

- The current version of HSDS has sufficient capabilities in the target domain. However, the domain is too narrow for preventive maintenance works at hydro power stations. The diagnostic domain must be expanded.
- Methods used for empirical diagnoses should be improved so that the methods can be applicable for other decision makings (Breuker, 1989).
- The development process and verification & validation (V&V) activities (Culbert, 1990; Terano, 1990) must be investigated to establish a knowledge system development methodology for integrated knowledge systems (Prerau, 1990).

REFERENCES

Breuker, J., Wielinga, B. (1989). Models of expertise in knowledge acquisition. In: Guida, G., Tasso, C. (Eds.). *Topics in expert system design*, (pp. 265–295). Amsterdam: North-Holland.

Chandrasekaran, B. (1986). Generic tasks in knowledge-based reasoning: High-level building blocks for expert system design. *IEEE Expert*, **1**, (3), 23–30.

Culbert, C. (ed.). (1990). Special issue: Verification and validation of knowledge-based systems. *Expert Systems with Applications*, **1**, (3).

Fikes, R., and Kehler, T. P. (1985). The role of frame-based representation in reasoning. *Comm. ACM*, **28**, (9), 904–920.

Prerau, D. S. (1990). *Developing and managing expert systems—proven techniques for business and industry*. Massachusetts, Addison-Wesley.

Saaty, T. L. (1980). *The analytic hierarchy process*. New York, McGraw-Hill.

Schorr, H., Rappaport, A., (Eds.) (1989). *Innovative applications of artificial intelligence*. Menlo Park, AAAI Press.

Terano, T., Sinohara, Y., Matsui, S., Nakamura, H. (1988). Dam gate diagnosing advisor—An expert system for steel structures. *Proc. IEEE/SICE Int. Workshop on Artificial Intelligence for Industrial Applications*, pp. 129–134.

Terano, T., Kobayashi, S. (1989). Problem analyses, tool evaluation, and verification & validation study: Three steps for knowledge-based systems development methodology. *IJCAI-89 Workshop on VV&T of Knowledge-Based Systems*.

Terano, T., Kongoji, H., Kaji, K., Yamamoto, K. (1990). Developing a guideline for expert system evaluation—A midterm report. *Proc. PRICAI'90*, pp. 164–169.

APPENDIX: SAMPLE SESSION AND OUTPUT FROM HSDS

In the Appendix, sample outputs of DGDA are shown with brief explanations. The samples are classified into character-based ones and graph-based ones. The character-based samples are both displayed on the terminal and printed out as diagnostic reports. Original reports are all written in Japanese; however, in the Appendix, the samples are translated into English. The graph-based samples are generated by the structural analyzer, and can be printed out via facsimile at any branches of electric utilities.

Figures 7A-1 and 7A-2 are the first and the second level menus of HSDS. For the convenience of the end users, the functions of HSDS are classified for each structure. So, the second menu says that DGDA has the functions of database retrieval, structural analyses, diagnoses, and report generation.

Figure 7A-3 shows a sample menu for database retrievals. The menus are designed so that the display images are similar to the format of field investigation reports.

Figure 7A-4 shows graphic images of a generated FEM model for a radial gate, and results of the structural analyzer by FEM. DGDA gets the main analytical values to compare with the measured values. These results are used for mechanical diagnosis.

In Figures 7A-5, 7A-6 and 7A-7, we show some parts of diagnosis reports. First, the results of the structural analyses are interpreted. In the report, data reliability and violation of permissible data values are carefully examined. The main results are shown first (Figure 7A-5); then the detailed reports follow (Figure 7A-6). Second, results of empirical diagnoses are given. The diagnoses are done based on the qualitative data in the field investigation (Figure 7A-7).

```
                  1         2         3         4         5         6         7         8
         12345678901234567890123456789012345678901234567890123456789012345678901234567890
         =================  < Hydro Steel Structure Diagnosing System >  ===============
 1
 2             SELECT ====>
 3
 4             1. Diagnoses of A Radial Gate
 5
 6             2. Diagnoses of A Roller Gate
 7
 8             3. Diagnoses of A Penstock
 9
10             4. Database for Hydroway Bridges
11
12             5. Database for Steel Screen
13
14             6. Miscellaneous
15
```

FIGURE 7A-1. First menu of HSDS.

```
                  1         2         3         4         5         6         7         8
         12345678901234567890123456789012345678901234567890123456789012345678901234567890
         =====================  < Dam Gate Diagnosing Advisor >  ====================
 1
 2             SELECT ====>
 3
 4             1. Investigation Report Input/Update/Retrieval
 5
 6             2. Structural Analyzer
 7
 8             3. Knowledge-Based System
 9
10             4. Report Output
11
12             5. Job Conditions
13
```

FIGURE 7A-2. Second level menu of HSDS (DGDA).

```
                  1         2         3         4         5         6         7         8
         12345678901234567890123456789012345678901234567890123456789012345678901234567890
         ====================  < Data Retrieval : Radial Gate Outline >  ================
 1
 2         Date:            1991 August, 19
 3         Company:              CRIEPI Electric Comp.
 4         Station:              ABIKO Station
 5         Dam-name:             ABIKO Lake
 6         River-name:           ABIKO River
 7         Gate-name:       A.111
 8         Width:           12.5 m  Height: 8.5 m    #Gates: 8
 9         Depth(Design):         10.2 m          Depth(Operation): 8.0 m
10         Earthquake Power:      0.2 g           Overflow Rate:    4400 m^3/sec
11         Weight:                44.0 ton
12         Material:              SS41 steel      Max. Stress:      1025 kgf/cm^2
13         Sealing:               Front 3-way Rubber
14         O/C Operation:         Electric Motor with Ropes
15         Operation Speed:       0.30 m/sec
16         Constructor:           CRIEPI Const. Corp.
17         Operation Start:       1958 April
18         Years Used:            33 Years        Replaced Date:
19
```

FIGURE 7A-3. Display for data input/update of DGDA.

GENERATED FINITE ELEMENT MODEL OF RADIAL GATE

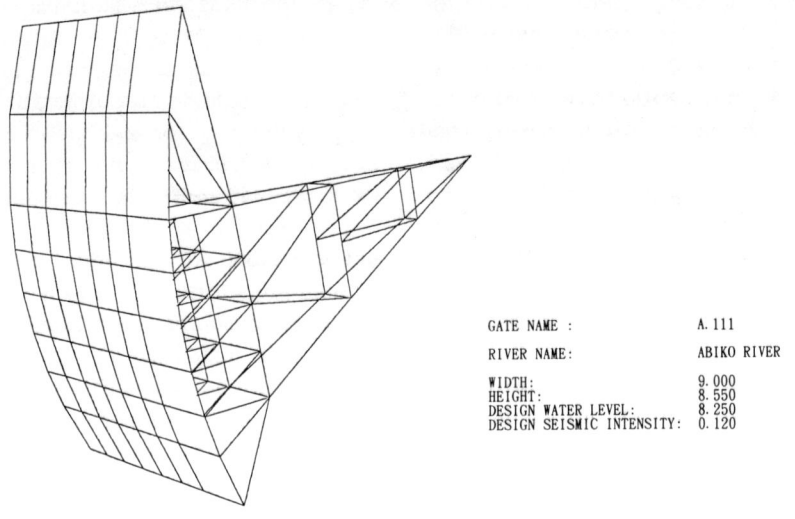

GATE NAME :	A.111
RIVER NAME:	ABIKO RIVER
WIDTH:	9.000
HEIGHT:	8.550
DESIGN WATER LEVEL:	8.250
DESIGN SEISMIC INTENSITY:	0.120

RADIAL GATE INSPECTION SYSTEM

RESULT OF STATIC ANALYSIS DISPLACEMENT

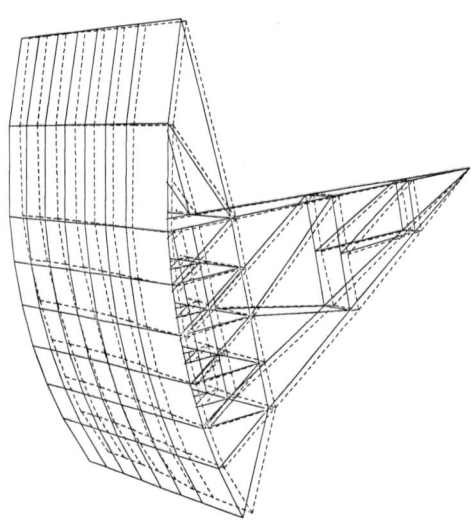

RADIAL GATE INSPECTION SYSTEM

FIGURE 7A-4. FEM model and the results of the structural analyzer.

```
*************************************************************************
*                 Start Diagnoses by Structural Analysis                 *
*************************************************************************
        Summary of Data Used by the Structural Diagnosis:
        Total # Data:   Measured: 21    Computed: 21
        Data Compared:          14 pairs
        High Reliable Data:      5 pairs (35% of the Total Pairs)
        Low  Reliable Data:      9 pairs (64% of the Total Pairs)

********** Diagnosis on the Displacements of Main Girders ************

        All displacements are within the permissibles (width/800).
        Max. displacement is found at the Hor. Direct. Center of the Upper
        Main Girder,   the value is (width/3050).

************* Diagnosis on the Stresses of Main Girders ***************

        All stresses are within the permissibles (compression/tension).
        Max. stress is found at the Low Str. Middle of the Lower Main
        Girder, the value is (0.54/permissible stress).

****************** Diagnosis on the Stresses of Arms ******************

        All stresses are within the permissibles (compression/tension).
        Max. stress is found at the Middle of the Lower Arm,
        the value is (-0.59/permissible stress).

****************** Diagnosis on the Buckling of Arms ******************

        The arms are sufficiently strong against buckling,
        the vertical buckling load is 22.1 times higher than the designed
        value.

                                  .....
                                  .....
                                  .....
```

FIGURE 7A-5. Diagnosing results of structural analyses (1).

```
*********** Detailed Report on the Reliability of the Data ************
[Displacement]
    The following data are high reliable, because the ratio between
    the measured and the analytical value is within 30%.
        Part            Var. Name              anal.   meas.   used
        Lower Arm       Hor. Direct. Center    0.182   0.159   Anal.

    The following data is low reliable, because there exists only
    the analytical value. The analytical values are used in the
    diagnoses.
        Part                Var. Name              anal.
        Upper Main Girder   Hor. Direct. Center    0.295
        Upper Main Girder   Ver. Direct. Center    0.06
        Lower Main Girder   Ver. Direct. Center    0.081
        Upper Arm           Hor. Direct. Center    0.15
        Upper Arm           Ver. Direct. Center    0.025
        Lower Arm           Hor. Direct. Center    0.014

    The following data is abnormal, because there two or more data
    whose ratio between the measured and the analytical value is
    not within 30%. The measured values are used in the diagnoses.
        Part                Var. Name              meas.   anal.   used
        Lower Main Girder   Hor. Direct. Center    0.268   0.42

                                . . . . .
                                . . . . .


****************** Graph of the Displacement Values *******************

    Width/800 = 1.125 cm

        -Width/800              0              Width/800
    ----------------+---------------+---------------+----------------
                    :               : @             :                  #1
                    :               : @             :                  #2
                    :               :       *       :                  #2
                    :               :    @          :                  #4
                    :               : @             :                  #5
                    :               : @             :                  #6
                    :               :@              :                  #7
                    :               : @             :                  #8
                    :               :  *            :                  #9
                    :               :@              :                  #10
    ----------------+---------------+---------------+----------------
    #1  Displacement of Upper Main Girder Hor. Direct Center (Anal.)
    #2  Displacement of Upper Main Girder Ver. Direct Center (Anal.)
    #3  Displacement of Lower Main Girder Hor. Direct Center (Anal.)
    #4  Displacement of Lower Main Girder Hor. Direct Center (Mea.)
    #5  Displacement of Lower Main Girder Ver. Direct Center (Anal.)
    #6  Displacement of Upper Arm Hor. Direct Center (Anal.)
    #7  Displacement of Upper Arm Ver. Direct Center (Anal.)
    #8  Displacement of Upper Arm Hor. Direct Center (Anal.)
    #9  Displacement of Upper Arm Hor. Direct Center (Mea.)
    #10 Displacement of Upper Arm Ver. Direct Center (Anal.)
    @: Data used for diagnoses, *: Data not used for diagnoses

                                . . . . .
                                . . . . .
```

FIGURE 7A-6. Diagnosing results of structural analyses (2).

```
**************************************************************************
*                        Start Empirical Diagnoses                        *
**************************************************************************

The Dam Gate is USABLE,
     because Appearance is Good,
             Operational_Condition is Good,
             Environmental_Condition is Good.
             Years_Used  is More_Than_40_Years

Detailed Qualitative Data and Explanation:

     Evaluation_Result        :         USABLE

     Appearance:
         Upper Main Girder    Frange Corrosion:    Fairly_Good
         Upper Main Girder    Web    Corrosion:    Not_So_Good
         Lower Main Girder    Frange Corrosion:    Fairly_Good
         Lower Main Girder    Web    Corrosion:    Not_So_Good
         Upper Arm            Frange Corrosion:    Fairly_Good
         Upper Arm            Web    Corrosion:    Not_So_Good
         Lower Arm            Frange Corrosion:    Fairly_Good
         Lower Arm            Web    Corrosion:    Not_So_Good
         Skinplate            Back   Corrosion:    Fairly_Good
         Stringers                   Corrosion:    Fairly_Good
         Cross Beams                 Corrosion:    Not_So_Good
         Trusses                     Corrosion:    Fairly_Good
         Water Leakage                          :  Little
         Standing Water                         :  Moderate
         Dusts                                  :  None
         Deformation                            :  None

     Operational_Condition:
         Unbalance                              :  None
         Vibration                              :  None

     Environmental_Condition:
         Flash Flood                            :  Little
         Influence                              :  None
         Past Troubles                          :  None
         Replace Plan                           :  None
         Sense of Safety                        :  Good
         Water Quality                          :  Good

     Years_Used                                 :  41 Years


                                  . . . . .
                                  . . . . .
                                  . . . . .
```

FIGURE 7A-7. Diagnosing results based on empirical knowledge.

DIAS2: A Diagnosing System for Automobiles with Electronic Control Units

SUK I. YOO AND IL KON KIM

Artificial Intelligence Laboratory, Dept. of Computer Science and Statistics, Seoul National University, Korea

1. INTRODUCTION

AS MICROPROCESSOR technology has been developed, some crucial parts of automobiles have been controlled by electronic devices using microprocessors. Such electronic devices, called Electronic Control Instruments (ECI), control the engine, transmission, cruise, suspension, and brake system to keep automobiles running in the optimal status. Although the performance of automobiles is greatly enhanced by means of these electronic devices, the diagnosis of automobiles becomes very hard. The components controlled by the ECI are so complicated related to one another that long experienced and well-trained mechanics with technical knowledge about the ECI are required for the correct diagnosis. Tiny actions based on the wrong diagnosis, due to a lack of expertise, may result in fatal damage to the ECI and its related components.

Hyundai Motor Service Company is responsible for diagnosing and fixing problems of all automobiles produced by Hyundai Motor Company in Korea. The problem that the HMSC has faced is that experienced and well-trained mechanics with technical knowledge about the ECI are few, and it takes a long time to train such qualified mechanics. To resolve this problem, the development of an expert system for diagnosing automobiles controlled by the ECI was suggested. Specially, an expert system for diagnosing engines controlled by one of the ECI, called Electronic Control Unit (ECU), was suggested to be developed at the first stage.

An expert system, called DIAS2, for diagnosing automobile engines controlled by the ECUs has been developed jointly by the Artificial Intelligence (AI) lab of Seoul National University and the AI team of Hyundai Electronics Industries Company in Korea.

2. DEVELOPMENT PROCESS

In this section, we describe the problems that the DIAS2 is developed to resolve and the approach for developing the DIAS2.

2.1. Problem Selection

Automobiles produced by Hyundai Motor Company have MPI engines controlled by the ECUs. As shown in Figure 8.1, the ECU consists of an 8-bit microprocessor, RAM, ROM, and I/O Interface (Hyundai, 1988).

Based on the information taken from the input sensors and switches, the ECU drives the output actuators to keep the engine in the optimal status. When those components related to the ECU or the ECU itself do not work properly, automobiles get in trouble, for example, engine starting problems, unstable idling, and poor driving force. Problems of automobiles are diagnosed by the mechanics based on data and symptoms observed either by an automatic self-diagnosis mechanism or manually. In either case, it is evident that the

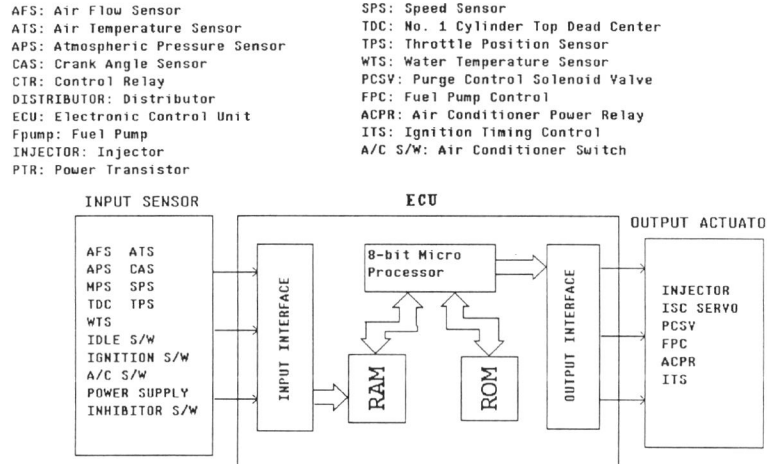

Figure 8.1. Diagram of ECU.

more experienced and well-trained mechanics are about the ECU the more accurately the problems are diagnosed. The efficiency of the diagnosing procedure varies depending on what action should be taken for fixing the detected problem. As one example, suppose that the self-diagnosis number associated with the Air Flow Sensor (AFS) is detected. If an automobile mechanic is a novice, he will simply check if the AFS works well by using the checking procedure from the shop manual. If the AFS seems not to work well, he will replace it with a new one and try to check whether any self-diagnosis code is detected. This action may solve the problem in some cases. However, it does not solve most cases because all of the input sensors, ECU, and output actuators are functionally related to one another, so that even if the AFS number is detected it may be from the other faulty part. Further, if the AFS seems to work well when the checking procedure is applied the mechanic may be in trouble. However, if the mechanic is experienced and has a deep knowledge of AFS and its related components, he will try several other approaches to find the exact faulty part.

To supply such qualified mechanics, however, is not easy, because knowledge about the ECU is too complicated and vast to be memorized in a short time. To overcome this difficulty the development of a computer system for diagnosing the MPI engines using knowledge about the ECU and expertise of the mechanics is required.

2.2 Knowledge Acquisition

The field of knowledge acquisition requires a methodological framework which logically supports the process of knowledge acquisition, identifies the characteristics of the products of knowledge acquisition, and offers a set of ordered assumptions about the nature of knowledge and its characteristics. The initial objectives of knowledge acquisition are to identify both the characteristics of the task situation and the method used by the problem solver to address the task. In developing the DIAS2, we first attended the mechanic's training program provided by the HMSC for a week to learn what parts are to be diagnosed and what actions should be taken for diagnosing those parts. From this program and discussions with the mechanics attending this program, we reached the conclusion that the difficult parts for the mechanics to understand and diagnose are those the electronic devices are used for like the MPI engine, the brake system, the cruise-control system, and the transmission system. We thus selected the MPI engine as the target for which the diagnosing expert system is developed at the first stage. The general knowledge about the MPI engine was taken from the shop manuals and related automobile texts, and the detailed procedure to detect feasible faults in the MPI engine was taken from the mechanic's training program and the well-trained mechanics. The knowledge taken was refined and represented using the formats required by the factbase of the SAILOR, discussed in the next section.

2.3 Knowledge Representation

A diagnosing system DIAS2 was developed using an expert system shell, called SAILOR (Kim et al., in press; Min & Yoo, 1990; Park & Yoo, 1990), that was designed and implemented by our lab. The SAILOR consists of five modules: a knowledge base, an inference engine, a user interface, a database interface, and an object module as shown in Figure 8.2.

The features of the SAILOR may be described by explaining briefly each component contained in it.

Knowledge Base. A knowledge base consisting of factbase and rulebase supports an object-oriented programming (Tello, 1989). Factbase describes the specific knowledge of objects by means of FACTCLASS, FACT, and METHOD. Each FACTCLASS defines one object class by declaring the types or the default values of the associated attributes, and each FACT represents one instance of one object class by specifying the related values of the attributes defined in the object class. METHOD gives an algorithm which implements operations defined on the types or the values of the attributes of an object. Property inheritance, which is well known to be one of the advantages of an object-oriented programming, can be done between two FACTCLASSes by specifying one FACTCLASS as the superclass of the other, or between a FACTCLASS and a FACT by specifying the FACT as one instance of the FACTCLASS.

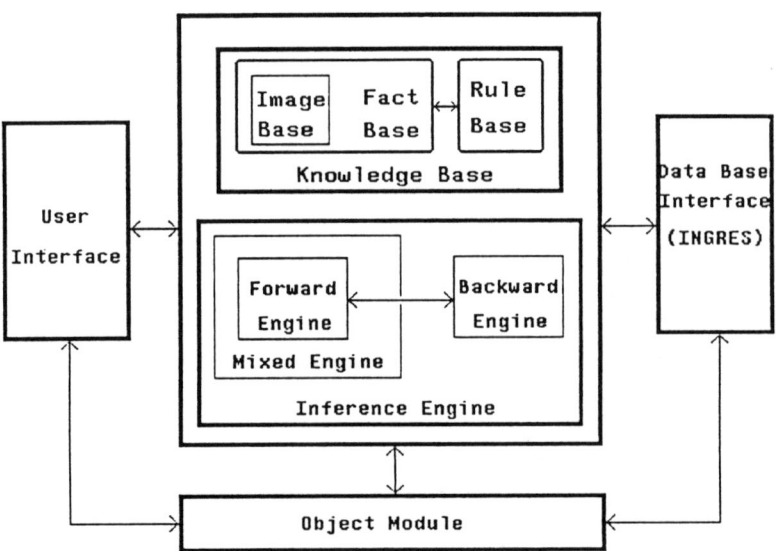

Figure 8.2. Diagram of SAILOR.

For example, the AFS implemented for the DIAS2 in the next section is defined by one FACTCLASS, as shown below, and ENGINE defined by another FACTCLASS is declared as its superclass. METHOD AFS following FACTCLASS AFS describes an algorithm by which the voltage meter is drawn on the window and the value represented on the voltage meter (called the active image), is retrieved to be stored into factbase of the DIAS2.

```
FACTCLASS AFS (ENGINE)
{
    voltage:        [valuetype float]
                    [inherit instance]
    state:          [valuetype
                    string{"good","broken"}]
                    [inherit instance]
    control_relay_afs_wire:
                    [valuetype
                    string{"good","broken"}]
                    [inherit instance]
    earth:          [valuetype
                    string{"good","broken"}]
                    [inherit instance]
    power:          [valuetype int]
                    [inherit instance]
    power_state:    [valuetype
                    string{"good","broken"}]
                    [inherit instance}
}
METHOD private AFS::get_from_
    voltage(object obj, ob)
{
    object ROUND_METER, WINDOW;
    object win1;
    int val;
    if (win1.open = = "no")
    {
        win1.open = "yes";
        WINDOW::win_open_method(win1);
    }
    if (obj.visible = = "no")
    {
        obj.visible = "yes";
        ROUND_METER::draw_round_
            meter(obj);
    }
    write ("Select Voltage on the Image. n");
    ob.voltage = ROUND_METER::get_value_
        from_meter(obj);
    write ("V = ", ob.voltage:2,". n");
}
```

Rulebase describes the general knowledge of objects by means of RULECLASS and RULE. One task may be completed by performing a sequence of subtasks, each of which may use its own inferring direction for achieving the goal. Each RULECLASS declares one of the three inferring directions: forward, backward, and mixed. Each RULE declares one RULECLASS as the one it belongs to. The following example is a part of rulebase of the DIAS2.

```
RULECLASS AFS_m (ENGINE)
{
DIRECTION :forward
}
RULE afs_1 (AFS_m)
{
    If : (car)
    do : (print "> Does engine start?
            (On/Off) \ n")
        (read en_st)
        (modify car start = en_st)
}
```

Inference Engine. An inference engine supports three different chaining directions: forward, backward, and mixed direction. Two matching algorithms developed for FORWARD and MIXED procedures in the SAILOR are expanded RETE algorithms, based on the Rete network algorithm which is well known to be an efficient matching algorithm (Forgy, 1982). Since the Rete was developed for processing the simple rule-based system in the forward direction, it cannot be applied directly to the object-oriented knowledge-based system either in the forward direction or in the mixed direction. Some augmentations are required to match object-oriented knowledge because Rete algorithm is appropriate for matching unstructured knowledge. Object-oriented knowledge designates the descriptions of objects and the relationships between objects. Rules handle both the objects and inter-relationships between objects. As an object may be either a factclass or a fact, the descriptions of both types of objects are used in rules. The inter-relationships are determined by the positions of objects in the inheritance lattice. Object-oriented paradigm directly supports the relationship notions of generalization, which is used to show families of similar objects. In one version of expanded Rete, two special nodes are introduced for matching object-oriented knowledge. These are the filter node, which distinguishes facts from factclasses, and the structure node, which discriminates inter-relationships between two objects. The other version, which is applied to the object-oriented knowledge base in the mixed direction, has been formulated by adding the hypothesis-nodes to the node network generated by the Rete. Finally, the matching algorithm developed for BACKWARD procedure is based on the backtracking algorithm using stack structure. The details of the three matching algorithm can be found in Kim et al. (in press).

User Interface. A user interface consists of four modules: a factbase browser, a rule browser, an explanation subsystem, and a graphic editor. A factbase browser is designed to show graphically the relationship between objects defined by FACTCLASS and FACT in the factbase. By allowing all operations on factbase to be done directly through the factbase browser, a knowledge engineer is able to maintain factbase easily. The graphical representation of the relationship between the objects is implemented by linking one FACTCLASS to another FACTCLASS (declared as its superclass) and a FACT to a FACTCLASS (declared as its class). A rule browser is designed to show graphically the sequence of rules fired during the inferencing process. The graphical representation of the sequence of the fired rules is implemented by linking the tokens generated by the node network when the rules are fired. An explanation subsystem is designed to explain why and how the current result is derived by giving the associated history. A graphic editor provides two mechanisms: one for showing the static image of the figure and the other for showing the active image of the figure. Further details can be found in Park and Yoo (1990).

Database Interface. A database interface is designed to provide two operations, UPLOAD and DOWNLOAD, for data transfer between factbase in SAILOR and database in INGRES (Stonebraker et al., 1986) database management system (Abarabanel et al., 1989; Kim et al., in press). The UPLOAD operation which transfers data from factbase to database is implemented by converting one FACTCLASS and its associated FACTs into one table in database and its tuples where each attribute of the FACTCLASS becomes one field of the table. Conversely, the DOWNLOAD operation which transfers data from database to factbase is implemented by converting one table and its tuples into one FACTCLASS and its associated FACTs (Abarabanel et al., 1989; Kim et al., in press). Figure 8.3 below shows one example of data transfer from database in INGRES to factbase in SAILOR.

Object Module. An object module provides a hierarchical data structure of factbase and a set of operations defined on factbase so that all the transactions required to access factbase are performed by means of these operations. The algorithms to formulate the hierarchical data structure by analyzing factbase, and to implement a set of operations can be found in Kim et al. (in press).

In the DIAS2, the forward inferring method is selected to take advantage of the fast matching time of the RETE. The knowledge bases of MPI, TESTER, DATA, SYMPTOM and ENGINE are thus refined in a way that the desired conclusion is always derived when the inference is done in the forward direction.

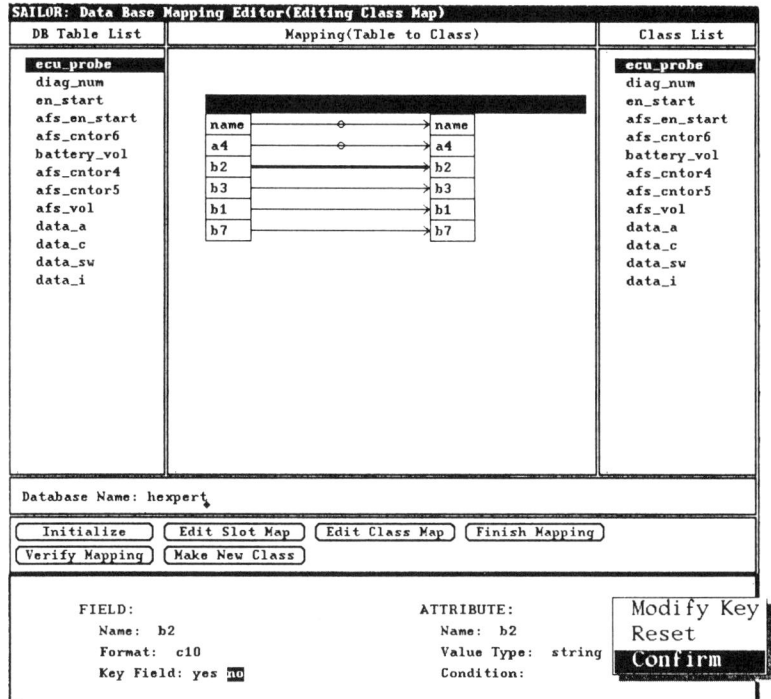

Figure 8.3. Mapping from INGRES to SAILOR.

2.4 Knowledge Encoding

The knowledge base of the DIAS2 was formulated based on the knowledge of an expert taken from his long field experience and technical knowledge about ECU and its related components. In formulating the knowledge base, the diagnosing knowledge of the expert mechanic and the technical knowledge about the ECU were refined and combined. The knowledge base formulated this way resulted in some new knowledge even the expert did not provide.

The DIAS2 was designed to diagnose two different types of automobiles: automobiles with Self-diagnosis Mechanisms, and automobiles without Self-diagnosis Mechanisms. We first present the overall design process of the DIAS2 and then illustrate its operations by three examples.

When there is a trouble in an automobile, the self-diagnosis mechanism allows the mechanic to assume the feasible faulty component related to the ECU. When there is a warning light indicating a problem in an automobile, the mechanic can detect one of twelve self-diagnosis numbers from the self-diagnosis probes of the MPI engine, where each self-diagnosis number indicates one of eleven input and output components of the ECU or the ECU itself. The feasible faulty component indicated by the self-diagnosis number, however, is often not correct because the indicated component itself may be good but some other part related to that component may be bad. To find the exact faulty part in this case, further detailed diagnosing process based on the technical knowledge about the ECU is required. For diagnosing automobiles with self-diagnosis mechanisms, the DIAS2 is designed to start with the observed self-diagnosis number, and based on this number keep asking the data for the actions necessary for further detailed diagnosing process until the exact faulty part is found.

Automobiles without self-diagnosis mechanisms may be diagnosed in two ways depending on the availability of the ECU-Checker. The ECU-Checker is a PC-based system where its tester is plugged into the ECU probes of the MPI engine and the measured data are automatically stored into database kept in the PC. When diagnosing automobiles using the ECU-Checker, the data measured from the ECU probes and the data assumed in the normal condition are compared. According to the difference, further diagnosing process is continued until the faulty part is detected. The DIAS2 is designed to store data collected by the ECU-Checker into a database contained in the INGRES database management system which is connected to the SAILOR, compare the stored data to the normal data, and continue based on the difference the diagnosing process until the conclusion is reached.

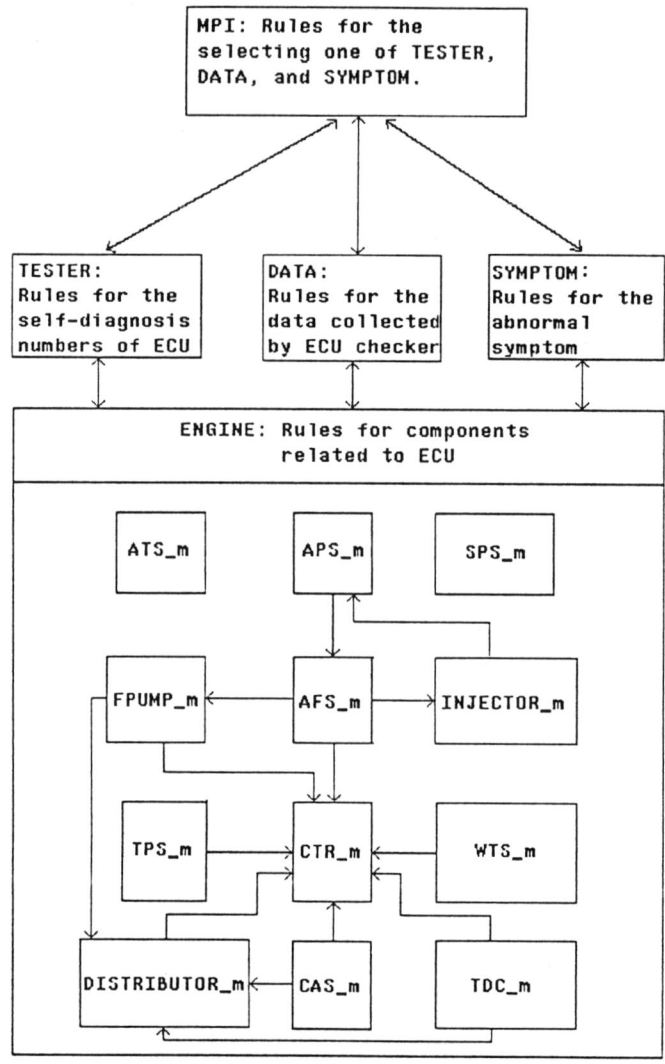

Figure 8.4. Rulebase of DIAS2.

Finally if the ECU-Checker is not available, the diagnosis of the automobile may start with a symptom claimed by the driver. The DIAS2 is designed to start with one of eight frequently claimed symptoms, and based on the claimed symptom keep asking for further information until the exact faulty part is found.

The diagnosing knowledge implemented in the DIAS2 was obtained from a long experienced and well-trained mechanic employed in the HMSC, the shop manual (Hyundai, 1988), and the related automobile texts (Choi, 1989). The knowledge taken has been formulated by five interrelated rulebases as shown in Figure 8.4. Rulebase ENGINE contains 12 ruleclasses with 240 rules which represent the knowledge for diagnosing the components related to the ECU. Rulebase TESTER contains one ruleclass with 30 rules, which process the observed self-diagnosis numbers and activate their associated rules contained in ENGINE for further processing.

Rulebase DATA contains one ruleclass with 50 rules which compare the data collected by the ECU-Checker to the normal data and activate their associated rules in ENGINE. Rulebase SYMPTOM contains one ruleclass with 70 rules which process the symptoms claimed by the drivers, ask further information, and activate their associated rules in ENGINE for further processing. Finally rulebase MPI contains one ruleclass with 5 rules which ask the types of automobiles diagnosed and activate one of the three rulebases, TESTER, DATA, and SYMPTOM, according to the given automobile type.

For each ruleclass defined in rulebase, one or more than one factclass is defined to declare the values or the types of the attributes of the object used in the rules contained in it. For each factclass, one fact is defined to accept the current status of the object given during the diagnosing process. As mentioned in the SAILOR, factbases represented by factclasses and facts can be formulated on the

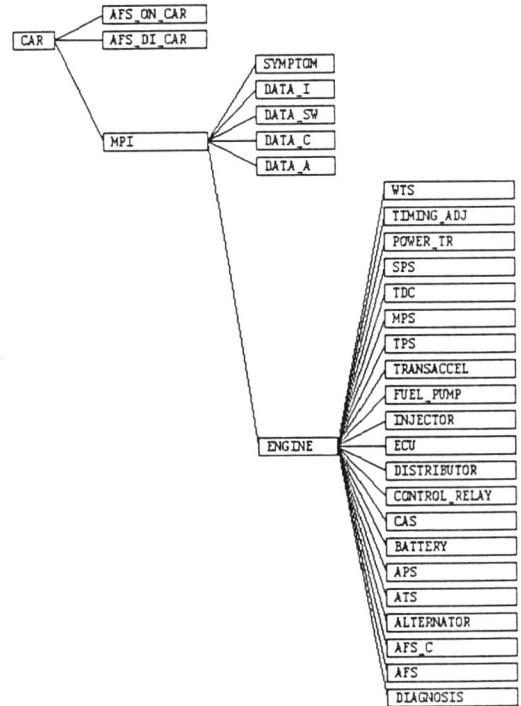

Figure 8.5. Factbase of DIAS2.

hierarchical structure so that all properties of an object defined at the higher level are inherited into an object at the lower level. Factbase of the DIAS1 is formulated on the 4-level tree structure as shown in Figure 8.5.

Diagnosis of Automobiles with Self-Diagnosis Mechanisms. When diagnosing automobiles with self-diagnosis mechanisms, the DIAS2 starts with a query about the detected self-diagnosis number by activating one rule contained in rulebase MPI. Rules contained in TESTER and ENGINE are then processed in the forward chaining direction until the conclusion is reached.

As one example, suppose that an automobile has some problem and the self-diagnosis number 12 is detected. The DIAS2 starts with the self-diagnosis number 12 entered through the active image window by the mouse and keeps asking the necessary questions following the answers given by the user until the conclusion is reached as shown in Figure 8.6.

Diagnosis of Automobiles without Self-Diagnosis Mechanisms. Automobiles without self-diagnosis mechanisms are diagnosed in two ways depending on the availability of the ECU-Checker.

When diagnosing automobiles using the ECU-Checker, the DIAS2 starts with the query about the availability of the data from the ECU-Checker in the INGRES database management system. If available, the data stored in database of the INGRES are transferred to factbase of the DIAS2 by activating one rule in MPI. Based on these data the DIAS2 keeps asking for further data and actions by processing rules contained in DATA and ENGINE in the forward chaining direction until the conclusion is reached. The following example shown in Figure 8.7 is the case that one of 40 data collected by the ECU-Checker, given by 4 as the voltage of the WTS, is not normal.

When diagnosing automobiles without using the ECU-Checker, however, the DIAS2 starts with the query about a symptom

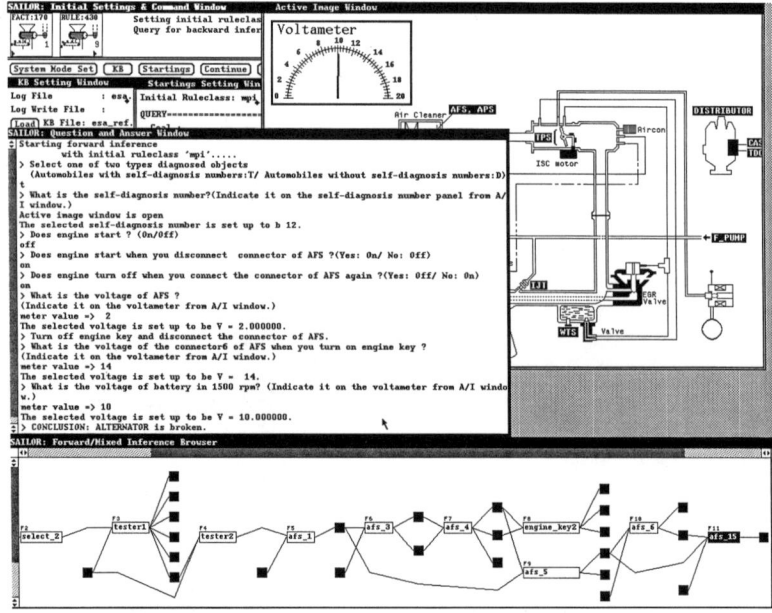

Figure 8.6. Diagnosis of automobile with self-diagnosis mechanism.

Automobile Diagnosing System

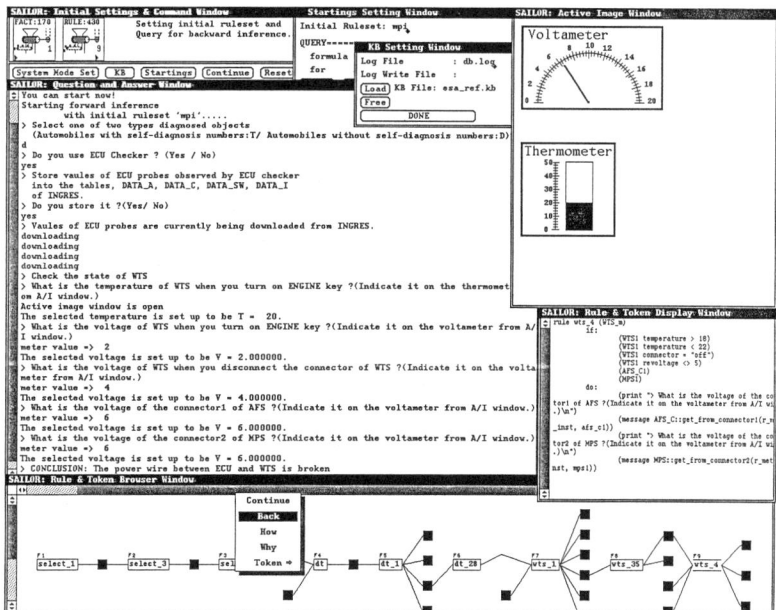

Figure 8.7. Diagnosis of automobile without self-diagnosis mechanism using ECU-checker.

claimed by the driver. Based on the claimed symptom, the DIAS2 keeps asking for further information by processing rules contained in SYMPTOM and ENGINE in the mixed chaining direction until the conclusion is reached. Figure 8.8 shown below is one example that an engine starting problem is claimed.

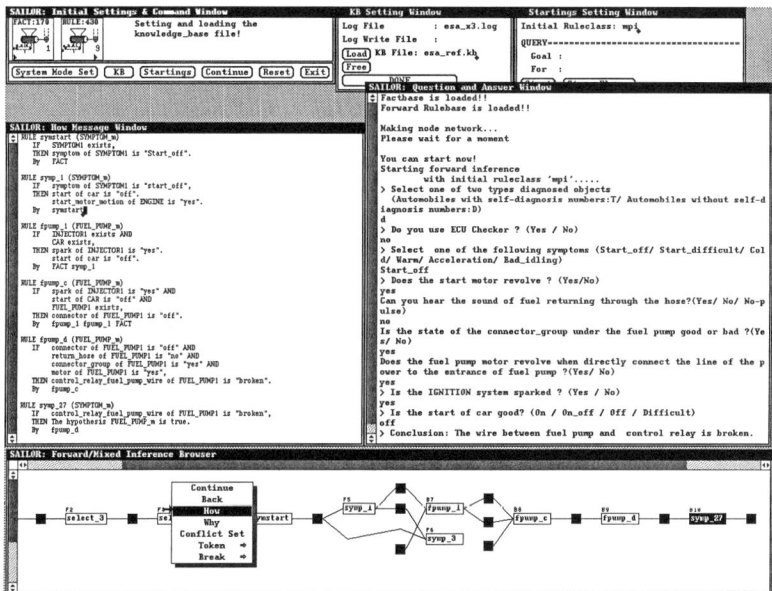

Figure 8.8. Diagnosis of automobile without self-diagnosis mechanism not using ECU-checker.

2.5 Knowledge Testing and Evaluation

To see the DIAS2 working correctly, the output printed from the Question & Answer Window was presented to the mechanic who had given us the diagnosing knowledge. He was satisfied with most cases from the output, suggesting minor modification on the output format. He also asked us to add a procedure for fixing up the faulty parts concluded from the diagnosing procedure, which was, however, decided to be added to the second version of the DIAS2.

Table 8.1 shows the 12 ruleclasses defined in ENGINE, the number of the related rules, and the number of faults diagnosed by those rules.

As shown in Table 1, the DIAS2 is able to detect 60 parts which are possibly broken in the MPI engine. Time taken to reach the conclusion to indicate the faulty part varies depending on the availability of the input data required by the system. If it is assumed that every input data is immediately given, it takes less than one minute to reach the conclusion through the sequence of ten rules.

3. IMPLEMENTATION PROCESS

3.1. Deployment Strategies

The DIAS2 has been developed to be used for educating mechanics in the training center of the HMSC as well as for diagnosing the MPI engines in the A/S branches of the HMSC. The DIAS2 can be delivered using the delivery system of the SAILOR:

As shown in Figure 8.9, the delivery system of the DIAS2 is completed as one package by filling up the appropriate names into Product_Name, Initial_Ruleclass_Name, Initial_Query, Output_Directory, and Making_tar_format, and by activating Start—Packaging button. The DIAS2 is currently operated on a Sun workstation using the SunView system for a single user. Figure 8.10 shows the initial screen of the DIAS2.

The DIAS2, currently designed for a single user, will be expanded to the new version for multi-users based on the Server-client model.

3.2. Technology Transfer and Maintenance Strategies

All detailed techniques used for developing the DIAS2 are described in the Appendix of Technical Report of SAILOR (Kim et al., in press) given to the AI team of the Hyundai Electronics Industries Co. In making the technical report, two engineers from the HEIC joined us to understand the technologies used in the SAILOR and the DIAS2. The DIAS2 is to be managed by two knowledge engineers from the HEIC who were involved in this

TABLE 8.1
Ruleclasses in ENGINE

Ruleclass	Number of Rules	Number of Diagnosed Faults
AFS	28	6
APS	20	5
ATS	15	3
CAS	22	7
CTR	16	6
DISTRIBUTOR	16	5
F-PUMP	13	4
INJECTOR	23	5
SPS	3	1
TDC	22	7
TPS	22	6
WTS	40	5

Automobile Diagnosing System

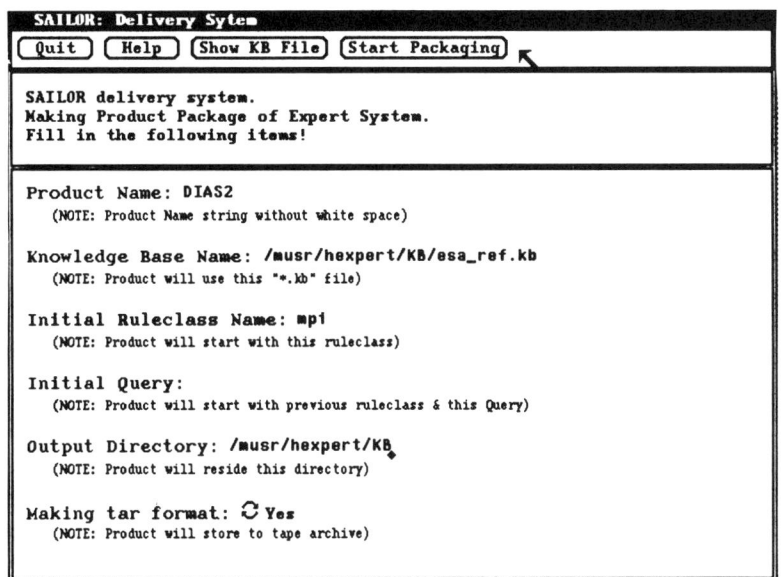

Figure 8.9. Delivery system.

project and one expert mechanic from the HMSC who gave us the diagnosing knowledge.

For easy maintenance and expansion of the knowledge base of the DIAS2, it consists of the 3-layered rulebase and the 4-level tree structured factbase as shown in Figures 8.4 and 8.5. The knowledge for diagnosing automobiles is then easily modified and expanded by editing the necessary parts directly through the factbase browser and the rulebase browser provided by the SAILOR. The factbase browser and the rulebase browser are designed to show graphically the 4-level tree

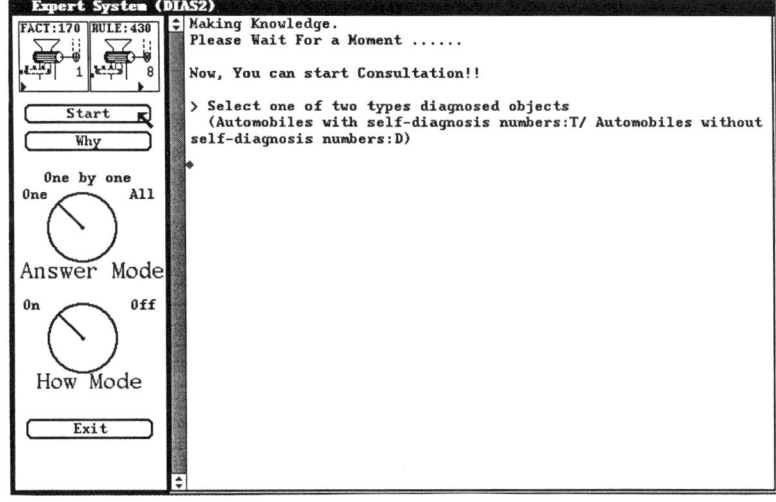

Figure 8.10. Initial screen of DIAS2.

structured factbase and the 3-layered rulebase, and to allow the knowledge engineers to edit their contents directly.

4. DISCUSSION

The DIAS2 developed jointly by the AI laboratory of Seoul National University and the AI team of Hyundai Electronics Industries Company in Korea is an expert system for diagnosing the MPI engines of automobiles with ECUs which are produced by Hyundai Motor Company in Korea. The DIAS2 is currently being reviewed by the top trainers in Hyundai Motor Service Company who educate and train mechanics working in many distributed branches of Hyundai Motor Service Company, and it will be soon released to those branches. The DIAS2, which currently diagnoses engines with ECUs, will be expanded to diagnose other parts of automobiles such as suspension, transmission, cruise, and brake systems.

REFERENCES

Abarabanel, R., Tou, F., & Gilbert, V. (1989). KEEconnection: A bridge between databases and knowledge bases. In M.H. Richer (Ed.), *AI tools and techniques*. Norwood, NJ: Albex.

Choi, I. (Ed.). (1989). *Automatic electronics instruments*. Seoul: Il-jin Press.

Forgy, C. (1982). Rete: A fast algorithm for the many pattern/many object pattern problem. *Artificial Intelligence*, **19**(1), 17-37.

HYUNDAI Motors Corporation. (Eds.). (1988) *HYUNDAI GRANDEUR, SONATA, and EXCEL shop manual*. Seoul.

Kim, I., Park, C., Chang, H., Kim, T., & Min, M. (in press). *Technical report of SAILOR*. Seoul, Korea.

Min, M. & Yoo, S. (1990). SAILOR: Design and implementation of an expert system shell. *Korea Information Science Society*, **17**(2), 163-172.

Park, C. & Yoo, S. (1990). Developing environment for building knowledge-based systems. *Korea Information Science Society*, **17**(1), 40-51.

Stonebraker, M., Kreps, P., Wong, E., & Held, G. (1986). The design and implementation of INGRES. In M. Stonebraker, (Ed.). *The INGRES papers: Anatomy of a relational database system*. Reading, MA: Addison-Wesley.

Tello, E. (1989). *Object-oriented programming for artificial intelligence*. Reading, MA: Addison-Wesley.

UNIK-PCS: A Crude Oil Delivery Scheduling System

JAE KYU LEE*, YONG UK SONG*, MIN SOO SUH*,
AND HAN SEONG YUN**

*Department of Management Science, Korea Advanced Institute of Science and Technology, Cheongryang, Seoul, Korea;
**Petroleum Business Operation Development Team, Yukong Ltd., Yoido, Seoul, Korea

1. INTRODUCTION

WE HAVE DEVELOPED an expert system, UNIK-PCS, which aids the crude oil delivery scheduling for refinery plants. UNIK-PCS was specifically developed for Yukong Limited. The system attempts to minimize each of the following cost factors individually: purchase prices, quality loss, delivery cost, and inventory cost. If a conflict occurs between the objectives, meta-knowledge based tradeoffs guide the solution toward the global optimum solution. We have described the scheduling procedure with an example. The schedule from UNIK-PCS was quite well accepted by field experts.

1.1. The Problem

Refineries in Far Eastern countries such as Korea and Japan purchase all the necessary crude oil via oil tankers from overseas oil producers. Therefore, the crude oil delivery scheduling (CODS) is very important. The CODS problem is very complex because: the vessel selection and routing have the integer programming feature; the blending has a nonlinear feature; some problem features (default decisions, disjunctive relationships) cannot be represented by a mathematical model; the necessity of heavy reactive controls during the contract causes the reactive scheduling feature. For these reasons, the traditional mathematical programming approach cannot effectively tackle this problem. Fortunately, the domain expert's scheduling strategies can reduce computational complexity while maintaining a satisfactory level of quality in the solution. Therefore, a knowledge-based approach seems to be an appropriate choice.

There are few literature about the integrated production planning and scheduling models. Concerning the integrated refined products planning models, read Klingman et al. (1987a, 1987b), and Chung (1989). For the literature about refinery planning, read Adams & Griffin (1972), and Wagner (1969); for unit process, Baker (1981); for blending, Arthur (1980) and DeWitt et al. (1989); for ocean transportation scheduling problem, Brown et al. (1987), and McKay & Hartley (1974). For the survey of models and problems for ship routing and scheduling, read Ronen (1983). For more information about UNIK-PCS, you may read Lee et al. (1989), Lee and the Associates (1989), Lee et al. (1990), and Song (1990).

In this chapter's specific case study, we attempt to solve the problem of Yukong Ltd. (one of the leading refineries in Korea), which has to generate a daily crude oil delivery schedule out of the lump-sum monthly optimal purchase amount provided by optimization packages such as Bonner & Moore Inc.'s Refinery and Petro-chemical Modeling System (RPMS). In the following sections, we

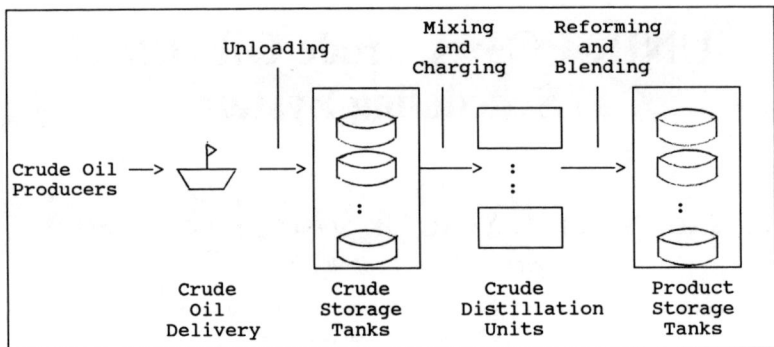

FIGURE 9.1. Flow of a crude oil refinery.

explain the nature of the CODS problem, the methodology behind the solution, and our experience with the knowledge-based scheduling system, UNIK-PCS, that was jointly developed by the KAIST and Yukong research teams.

2. NATURE OF REFINERY AND CRUDE OIL DELIVERY

2.1. Nature of the Problem

1. *Crude Oils.* The general flow of a crude oil refinery is depicted in Figure 9.1. Crude oils are produced at various places throughout the world. The oils consist mainly of a complex mixture of hydrocarbons. Although the assay of each crude oil—the contents of the mixture—differs from origin to origin, the typical assay is specified by the yield of the reduced crude oil, the proportion of sulfur, viscosity, pour point, etc. According to their assays, crude oils can be classified into the following crude groups: high sulfur, low sulfur I, low sulfur II, condensate, and high pour. The crude oil producers set a minimum selling quantity for each purchase.

2. *Tankers.* Crude oils can also be grouped by their regional origin: Middle East, South East, Red Sea, North Africa, West Africa, North Sea, North America, Middle America, and South America. Since the crude oils are delivered long distance from these nine regions via oil tankers and since the purchase contract takes time, the crude oil delivery should be scheduled about three months in advance.

As a means of delivery, there are several types of oil tankers with different capacities. Since the fixed cost portion of leasing a vessel is so large, a larger size is in general more economical so long as we effectively utilize this capacity. However, port and canal sizes restrict the vessel sizes allowed in each region. Therefore, a default decision is to use the vessel of the largest allowable capacity for each region. Another important factor to be considered is that one to four types of crude oils should be delivered together by a vessel to support the operations in a refinery.

3. *Unloading.* When a vessel anchors at the port of an oil refinery, the crude oils are unloaded from the buoy on the sea to the crude oil storage tanks through pipelines. Thus, the number of buoys restricts the maximum number of vessels that can anchor at one time. The unloading usually takes two days. Since there are a limited number of crude oil storage tanks, different crude oils may have to be mixed together within a tank. If we mix the crudes during the unloading in chargeable composition for distillation, we can utilize the crudes without extra mixing.

4. *Distillation.* The chargeable crude oils are charged to a Crude Distillation Unit (CDU), yielding a primary stream which can be upgraded by reforming. The reformed oils are finally blended into marketable products. Each CDU may be dedicated to a high or low sulfur crude oil distillation, but a certain CDU

may be used alternately for both types of crude oils. When the CDU is used alternately, the minimum switching interval between the two different crudes should be at least two days, because overly frequent alternation deteriorates the quality of the output stream. Although the chargeable crude oils must satisfy assay constraints (for instance, the sulfur contents in low sulfur oils should be less than 1.5%), excessive quality means *quality loss* because customers do not pay for this extra quality.

Each CDU has a maximum processing capacity, minimum requirement, and recommended processing level. Sometimes a CDU must be shut down for cleaning or repairs. Safety stocks of products are necessary to cope with the unexpected delays in delivery that may be caused by bad weather or a seller's political situation.

2.2. Definition of Crude Oil Delivery Scheduling

Let us define the scope of the CODS problem formally. The monthly purchase amount is given by an optimization model. To transform the monthly plan into a daily basis delivery schedule, we have to consider not only the purchase price but also the delivery and inventory costs. We can summarize the characteristics of CODS as follows:

1. Objectives
    a. Minimize purchase price
    b. Minimize quality loss
    c. Minimize delivery cost
    d. Minimize inventory cost
2. Decisions
    a. Scheduling of vessel arrival date
    b. Vessel type selection
    c. Assignment of crude oils to each vessel
    d. Vessel routing
3. Constraints
    a. Operation of CDUs
    b. CDU capacity limits
    c. CDU shutdown schedule
    d. Minimum switching interval for alternately used CDUs
    e. Minimum selling quantity for each crude oil
    f. Scale of producer's port
    g. Vessel capacity limits
    h. Minimum difference in the arrival times of two successive vessels at refiner's port
    i. Minimum chargeable inventories of high and low sulfur crude oils
    j. Maximum total inventory of crude oils
4. Input from Monthly Lump Sum Purchase Plan
    a. Monthly purchase amount of each crude oil
    b. Monthly charge amount of each crude oil to each CDU

3. SOLUTION METHOD

To reduce complexity, we decompose the problem into three distributed problems:

TABLE 1
Problem Decomposition

Subproblem	Constraints	Objectives	Decision
CDU Charge Scheduling	Minimum switching interval CDU capacity CDU shutdown schedule	—	—
Crude Oil Consumption Scheduling	Minimum chargeable inventory	Minimize quality loss	Vessel arrival date
Crude Oil Supply Scheduling	Minimum selling quantity Vessel availability Capacity of vessel Minimum difference in the arrival times of vessels Maximum total inventory	Minimize purchase, delivery, and inventory cost	Vessel type selection, Assignment of crude oils to a vessel, Vessel routing

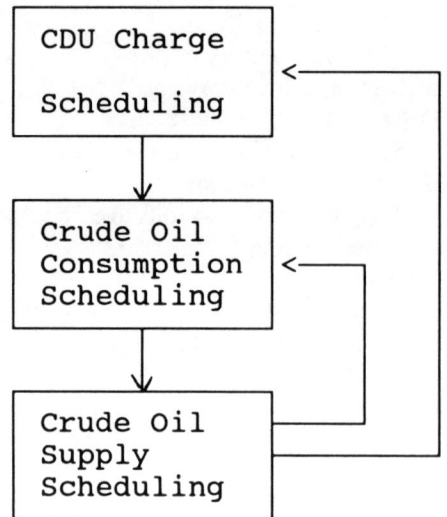

FIGURE 9.2. Interactions between subproblems.

CDU charge scheduling, crude oil consumption scheduling, and crude oil supply scheduling as listed in Table 9.1. The interactions between subproblems are depicted in Figure 9.2.

3.1. CDU Charge Scheduling

The CDU charge schedule subproblem can be easily solved by assigning the monthly total charge amount into the daily charge amount for each CDU without violating the constraints associated with the minimum switching interval, CDU capacity and shutdown schedule. In the Yukong case, CDU1 is dedicated to high sulfur crudes, CDU2 to low sulfur crudes, and CDU3 to both types of crudes. An example of a CDU charge schedule is shown in Figure 9.3. CDU1 was shut down from 08/01/90 to 08/09/90.

3.2. Crude Oil Consumption Scheduling

A chargeable crude oil inventory should be maintained at a level so as to avoid any quality loss due to the unavailability of a timely supply of necessary crude oils. The consumption schedule comes from the CDU charge schedule. The inventory levels of chargeable crude oils are reduced daily according to the CDU charge schedule so long as there is enough inventory left for the day's charge. If we do not have sufficient inventory—which is detected when the minimum chargeable inventory level is violated—it is time to send a message to the Crude Oil Supply Scheduling subproblem so that a vessel can arrive two days earlier than the violated day, since two days are normally required for unloading. In this manner, the chargeable inventory level can be increased following the delivery. The consumption and supply are iterated on a daily basis until the last day of the month. For the calculation of consumption amount, we have applied the monthly standard consumption ratio among five crude oil groups. Figure 9.4 shows the chargeable inventory levels of high sulfur and low sulfur crude oils with a violation report.

CDU charge Schedule				
Date	CDU1	CDU2	CDU3H	CDU3L
08/01/90	0	100,002	115,643	0
08/02/90	0	100,002	0	122,749
08/03/90	0	100,002	0	122,749
08/04/90	0	100,002	0	122,749
08/05/90	0	100,002	0	122,749
08/06/90	0	100,002	115,643	0
08/07/90	0	100,002	115,643	0
08/08/90	0	100,002	115,643	0
08/09/90	0	100,002	0	122,749
08/10/90	55,000	100,002	0	122,749
08/11/90	55,000	100,002	0	122,749
08/12/90	55,000	100,002	0	122,749
08/13/90	55,000	100,002	115,643	0
08/14/90	55,000	100,002	115,643	0

FIGURE 9.3. CDU charge schedule.

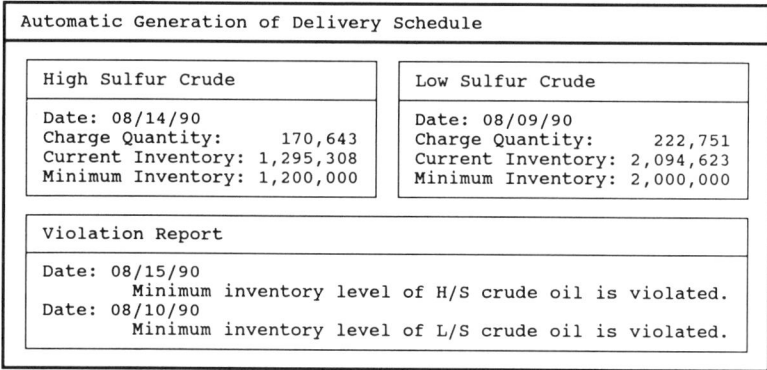

FIGURE 9.4. Checking chargeable inventory.

3.3. Crude Oil Supply Scheduling

As mentioned earlier, crude oils must be delivered whenever the minimum chargeable inventory level is violated. For each violation, the vessel size should be selected, and the combination of crudes with their amounts for the vessel should be determined.

During the vessel allocation, the monthly purchase amount may have to be adjusted because of the "tiny-amount" problem. The tiny amount problem occurs when the remaining purchase amount is less than the minimum selling quantity. To handle the tiny amount problem, we can consider several strategies. First, if we have sufficient inventory for the month, do not buy for this month. Second, if the inventory cost is more economical than the substitutional cost, buy as much as the minimum selling quantity and use for more than one month. The last strategy is to replace the tiny oil with other oil(s), even if it may be a little bit more expensive in terms of oil price, should the saving in inventory holding cost exceed the extra cost caused by the higher price. In Figure 9.5, the crude oils ARH, MUR, YEM and BAL have tiny amount problems. In this example, the amount of YEM is adjusted to 540,000. The adjustment may be done either manually or automatically by rules.

We may deliver crude oils for each violation of the minimum inventory level. If we can deliver all of the monthly purchase amount by the iteration of consumption and supply, a feasible schedule is found. However,

Tiny Amount Adjustment	Crude Oil	Quantity	
		Remained	Minimum
Current Vessel Assignment			
Vessel : LR2-RSEA	ARH	109,058	500,000
(900,000 - 1,200,000)	ARM		500,000
Crude Oils :	ARN		500,000
(GSM 305,753)	DKN		450,000
(YEM 510,291)	KWT	944,043	200,000
Total : 816,044	LZK	509,578	450,000
YEM(510,291) is tiny !	MUR	288,300	450,000
	USF		400,000
Press 's', or 'q' !	OMN	300,000	300,000
	SJH		400,000
{{ Blackboard	YEM	510,291	540,000
Crude : YEM	BAL	419,368	500,000
-->Remained-qty : 540,000	GSM	305,753	300,000
Purchase-p : YES	RBD		300,000

FIGURE 9.5. Tiny amount adjustment during scheduling.

Generated Delivery Schedule : August 1990					
Date	CDU Charge Q.			Inventory	Total
	L/S	H/S	L/S	H/S	
1	90	190	3059	3421	6480
2	90	190	2969	3231	6200
3	90	190	2879	3041	5920
4	((ABK 509)	(OMN 921)	(MUR 288))	{VLCC}	
	230	50	2789	2851	5640
5	230	50	2559	2801	5360
6	((ARN 435)	(CHN 417))		{LR2-SE}	
	230	50	2329	2751	5080
7	230	50	2099	2701	4800
8	90	190	2319	3801	6120
9	90	190	2229	3661	5840
10	((GSM 400)	(YEM 540))		{LR2-RSEA}	
	230	50	2139	3421	5560

FIGURE 9.6. A generated delivery schedule.

if it is not possible, we have to backtrack to previous vessels for adjustment. Because of this characteristic, delivery scheduling is a kind of search problem. Since performing a blind search for all combinations of crude oils expands the computational amount exponentially, we must utilize expert advice to decide the reasonable combination of crude oils for each vessel. During the search process, the purchase amount is also adjusted to fit the vessel's capacity: if the vessel has empty space and the inventory cost is less than the delivery cost, we should deliver at full capacity.

3.4. Generated Delivery Schedule

By resolving conflicting objectives among distributed problems, we seek the near optimal delivery schedule, as in Figure 9.6. The figure shows the charge schedule, inventory, and delivery schedule (date, composition of crude oils and vessel type).

The vessel is selected with the largest size within the producer's port scale limitation. The most needed crude oil determines the major producer for the vessel. As a next step for the given vessel, a route is determined considering the transportation of the other complementary oils. According to the expert's experience, the relationship between vessel type, production region of the major crude oil, and route are recommended as in Table 9.2.

4. UNIK-PCS: A KNOWLEDGE-BASED CRUDE OIL DELIVERY SCHEDULER

To realize the approach mentioned above, a knowledge-based system UNIK-PCS (Uni-

TABLE 2
Example of Vessel Routing Knowledge

Vessel	Route by Region
VLCC	Red Sea* → Middle East → Korea
LR2-RSEA	Red Sea → Korea
LR2-SE	South East → Korea
LR2-AFR	North Sea ⌐→ North Africa → Korea West Africa ⌙
LR2-ED	South America → Middle America → North America → Korea

* For BAL and YEM crude oils only.

fied-Knowledge Purchase) was developed by the KAIST research team. The overall architecture of UNIK-PCS is depicted in Figure 9.7. The key components are fact base, generated schedule, and rule base.

4.1. Tools

Knowledge in the fact base, schedule base, and the crude consumption model are represented in *frames,* while the rule base is represented in *production rules.* For implementation, the proprietary tools UNIK-FRAME and UNIK-FWD are used respectively.

4.2. Knowledge in the Fact Base

The fact base contains the domain description and constraints: crude specification (charge type, crude group, minimum selling quantity, region), crude purchase plan (monthly purchase amount and charge amount to each CDU, dates when the crudes become unavailable), vessel (region, vessel capacity, dates when the vessels are unavailable), CDU (assay constraints, minimum chargeable inventory, maximum total inventory, shutdown interval, CDU capacity), and prefixed delivery schedule (prefixed crude oils, quantities, and delivery date). Sample constraints are shown in

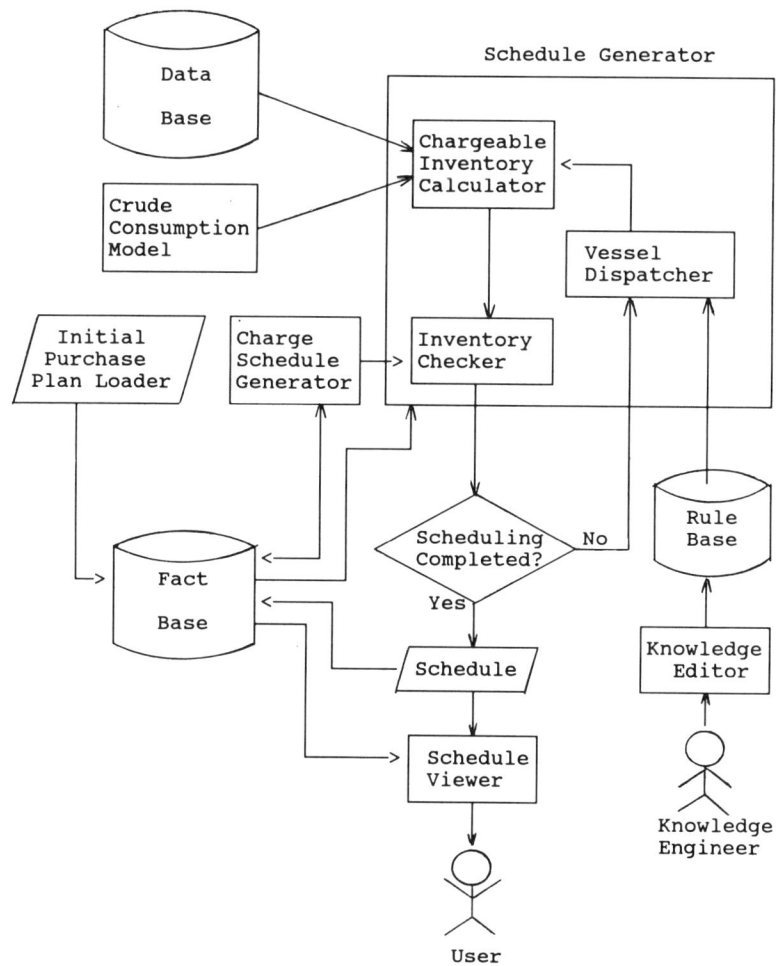

FIGURE 9.7. Overall architecture of UNIK-PCS.

```
{{ Crude                                    {{ P-Crude
   Is-a+INV : ABK SJH ... }}                   Instance+INV : P-ABK ... }}

{{ ABK
   IS-a : Crude
   Charge-to : H/S-CDU
   Crude-group : H/S
   Min-selling-quantity : 450,000
   Region : ME   }}

{{ P-ABK
   Is-a : ABK
   Instance : P-Crude
   Monthly-Quantity : 540,000
   CDU#1-quantity : 200,000
   CDU#2-quantity : 0
   CDU#3-H/S-quantity : 340,000
   CDU#3-L/S-quantity : 0   }}
```

FIGURE 9.8. An example of frames in the fact base.

Figure 9.8. In Figure 9.8, the frame ABK represents a crude oil, while the frame P-ABK represents a purchase plan of the crude oil ABK for this month. The frame P-ABK inherits all the slot values of frame ABK such as charge-type, crude group, min-selling-quantity, and region via the IS-A relationship.

4.3. Generated Schedule

The generated CDU charge schedule is also represented in frames. Likewise, the generated delivery schedule is represented in *tree structure*, whose nodes are represented in frames. Our search heuristic is conducted with this tree.

```
(RULE Select-crude-for-ME-I

    "This rule selects a crude oil from region ME with
    highest priority"

    [necessity first]
    [region same-region]
    (rule-control
       ^frame-name 'p-rule-control
       ^active-rule-group 'slack-usage
       ^current-region 'ME)
    (p-crude
       ^frame-name <new-crude>
       ^vessel-status 0
       ^region 'ME)
    (rule-control
       ^frame-name 'p-rule-control
       ^priority-flag (p-purchase-priority-I <new-crude>))
    ——>
    (p-register-new-crude <new-crude>)
    (new-value 'p-rule-control 'active-rule-group 'tiny-adjustment))


(META-RULE Slack-usage-necessity-I
    (RULE
       ^name <rule>
       ^necessity 'first)
    ——>
    (fire <rule>))

(META-RULE Slack-usage-region-I
    (RULE
       ^name <rule>
       ^region 'same-region)
    ——>
    (fire <rule>))
```

FIGURE 9.9. An example of production rules.

4.4. Knowledge in the Rule Base

Illustrative production rules and meta-rules are shown in Figure 9.9.

The rule Select-crude-for-ME-I shows how to assign a vessel. The rules are categorized into four rule groups: selection of crude oil, determination of vessel, adjustment of tiny crude oil, and combination of crudes for a vessel. When a rule in a rule group is fired, a corresponding rule in the next rule group is fired accordingly. This process continues until a vessel assignment is accomplished. When there are conflicts between rules, the conflicts are resolved by *meta-rules*, which identify the priority among rules. The conflicts usually occur when several crude oils are selected for a vessel. In this case, the most needed crude oil is selected, as illustrated by the meta-rule in Figure 9.9.

5. RESCHEDULING

After the generation of the crude oil delivery schedule, the oil refiner will buy the crude oils as recommended by the schedule. However, some crude oils may not be able to be purchased due to the producer's predicament. Some vessels may not be able to be hired. In such cases, the data-driven UNIK-FWD is

Crude Oil Rundown

89.10   Crude Oil & Products Dept. (UNIT : MBBL)

Day	Vessel	Cargo Grade	Cargo Volume	Charge L/S	Charge H/S	Inventory L/S	Inventory H/S	Inventory Ttl.
1				170	146	2808	2438	5248
2						↓	↓	↓
3								
4	TBN*	⌈ SJH	400			2298	2000	4298
5		H/S	600			↓	↓	↓
6		⌊ OMN	500			2858	2308	5166
7						↓	↓	↓
8	TBN	⌈ KFJ	800			2518	2016	4534
9		UZK	500			↓	↓	↓
10		⌊ OMN	500			2678	3024	5702
11						↓	↓	↓
12	TBN	L/S	800			2338	2732	5070
13						↓	↓	↓
14						2798	2440	5238
15						↓	↓	↓
16	TBN	SEN	390			2458	2148	4606
17						↓	↓	↓
18	TBN	⌈ H/S	1000			2508	1856	4634
19		⌊ MRB	620			↓	↓	↓
20						2788	2564	5352
21	TBN	⌈ BN2	550			2618	2418	5036
22		⌊ COL	300			↓	↓	↓
23						3128	2126	5254
24						↓	↓	↓
25	TBN	⌈ H/S	1000			2788	1834	4622
26		⌊ L/S	500			↓	↓	↓
27						2948	2542	5490
28						↓	↓	↓
29	TBN	⌈ KWT	800			2600	2250	4850
30		⌊ OMN	920			↓	↓	↓
31						3188	2758	5946

Average   170   146

* TBN : To Be Named

FIGURE 9.10. A schedule by experts three-months-ahead.

invoked for rescheduling in the light of the situation. During rescheduling, the unavailable crude oils and vessels are excluded from the candidate list.

6. PERFORMANCE EVALUATION

We cannot compare the performance of UNIK-PCS with the global optimum solution which we never know. However, we can evaluate it in contrast with the performance of the human scheduler. The quality of the schedule generated by UNIK-PCS is at least as good as the one provided by the human schedulers with a partial computing aid. The information that can be generated by UNIK-PCS is also more comprehensive. The outputs by UNIK-PCS were well accepted by the human schedulers, who could easily reschedule within a few minutes during the contract process.

For instance, compare the three-months-ahead and one-month-ahead schedules by a human scheduler (Figures 9.10 and 9.11) and the three-months-ahead schedule by the UNIK-PCS (Figure 9.12). The UNIK-PCS

<u>Crude Oil Rundown</u>

1989.09.22
Crude Oil & Products Dept.
(UNIT : MBBL)

89.10

Day	Vessel	Grade	Cargo VolumeH	VolumeL	Charge L/S	H/S	Inventory L/S	H/S	Ttl.
1					250	60	4907	3114	8021
2					250	60	4657	3054	7711
3	TBN	SEN*	390		250	60	4407	2994	7401
4					250	60	4157	2934	7091
5	Narica	BN2ᵖLBN*394/450			100	220	4297	2874	7171
6					100	220	4197	2654	6851
7	Y.Winner	TAP#CHN 276/600			250	60	4941	2434	7375
8					250	60	4691	2374	7065
9					250	60	5317	2314	7631
10					100	220	5067	2254	7321
11					100	220	4967	2034	7001
12					100	220	4867	1814	6681
13					250	60	4767	1594	6361
14					250	60	4517	1534	6051
15					250	60	4267	1474	5741
16	Y.Pioneer	CHN(#/*)500/500			250	60	4017	1414	5431
17		FAO*		300	100	220	3767	1354	5121
18					100	220	4667	1934	6601
19					250	60	4567	1714	6281
20					250	60	4317	1654	5971
21	Y.Fron	SJH	400		250	60	4067	1594	5661
22		KFJ#/UZK(M)		800/500	100	220	3817	1534	5351
23					100	220	4117	2614	6731
24					100	220	4017	2394	6411
25	Y.Comm.	LZK#ARM*/KWT 350/400/500			250	60	3917	2174	6091
26		OMN#	500		250	60	3667	2114	5781
27					250	60	3917	3304	7221
28					100	220	3667	3244	6911
29					100	220	3567	3024	6591
30	TBN	COL*		400	100	220	3467	2804	6271
31					100	220	3367	2984	6351
				Average	182	132	4289	2300	6589

*SK ᵖPOLICY #SPOT

FIGURE 9.11. A schedule by experts one-month-ahead.

Crude Oil Rundown

89.10   (UNIT : MBBL)

Day	Vessel	Grade	Cargo Volume LS/HS	Charge L/S	Charge H/S	Inventory L/S	Inventory H/S	Inventory Ttl.
1				235	64	5150	2604	7755
2				235	64	4916	2541	7456
3				235	64	4681	2477	7158
4				100	234	4581	2244	6825
5				100	234	4481	2010	6491
6				100	234	4381	1777	6158
7	LR2-SE	BN2 TAP CHN	394 300 206 / - - -					
8				235	64	4146	1713	5859
				235	64	3911	1650	5561
9	VLCC	KFJ OMN UZK	800 170 500 / - 283 -					
10				235	64	4577	1586	6163
11				100	234	4477	1353	5829
12				100	234	4660	2436	7096
13				100	234	4560	2203	6762
				235	64	4325	2139	6464
14	LR2-SE	CHN LBN	394 506 / - -					
15				235	64	4090	2076	6166
16				235	64	3855	2012	5867
				100	234	4655	1779	6434
17	VLCC	OMN MUR LZK KWT	17 450 450 600 / 283 - - -					
18				100	234	4555	1545	6100
				100	234	4455	1311	5767
19	LR2-ED	ORI	325 / 325					
20				235	64	4504	2765	7269
				235	64	4269	2701	6970
21	LR2-SE	SEN HAN	400 400 / - -					
22				235	64	4359	2963	7322
				100	234	4259	2729	6988
23	VLCC	SJH KWT DKN ARM	327 400 450 500 / 28 - - -					
24				100	234	4959	2496	7455
				100	234	4859	2262	7121
25	LR2-AFRICA	KOL	959 / -					
26				235	64	4652	3921	8573
27				235	64	4417	3858	8275
28				235	64	5142	3794	8936
29				235	64	4907	3731	8637
30				100	234	4807	3497	8304
31				100	234	4707	3264	7970
				100	234	4607	3030	7637

FIGURE 9.12. A schedule by UNIK-PCS three-months-ahead.

provides a more comprehensive schedule that satisfies all the constraints.

7. IMPLEMENTATION PROCESS

7.1. Deployment Strategies

For the first version of UNIK-PCS, LISP versions of UNIK-FRAME and UNIK-FWD were used. The LISP version was effective for the development process, but its speed was too slow for use in the field. Thus, we have converted the LISP versions to C. The speed was enhanced about 10 times, so that a schedule could be made within a few minutes.

7.2. Knowledge Acquisition

Human schedulers very sincerely explained the nature of the domain, their experiences, and expertise for codification by knowledge engineers. Nevertheless, a large portion of heuristic knowledge should have been normatively developed by knowledge engineers due to the nature of the scheduling problem. This means that to reduce computational complexity in expert systems, we not only have to collect expertise from experts, but also have to devise heuristic rules normatively. This seems to be a general principle for the knowledge-based scheduling systems.

7.3. Technology Transfer

We kept in close communication with the Yukong research team from the beginning of the project's development. Comprehensive education in expert system tools and approaches were conducted for the Yukong team. The Yukong team also participated in the coding stage so that they could both help the development and enhance maintenance capabilities.

8. CONCLUSION

In this chapter, we have explained how the knowledge-based system UNIK-PCS has solved the crude oil delivery scheduling problem. UNIK-PCS provides a quality schedule with comprehensive information and rapid reactivity.

Although the current version of UNIK-PCS is already realistic enough to be used in the field, the enhancement of knowledge is an on-going concern. We need to simulate a variety of heuristic knowledge before we reach the best knowledge we can get.

ACKNOWLEDGEMENTS

We owe the success of the UNIK-PCS project to many people: particularly, members of the Yukong Ltd. (Director Se Jong Wang, Manager Sang Jin Joo, Manager Chang Kuk Kum, Manager Yun Sung Lee, and Mr. Mun Hag Kwon) and the members and graduates of the DSS/ES Laboratory of the Korea Advanced Institute of Science and Technology (Mr. Sung Man Ahn, Mr. Byung Kwon Park, Mr. Jae Bu Chung and Mr. Min Yong Kim).

REFERENCES

Adams, F.G., & Griffin, J.M. (1972). Economic-linear programming model of the U.S. petroleum refining industry, *J. Amer. Statist. Assoc., 67,* 542–551.

Arthur, J.L., & Lawrence, K.D. (1980). A multiple goal blending problem, *Comput. and Ops. Res., 7,* (3), 215–224.

Baker, T.E. (1981). A branch and bound network algorithm for interactive process scheduling, *Math. Programming Study, 15,* 43–57.

Brown, G.G., Graves, G.W., & Ronen, D. (1987). Scheduling ocean transportation of crude oil, *Management Sci., 33,* (3), 335–346.

Chung, J.B. (1989). *A Knowledge-Based Production Scheduling System for Oil Refinery.* Master's Thesis, KAIST.

DeWitt, C.W., Lasdon, L.S., Waren, A.D., Brenner, D.A., & Melhem, S.A. (1989). OMEGA: An improved gasoline blending system for Texaco, *Interfaces, 19,* (1), 85–101.

Klingman, D., Phillips, N., Steiger, D., & Young, W. (1987a). The successful deployment of management science throughout Citgo Petroleum Corporation, *Interfaces, 17,* (1), 4–25.

Klingman, D., Phillips, N., Steiger, D., Wirth, R., Padman, R., & Krishnan, R. (1987b). An optimization based integrated short-term refined petroleum product planning system, *Management Sci., 33,* (7), 813–830.

Lee, J.K., Suh, M.S., Song, Y.U., & Yi, Y.S. (1989). Toward the knowledge-based optimization and knowledge-based relaxation of complexity: A case of crude oil delivery scheduling for refinery plant, *Workshop on Manufacturing Production Scheduling,* IJCAI Detroit.

Lee, J.K., & the Associates (1989). *Development of UNIK for the Integration of Knowledge and Optimization Models and its Application to Petroleum Industry,* Technical Report N486-3509-7, KAIST.

Lee, J.K., Oh, S.B., Suh, M.S., Kim, M.Y., & Song, Y.U. (1990). Knowledge network for planning and control of refinery industry: UNIK-R project experience, *The Fourth International Conference on Expert Systems in Production and Operations Management,* 16–32.

McKay, M.D., & Hartley, H.O. (1974). Computerized

scheduling of seagoing tankers, *Naval Res. Quart.*, **21,** 255–264.

Ronen, D. (1983). Cargo ships routing and scheduling: Survey of models and problems, *Euro. J. of Oper. Res.*, **12,** 119–126.

Song, Y.U. (1990). *A Knowledge-Based Approach to Crude Oil Delivery Scheduling,* Master's Thesis, KAIST.

Wagner, H. (1969). *Principles of Operations Research with Applications to Managerial Decision,* Prentice-Hall Inc., Englewood Cliffs, N.J.

A Scheduling Expert System for Paper Production

SHOICHI KOJIMA*, HIROATSU HARA*, NOBUO MATSUDA*,
YOSHITATSU MORI**, MICHIAKI NISHIMURA**, AND YASUHIKO YASUDA**

*Toshiba Corporation, **Oji Paper Co., Ltd.

1. INTRODUCTION

THIS CHAPTER describes an expert system for paper production in the Tomakomai Mill of the Oji Paper Co., Ltd. The system is a subsystem of a millwide production management system. The millwide system includes scheduling systems and controlling systems for all plants in the mill. The paper production machines are scheduled by an expert system, while other plants are scheduled algorithmically according to the paper production schedule. The millwide production management system is introduced in Section 2.

The expert system development required 27 months. The development consisted of 3 stages: feasibility model, prototype model and operational model. The development process is described in Section 3.

In the paper production scheduling system, there are several problems to be solved. They are huge search space, countermeasures for no solution and maintenance of the system.

To schedule efficiently, pruning the search space is essential. Two pruning strategies are introduced in this system. One is the hierarchical approach. The scheduling system is broken down to three subsystems, where each subsystem has different granularity. The first subsystem schedules in the product group unit, the second subsystem schedules in the individual product unit, and the last subsystem adjusts resources balance. This approach is described in Section 5, and individual subsystems are described in Section 6. The other pruning strategy is ordering alternatives and evaluating with satisfactory criterion. In ISIS (Fox & Smith, 1984), the ordering concepts are introduced. However, the authors' proposed ordering method is different from that for ISIS, which the authors called the "most-constrained strategy." This method is described in Section 7.1.

It is not a special case, wherein no solution is found. For no solution countermeasures, a goal modification technique is introduced. The strategy for severe constraints is to step up the temporary goal to the final goal. This strategy is described in Section 7.3.

Maintenance is the one of the most important aspects in practical use. The authors' standpoint for maintenance is that a suitable maintainer should be assigned according to frequency of knowledge change, and that suitable level support tools should be prepared. For example, frequently changed knowledge is maintained by end users with a spread-sheet like editor. This strategy is described in Section 9.

Evaluation of the system is described in Section 10.

2. SYSTEM OVERVIEW

2.1. Tomakomai Mill

The Tomakomai Mill has 10 paper making machines, energy supply plants and pulp supply plants. Two hundred paper products are produced a month. Each product has a specified production volume and due date. It requires a specific machine to produce. There are 25 kinds of pulp, and products are made from several mixtures of the pulp. The mixture ratio characterizes some of the product nature.

2.2. Millwide Production Management System

In the Tomakomai Mill, a millwide production management system is built. It supports all of the production activities, such as energy supply, pulp supply, paper making and shipping. The system has a planning level and a control/operation level. This scheduling system is situated on the planning level for paper making. It receives product orders from the headquarters office, makes a schedule and delivers it to the other planning systems. Each system schedules and optimizes their operations, based on the paper making schedule. For example, the energy supply plant planning system schedules with non linear programming techniques and the pulp plant planning system schedules with linear programming techniques. Each system has computers. All of them are connected by local area networks.

2.3. Paper Production Scheduling System

The paper production scheduling system consists of an expert system for automated scheduling and a data management system.

The expert system consists of three subsystems: product group scheduling system, individual scheduling system, and balancing scheduling system. The group scheduling system makes a rough schedule, the individual scheduling system details the result of the rough schedule, and the balancing schedule system optimizes the result of the individual system.

In practical use, it is important to modify the schedule created by the expert system or to reschedule after modification. The scheduling expert system has a schedule editor. Users can edit the schedule on a Gantt chart. The editor can add, delete, shift and swap products. It can check all constraints. Rescheduling is executable after modifying final or intermediate results.

The data management system is a database system for various products data. For example, mixture ratio and production volume are included. This system has spread-sheet-like editors.

3. DEVELOPMENT PROCESS

This scheduling system required 27 months to develop. The data management system was developed at the same time. There were 3 stages for developing the system, which were feasibility model stage, prototype stage and real model stage. In this project, there were 3 domain experts and 3 knowledge engineers.

3.1. Feasibility Model

The first phase of the development involved requirements definition and knowledge analysis. At first, domain experts explained a scheduling process, input/output for the system and constraints. After the explanation, knowledge engineers observed the real scheduling processes of the domain experts. The knowledge engineers could question the domain experts whenever they wanted. All dialogues were recorded with a tape recorder. The knowledge engineers analyzed the explanation observation results, and made a basic structure of the expert system, which included system hierarchy, constraints and arrangement rules.

A feasibility model was built according to result of the knowledge analysis. The model was constructed with OPS5. The model was made only for the group product scheduling. The reason was that the group product scheduling and individual scheduling had almost the same knowledge, without granuality. The authors thought that they were more difficult than balancing scheduling. In this model, knowledge representation, was the only production rule.

In this stage, functional feasibility and knowledge existence were checked. This stage required 4 months.

3.2. Prototype Model

In this stage, knowledge engineers acquired all the knowledge they could, and checked it. All scheduling subsystems were implemented. The object in building these subsystems was to check scheduling performance and to acquire sufficient knowledge to schedule successfully. The schedules created by the prototype model were compared with the schedules created by the domain experts. If there was any difference, then knowledge engineers interviewed the domain experts to correct the implemented knowledge. A simplified Gantt chart display system was implemented to check the schedule easily.

The tool for building the expert system was changed to ASIREX, which had a frame system and production system. Structural knowledge was described with the frame system, and heuristic knowledge was described with production rules. Using the tool, description making capability increased and the debugging environment was improved.

In this stage, knowledge was structured. Several categories were available for maintenance.

Many kinds of real data were used to check knowledge, and much knowledge was revised. While the schedules created by the expert system were mostly valid, the system performance was not sufficient to allow its use practically.

This stage required 11 months.

3.3. Real Use Model

There were 2 problems in the prototype; one was performance, the other was maintenance.

The authors thought that the performance problem was caused by insufficient strategic knowledge. The scheduling process was carefully analyzed again. Then, the "most-constrained strategy" was identified. It is described in Section 7.1. in detail.

The maintenance problem was that revising frames or rules was difficult for the domain experts. The degree of freedom and frequency of the revision were investigated. For frequently revised knowledge, specific editors were prepared.

In this stage, human computer interfaces were also designed and implemented. Scheduling expert systems were integrated into the total scheduling system. In other words, they came to access the same databases, which were managed by the data management system, and to be controlled by the same controller.

This stage required 11 months.

4. PAPER PRODUCTION SCHEDULING

The scheduling task is defined as arranging all given jobs to appropriate resources, satisfying all constraints. In this chapter, jobs are paper product, and resources are paper production machines with usage periods. The result is represented with a Gantt chart.

In this scheduling there are two kinds of constraints. One is product combination constraint and the other is balancing constraint. The product combination constraints arise from quality requirements. For example, thin colored paper should not be produced after thick colored paper. Some of these constraints are pertinent for the same machine, and others are pertinent for cross-machinery. There are hundreds of constraints of this type. The balancing constraints are energy balance and pulp balance. While the combination constraints are checked locally, these balancing constraints are checked globally through all machines. The balancing constraints arise from their supply ability. Energy and individual pulp are manufactured in other plants and supplied to the paper making machines. The supply ability and shutdown schedule for the paper making machines are determined out of the scheduling system in advance.

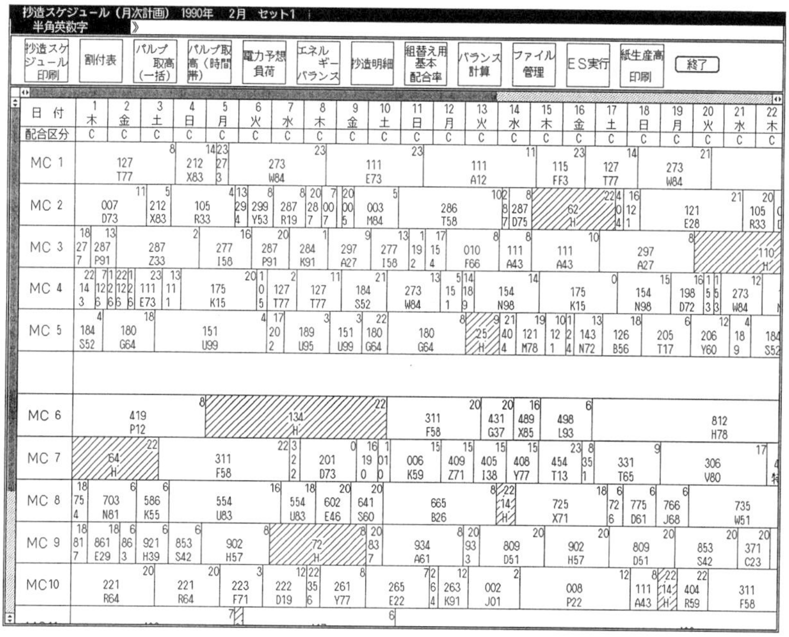

Paper Production

FIGURE 10.1. A scheduling result example.

5. HIERARCHICAL SCHEDULING APPROACH

The combination constraints involve relations between kinds of products. They are evaluated whenever the related products are arranged to the Gantt chart. In contrast, the balancing constraints can't be evaluated until all machines are assigned to products. The reason is that energy demands at each time are calculated by summing up the demands for all assigned products to be produced at the same time. Pulp balance faces the same situation. The authors broke down the system into a combination constraint satisfaction subsystem and a balancing constraint satisfaction subsystem.

It is important to prune search space, in order to achieve efficient scheduling. In the combination constraint satisfaction subsystem, there is a large search space for scheduling. The authors segregated the subsystem into two smaller subsystems again, in order to prune its search space. One is product group scheduling, and the other is individual scheduling. Product group scheduling handles the scheduling for product groups, which consist of products with almost the same constraints. Products in the same group can be identified with a similar mixture ratio for pulp and near due date. After group product scheduling, individual scheduling arranges individual products, according to the result of the product group scheduling. In other words, individual scheduling divides the arranged product group into individual products. The result of this scheduling satisfies all combination constraints and allows meeting all product due dates.

This approach does not guarantee a globally optimal solution, but guarantees a locally optimal solution.

6. KNOWLEDGE REPRESENTATION

In each scheduling subsystem, knowledge is classified into 3 groups: task control knowledge, domain knowledge and strategic knowledge.

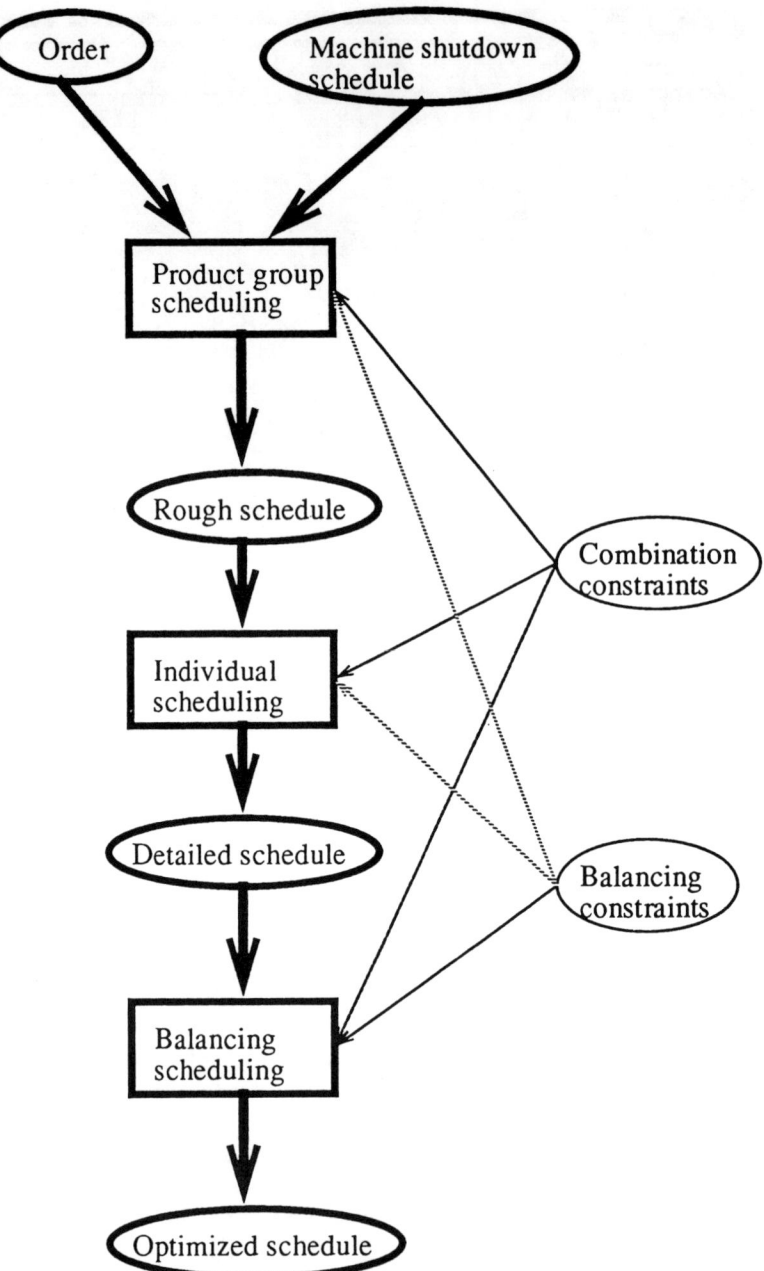

FIGURE 10.2. Scheduling general flow.

6.1. Task Control Knowledge

Each scheduling consists of several tasks. Each task is concerned with domain knowledge and strategic knowledge. Task control knowledge defines the general flow of the scheduling. This knowledge arises from problem solving behavior exhibited by the human experts. This knowledge is robust to withstand environment changes.

TABLE 1
Summary of Knowledge

Knowledge category	Subsystem				
	Quality satisfaction		Balancing	Representation	Maintainer
	Product group	Individual			
Task control	FIGURE 10.2	FIGURE 10.2	FIGURE 10.3	production rule	developer
Domain	combination constraint	combination constraint	combination constraint	frame + production rule	end user computer specialist
			pulp mixture ratio energy consumption ratio	table	end user
Strategic	job ordering	job ordering		evaluation function	knowledge engineer
	initial placement backtracking	initial placement backtracking		production rule	knowledge engineer
				production rule	knowledge engineer
			swap target search	procedure	computer specialist
			goal shifting	procedure	knowledge engineer

This knowledge is represented by production rules.

6.2. Domain Knowledge

Domain knowledge represents problem characteristics. In the considered problem, domain knowledge consists of pulp mixture ratio, energy consumption rate for an individual product and combination constraints.

Some of the knowledge is acquired from the product database. For example, the mixture ratio data can be acquired directly from the products database. This knowledge is represented by tables. Product combination constraints, in which products consuming the same pulp are largely constrained not to be produced at the same time, are acquired by interpreting product database. Other parts of knowledge are acquired from human expert heuristics. For example, low quality paper should be produced just after the shutdown period.

In the considered problem, it was found that the combination constraints can be classified into several categories. Moreover, the constraints can be represented by the relation between two products only.

The constraints are represented by frames.

6.3. Strategic Knowledge

Strategic knowledge affects the scheduling efficiency. In the group product scheduling and individual scheduling, job ordering knowledge is one of the most important kind of knowledge. This knowledge is represented by evaluation functions. The initial arrangement strategy, which determines the initial place for selected jobs according to job ordering knowledge, is represented by production rules. Backtracking strategies are also represented by production rules. Some constraints are regarded as strategic knowledge. They prevent wasteful backtracking. They are represented by frames, the same as constraints in the domain knowledge.

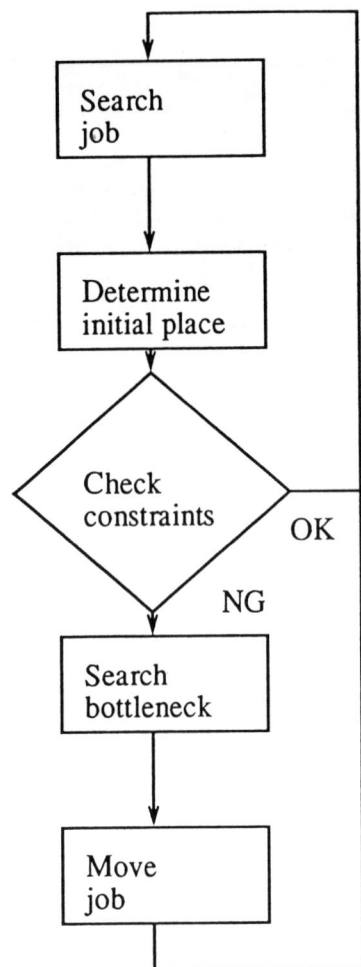

FIGURE 10.3. Product group scheduling task flow.

In the balancing scheduling, swapping target search knowledge is the most important. This knowledge is represented by production rules. The rules have a fixed format. The format is concerned with the pulp and/or energy condition and the two products to be swapped. Other important knowledge is goal shifting knowledge. In the scheduling, there may be no solution for required products. So, a goal is set up at an intermediate point between current situation and the final goal. This shifts the goal to a final goal, when the goal is satisfied. Knowledge needed to determine the improvement size is represented by the pertinent procedure.

7. INFERENCE METHOD

This section describes the scheduling method for each scheduling subsystem.

7.1. Product Group Scheduling

This scheduling is regarded as a constraint satisfaction problem (King & Yun, 1989). Tasks for solving this problem, and their relations are as follows.
1. Select one job from unarranged jobs, according to the room ratio.
2. Determine the temporary location for the selected job, by specifying the start time.
3. Check all constraints (calculate room ratio).
4. If all constraints are satisfied, go to (1).
5. Search any bottleneck job for constraints violation.
6. Move the searched job to other place.
7. Go to (1).

In this scheduling, the job selection task is the most important. Because there are many constraints, backtracking tasks are very expensive. So, reduction of backtracking makes this scheduling efficient. In this task, the "most-constrained strategy" is employed. The degree of constraint for a job is defined as a room ratio, which is calculated as follows,

room ratio = arrangeable time area/load time

When the room ratio for a job is near 1.0, it is strictly constrained. When room ratio is smaller than 1.0, at least one of the constraints are violated. The arrangeable time area is an intersection of the area that does not violate individual constraints. These areas are easily identified, because the constraints are limited to 2 products relations and the relation categories are fixed.

The selected job are arranged according to the initial arrangement strategy, and the room ratios for unarranged jobs are calculated again. If the room ratio is smaller than 1.0, the violated constraints are identified, as are the products that are included in the constraints to be rearranged.

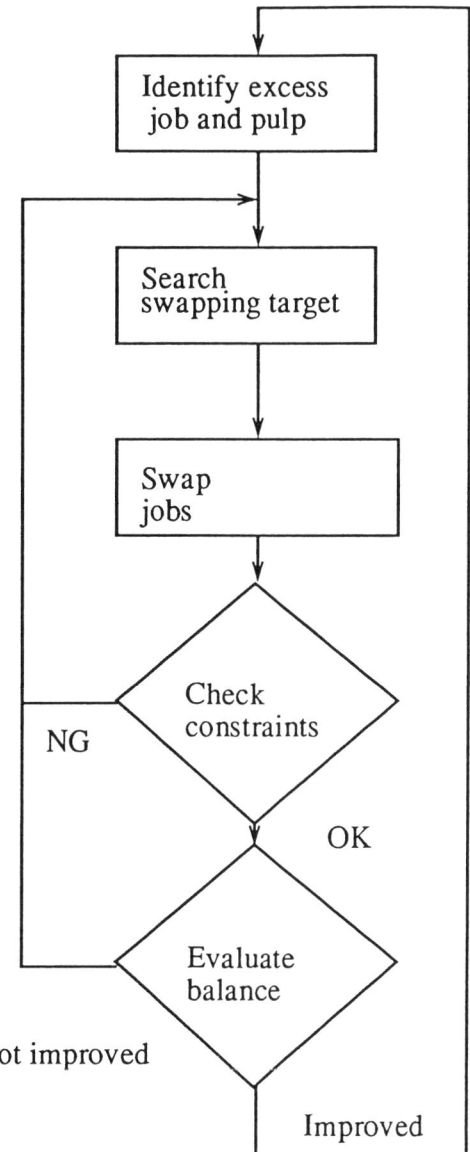

FIGURE 10.4. Balancing scheduling task flow.

When all jobs are arranged, this scheduling terminates.

7.2. Individual Scheduling

The individual scheduling is the same as product group scheduling. The differences between them are the scheduling granularity and the arrangeable area range for each job. In this scheduling, the job is a product and is restricted by the product group scheduling result. This means room ratio calculation is different from the product group scheduling.

7.3. Balancing Scheduling

In the balancing scheduling, total usage of all pulp and energy consumption should retain their limits. However, even a human expert often cannot delete the excess from the limits.

This means that there may be no solution for this problem. The authors employ a stepwise improvement approach. At first, the goal is not the final goal, but only a somewhat improved situation. When the goal is satisfied, a new goal, improved to a point better than the previous goal, is created. The improvement speed is determined according to the human expert experiences.

In each step, tasks for this problem and their relation are as follows.
1. Swap two products with heuristic knowledge.
2. If there are no heuristics, swap with most-over least-usage swapping strategy.
3. If the goal is satisfied, create a new goal and go to (1).
4. If there are swapping alternatives, then go to (1), or else terminate.

Swapping by heuristics is the main operation in this problem. If there are no heuristics to be applied, then the most-over least-usage swapping strategy is operated. The most-over least-usage swapping strategy is as follows.
1. Identify a job and pulp that has the most excess to the limit. If no excess is found, terminate.
2. Find a job that has the least pulp usage.
3. Swap them and check all the constraints.
4. If there is constraint violation, backtrack to (2).
5. Go to (1).

High priority is given to the heuristics, because the most-over least-usage swapping requires much computational resource.

7.4. Scheduling Relation

The final goals in the proposed system are to arrange the jobs satisfying all quality constraints and to balance all resources. The former goal is satisfied by group product scheduling and individual scheduling. The latter goal is satisfied by balancing scheduling. This separation drastically reduces the required search space. However, if the balancing goal is not considered at satisfying quality constraints, it is difficult to balance resources. Therefore, it is effective that balancing resources conditions are propagated to the quality constraints phase. So, the condition for leveling required resources is translated to the product or product group combination constraints. For example, some combinations of products can't be produced at the same time or sequentially, and other combinations of products are suggested to be produced sequentially.

8. IMPLEMENTATION

The scheduling systems are implemented with expert shell ASIREX. The main considerations are as follows.

1. Human expertise should be converted smoothly to the system.
2. For maintenance, a frame is a more desirable knowledge representation than a production rule, and a production rule is more desirable than procedure.
3. Flexibility is required for frequently changing items.

According to the consideration above, four implementation methods are employed, as follows.

| 抄紙機1 | 抄物1 | | 抄紙機2 | 抄物2 | | 期間 |
	品番	大枠名称		品番	大枠名称	
MC 3	322	ZP958	MC 3	278	QE33256	1.0
MC 8 MC10	264	RL6543	全M/C	280	QE33256	96.0
全M/C	452	FI3832	MC 2 MC 3 MC 4	326	AJ39289	120.0
MC 1 MC 2 MC10	350	YQ38912	MC 1 MC 2 MC10	407	DK8493	96.0
MC 3 MC 4 MC 5	466 405	GE9533 DK8493	MC 3 MC 4 MC 5	331	DP93822	120.0
MC 3 MC 4 MC 5 MC 6 MC 7	407	DK8493	全M/C	271	ZI539	168.0

一定期間後抄造ルール

(抄紙機1の抄物1)の抄造後、(期間)以内、(抄紙機2の抄物2)を抄かない

FIGURE 10.5. Knowledge editor.

1. Knowledge with fixed format and fixed number of arguments is implemented by frames for individual knowledge and production rules for interpreting knowledge. This method is applied to the frequently updated knowledge, but its interpretation is rarely modified. The product combination constraints are implemented with this method.

2. Knowledge with fixed format and variable number of arguments is implemented by fixed formatted production rules. This method is applied to knowledge which is updated frequently and interpretation is rarely modified, but various conditions exist in them. The swapping target search knowledge is implemented by this method.

3. Knowledge, which needs global comparison with a unique criterion, is implemented with production rules and procedural evaluation functions. When the comparison makes it difficult to describe the procedure, all knowledge is implemented with production rules. Job ordering knowledge is implemented with this method.

4. Unformatted and modifiable knowledge is implemented with production rules. The task control strategies are implemented with this method.

5. Fixed functions are implemented with procedures.

9. MAINTENANCE STRATEGY

Maintainability is one of the most important aspects of expert systems. In the proposed expert system, many kinds of knowledge are implemented. When the environment changes, the knowledge should be maintained. In practical use phase, the knowledge engineer can't maintain the knowledge so rapidly. Moreover, there may be no knowledge engineer available, when maintenance is needed. In the proposed approach, for ordinary and not structural changes, the end users of the expert system, who have little knowledge about computer technique, can maintain the knowledge base by themselves. For changes which are not structural, computer specialists can maintain the knowledge base. For structural changes, the knowledge engineers should maintain the knowledge base.

In order to develop maintenance support tools or methodology, knowledge is classified according to change frequency and maintenance difficulty. For each knowledge class, pertinent maintenance tools or maintenance methodology were prepared.

The end users of the expert system can maintain frequently updated knowledge. In this class, there are product combination constraints. When a new kind of product is added, then new constraints should be added. When a new machine is added, new constraints should be added, also. Because end users may not be familiar with using a computer, a spread-sheet-like editor for the product combination constraints was developed.

Computer specialists can maintain two kinds of knowledge. One variety involves product combination constraints. While end users can maintain the predefined type of product combination constraints, computer specialists can add a new type of product combination constraints. The computer specialists add the production rules for the new type. The production rule formats for the constraints are fixed, so the rules can easily added. The other type of knowledge, maintained by the computer specialists, involves search strategy for swapping products. This knowledge is also implemented by production rules. It doesn't have a completely fixed format. However, their condition parts are a combination of pulp condition and/or energy conditions, and operation parts have a fixed format. So, the computer specialists can easily maintain these bits of strategy by the ordinary editor, too.

The other kind of knowledge should be maintained by a knowledge engineer. For example, the task control knowledge should be maintained by them. This knowledge influences the entire system. So, local maintenance operation could be potentially dangerous to the whole system. Another example is initial placement strategy. It is embedded in the task operation and can't be maintained separately. Because the knowledge is seldom modified, it involves no trouble for daily use. The authors think that the maintenability for the user trades off in proportion to the descriptionability. So, the degrees of maintenability are determined by the balance with regard to the descriptionability and the maintenance activities frequency.

10. EVALUATION

There are 3 scheduling subsystems. Each subsystem has almost 50 production rules and hundreds of constraints.

The greatest advantage of this system is scheduling speedup. The scheduling time for a monthly schedule was reduced to 2 hours from 3 days, when done by a human expert. When human experts scheduled manually, a schedule with unsatisfied constraints or lack of balance occasionally resulted. Now, all constraints are always satisfied. Also, the schedule can be changed whenever necessary, for example adding urgent orders.

11. CONCLUSION

This paper describes the scheduling expert system for a paper making mill. There are two important problems about the scheduling system in the practical use level. One problem is efficiency, the other problem is maintainability.

In the scheduling system, there is almost infinite search space. The system prunes its search space in several ways. First, the scheduling process is segregated into three sub-scheduling systems. This breakdown uses the nature of goals and the jobs to be scheduled. The system has two kinds of goals. One is a quality goal, and the other is balancing resource usage. The authors break the process down into two subsystems, according to the kind of constraints involved. The quality requirement satisfaction subsystem schedules first. Then, the resource balancing subsystem revises the result. To prevent backtracking between subsystems, part of the resource balancing requirements are translated into the constraints in the quality satisfaction subsystem. Furthermore, the quality satisfaction subsystem is then segregated into two subsystems. The jobs, that is paper products, can be categorized into product groups. All products in the same group have almost the same characteristics, so that the scheduling can be broken down into the scheduling in the product group unit and the scheduling on each product group placement in the individual product unit. Second, in the quality satisfaction subsystem, the most-constrained strategy is effective for pruning the search space. The constraints are limited to several kinds of two product relations, so that the constraint degree calculation becomes very simple and efficient.

In this system, knowledge is classified according to the change frequency. Maintainers are assigned to a pertinent knowledge class. Maintenance supports are prepared according to the skill of the maintainer. In general, the flexibility trades off maintainability. They are related to the restriction to the knowledge description format. In practice use, the description formats are sufficient for this assignment.

This scheduling system has run since January, 1989, in practical use. The scheduling time for a monthly schedule was reduced to 2 hours from 3 days, when done by a human expert.

REFERENCES

Fox, M.S., & Smith, S.F. (1984). ISIS: A knowledge-based system for factory scheduling, *Expert Systems,* **1**(1), 25–49.

King, N., & Yun, D.Y.Y. (1989). A planning/scheduling methodology for the constrained resource problem, *Proc. IJCAI '89* 998–1003.

Cockpit Crew Scheduling and Supporting System

KIYOTO ONODERA AND AKIRA MORI

NEC Corporation, Tokyo, Japan; Japan Airlines, Tokyo, Japan

1. INTRODUCTION

THE APPLICATION of Artificial Intelligence (AI) to scheduling problems has recently become the focus of attention. The airline industry is no exception, and several scheduling systems have reportedly been developed in the industry. The system herein described has been developed by Japan Airlines and NEC Corporation. It is a planning type expert system designed for a preparation of monthly schedules for captains, co-pilots, and flight engineers using knowledge engineering techniques. The development of this system started in the summer of 1986 and entered the test-run stage in the summer of 1988. The system has gone into a formal operation since February, 1990.

1.1. Cockpit Crew Scheduling

Cockpit crew scheduling is very complicated work. This work needs specialized knowledge and sufficient experience. Flights, check-ups, trainings, meetings and other ground jobs must be assigned without any omission or duplications while closely observing various restrictive conditions, including the governing law, company regulations and labor management agreements. Moreover, it is not just a process of preparing a machinery schedule, but a schedule for cockpit crew, that is, a schedule for human activities. For this reason, the quality of schedule, including the balanced assignment of flight routes, the balanced arrangement of flights and other items, and impartial flight hours, must be taken into consideration. Before the realization of computerized scheduling, 24 experts, called "schedulers," were engaged in manual scheduling work over a period of about two weeks each month.

In many cases in the past, Operations Research (OR) was generally used to cope with a various combination problems such as scheduling. But the difficulties in formulating problems, and maintaining and managing software, had made it extremely difficult to achieve satisfactory results using OR techniques if problems became somewhat complicated. Attempts to develop a system using OR techniques had been made several times in the past, but it was not successfully developed as a viable system. Computerization of those restrictive conditions presented various difficulties and the system was required to keep up with ongoing changes in the external environment, such as introduction of new types of aircraft, changes in labor management agreements, and major events occurring all over the world.

In computerizing this scheduling work, schedulers' expertise was incorporated into the system to ensure software flexibility which is necessary to keep up with the oft-occurring changes. The major features of this system, called Crew Operation & Schedule Management Online System/AI (COSMOS/AI), are as follows:
1. Distributed expert system:
2. Cooperative inference applicable to scheduling problem: and
3. Intelligent backtracking reflecting the expertise of schedulers.

By realizing these features, we succeeded in the development of a practical, large-scale expert system which can handle a large volume of data and restrictive conditions. The system has 45,000 frames, 7,000 rules, 1,500 constraints, and 300,000 program lines as of October, 1990.

2. THE OUTLINE OF OPERATION

Japan Airlines (JAL) had approximately 2,300 cockpit crew members for 3 types of aircraft, Boeing 747 (B747), and Boeing 767 (B767), products of Boeing Company and DC-10, a product of Mcdonnell Douglas Corporation, on its payroll in 1990. A flight schedule for each individual is prepared on a monthly basis. The goal of the schedule is to satisfy the corresponding requirements for governing law, company regulations, labor management agreements, and other restrictive conditions based on a flight operation diagram, which varies with the qualifications of each crew. These pilots and flight engineers often spend many days away from home. Although a certain number of off-duty days are ensured, they have to work on a highly irregular schedule.

The flight schedule should also satisfy additional requirements for days of training and check-ups on the simulators and aircraft, classroom lectures, emergency rescue training, flight physical examinations (PE) and various meetings. Each of these must be properly assigned according to crew qualifications. Among crew members, captains are required to meet the most complicated qualifications, and have the heaviest restrictions.

2.1. Former Work-flow

In the past, manual scheduling work began in the middle of each month and continued to the day when schedules were distributed to each crew member at the end of each month. It took about two weeks. The expiration date for training and check-ups which must be performed in the next month and various qualifications for each individual crew member were checked first. When vacation was requested by crew, such dates were to be definitely kept. Then, dates for attendance at various meetings, seminars, etc. requested by management were booked on the schedules.

Flight patterns were prepared after the original plans of flights and equipment in the next month were acknowledged. A flight pattern consists of several flight routes from a base airport (Haneda and Narita in Japan; Anchorage, Los Angeles and Athens in foreign countries), back to the base airport via other airports, and several stay days and rest days, the number of which depends on the length of duty days, flight routes and job title. The length of flight patterns varies from one day to 14 days. As many as about 7,000 flights per month (as of October, 1990) must be assembled in this flight pattern without any omission, duplication or errors. This work was a great strain on schedulers.

The timetable for simulator training must also be prepared and the slots of the table must be ensured for several check-ups and training. The combination of checkers and crew for check-ups, and captains and co-pilots for training are to be assigned in advance.

After the required items for scheduling were prepared and mandatory assignments were made, the other parts of schedules were prepared, taking into account qualifications, experience and any other items of each crew, and making sure that scheduling items such as flight patterns were not assigned incorrectly. This difficult and time-consuming work was manually done on paper.

Schedulers input the assigned schedules on paper into the JAL Flight Operation System (JALFOS), and then the schedules were distributed to each crew member after having corrected errors by hand.

2.2. Present Work-flow

Since COSMOS/AI went into trial use, information about the changes of crew qualification, flight data, and other flight operation can all be automatically gathered and updated.

As a result, it is no longer necessary to re-examine the expiration dates of training and check-ups, since necessary training and check-ups can be scheduled automatically. The vacation request of each crew can be input through OCR. Flight patterns are automatically prepared. Important meetings and educational activities requested by managers are booked in advance on the system.

After rough assignment is completed as described above, automatic scheduling and adjustment of schedules are repeatedly conducted for further tuning. Unlike the former manual system, the schedules which are finished are sent to JALFOS automatically.

3. SYSTEM CONFIGURATION

The hardware configuration of COSMOS/AI is shown in Figure 11.1. MS4110 has a gateway function between SNA[1] network and B4680 network. EWS4800s are the nucleus of this scheduling work. Scheduling is done on the machine. Some EWS4800s contain an AI-processor as a back-end processor. AI-processor is a LISP machine based on CHI-2, which was developed as part of the FGCS (Fifth Generation Computer Systems) project in Japan.

The software environment of EWS4800 is shown in Figure 11.2. The os of EWS4800 is UNIX[2] and the used languages are UTILISP[3] and C.

4. THE OUTLINE OF SYSTEM

4.1. Automatic Scheduling

The scheduling items covered by automatic scheduling include not only flight patterns,

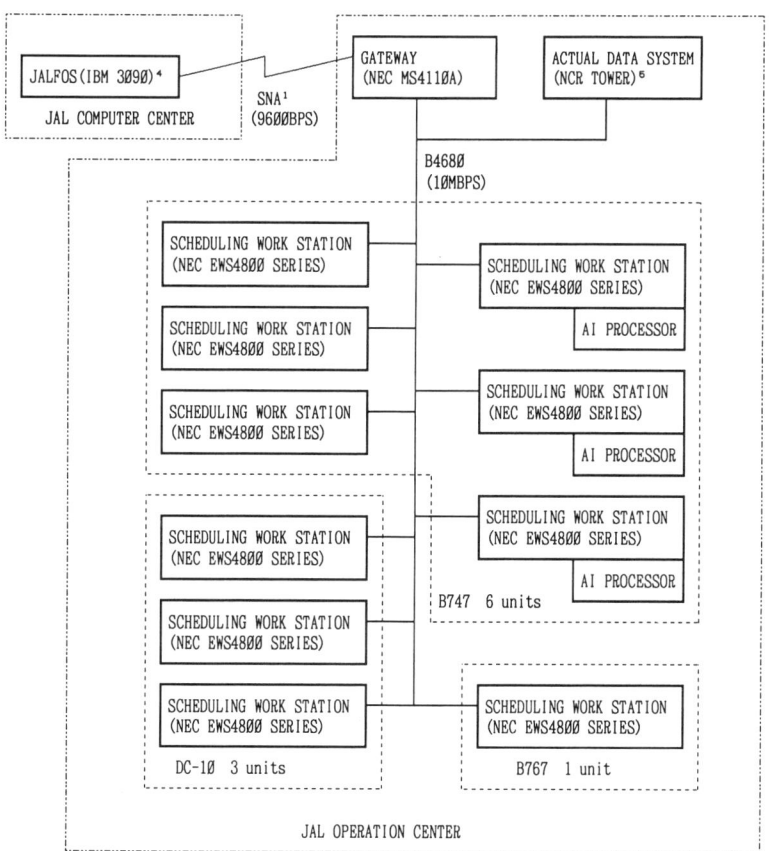

FIGURE 11.1. Hardware configuration.

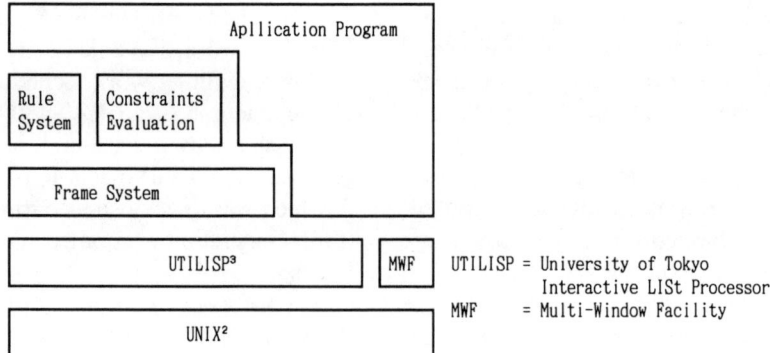

FIGURE 11.2. Software environment.

but check-ups, physical examinations, trainings, education, meetings, rest days, stand-by duties for flights, and almost all items related to the schedules of pilots and flight engineers. The components consisting of automatic scheduling process are shown in Figure 11.3.

4.1.1. The Execution of Automatic Scheduling. The timing for starting automatic scheduling is not limited. It can be freely executed according to the purpose. This is because automatic scheduling items and the period, i.e., the range of pilots or flight engineers to be processed in automatic scheduling, the range of flights, scheduling period, scheduling items can be set freely. Therefore, automatic scheduling can be done depending on the status of flight pattern preparation and the progress of required manual work, including assignment of each crew member's holidays, meetings, etc. For example, only certain types of training are assigned by automatic scheduling when flight patterns are not prepared yet, or automatic scheduling for certain section's crew members is done because required manual work for this section has been finished earlier than that for the other sections.

Automatic scheduling can be made several times for the same items. Trials can be done by varying schedule conditions. The results

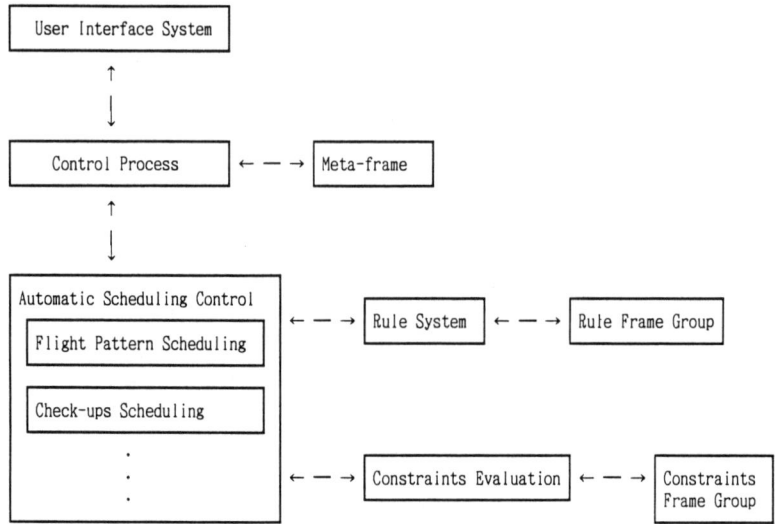

FIGURE 11.3. Automatic scheduling process components.

of automatic scheduling can also be deleted using deleting function. In this case, the items to be deleted can be designated in the similar way to the designation of applicable items and range in automatic scheduling.

Automatic scheduling is started from the window for the execution of automatic scheduling and deleting.

4.1.2. Scheduling Strategy. When a scheduler prepares a schedule, he or she sometimes wants to emphasize certain items or conditions. For example, when the personnel situation is very tight, assignment is done as effectively as possible, or the averaging of yearly flight hours is rather strongly taken into account during the end of year. Several types of rule groups are prepared for this emphasis. The desired group of rules can be selected at starting time. These groups of rules is called "Scheduling Strategy" in this system.

4.1.3. Constraints. As mentioned above, there are many restrictions, and they range from those which must be observed to those which are merely desirable for a better schedule. The strictness of these restrictions often changes depending on the situation.

Almost all restrictions are represented as "Constraints" in the system. The constraints are made up separately with aircraft type, job title and route group.

4.1.4. Rule. Rule system is used on a limited basis. System control such as process starting, process order, back-track level, etc. is defined in the system control frames, not in rule frames. To ensure efficient execution of rule, the rule system was designed to be suited for automatic scheduling of this system.

4.1.5. Trimming. In the large-scale planning-type expert system, the size of searching space affects time required for processing. In order to reduce the searching range in this space and to shorten processing time, a process called "Trimming" is done when the system situation changes.

Trimming is the process of cutting the searching tree branches which had no possibilities after the situation changed, based on the contents of systems situation. It is useless or sometimes harmful to execute this process if it consumes a lot of time. Therefore, relatively easy checks are performed. For this reason, tree branches which have not possibility to be selected any more in new situation are sometimes not trimmed.

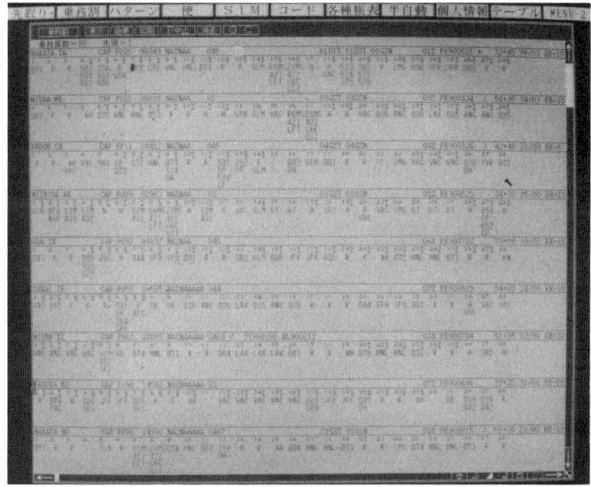

FIGURE 11.4. Main window (schedule table window).

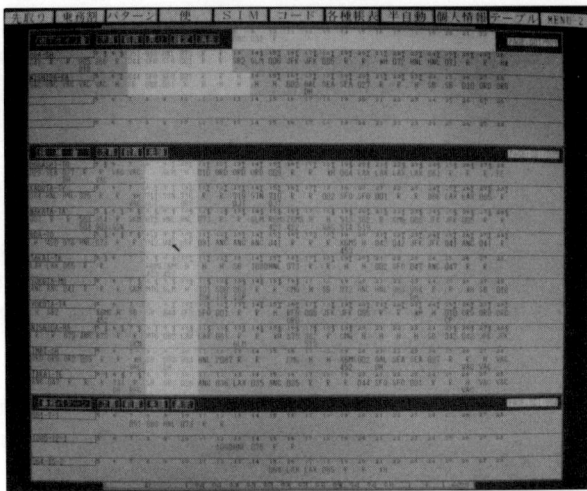

FIGURE 11.5. Semi-automatic scheduling window.

4.2. User Interface

In general, it is important to provide special means to use the system easily. Therefore, we developed multi-window interface so that a scheduler could easily operate COSMOS/AI.

The main window which displays a schedule table was designed to resemble the scheduling worksheet which was used for previous manual scheduling by schedulers. The window, with the cockpit crew taken as vertical axis and the date as horizontal axis, plays a principal role in scheduling work. An example of this window is shown in Figure 11.4.

Figure 11.5 shows a "Semi-Automatic Scheduling" window. Schedulers can simulate the assignment of flight patterns and crew on the window without changing the system situation. On this window, the system displays preferable candidate crew for a certain flight pattern which a scheduler selected from the lower part of the window, then the scheduler selects one of crew for the pattern. The system then gathers preferable candidate crew for the flight pattern which was deassigned from the selected crew.

The system has 80 windows as of October, 1990. Schedulers can operate almost all works for preparation of crew schedules on these windows.

5. USE OF KNOWLEDGE

5.1. Knowledge Acquisition

The system has various kinds of knowledge, which are divided broadly into three categories. One is based on the expertise of schedulers, another is based on EDP data on other computers such as JALFOS, and the other is based on the data which is not computerized.

To acquire knowledge based on the expertise of schedulers, we interviewed several schedulers, most of whom have longer career as a scheduler, and conducted questionnaire survey for all schedulers. We also inspected actual scheduling work and analyzed schedule tables finished by schedulers. Furthermore, several development personnel took OJT (on-the-job training) under the guidance of schedulers. The results obtained through the above were analyzed and verified by schedulers' evaluation. We could extract certain knowledge which could not have been acquired only through such indirect means as interviews or questionnaire surveys. As a result, we discovered several types of knowledge which was necessary for computerizing of the scheduling work and which was used by schedulers in their daily routine almost unconsciously.

The above process was repeated several times, while the knowledge thus acquired was encoded by knowledge engineers (KEs). We did not use any knowledge acquisition tools because there *was* no proper tool.

To acquire the knowledge based on EDP data, the system has been designed to acquire and update the knowledge automatically. This makes it easy to maintain a vast amount of knowledge required for scheduling work. This subject will be discussed in more detail in the Section 5.3 on Knowledge Encoding.

The knowledge based on non-computerized data (raw data) is quite small in volume, and is not frequently updated in most cases. Therefore, the input and update of the knowledge is conducted with using the frame editor and application windows.

5.2. Knowledge Representation

All knowledge is represented in frames. Rules and constraints are some of the frames. In this system, frames are divided into class units, and each class was designed to be handled independently one another.

5.3. Knowledge Encoding

The system has a function to encode EDP data into knowledge. Most of knowledge is automatically updated by use of this function. The function, called Knowledge Base (KB) conversion, is usually executed daily. The execution schedule, which may be changed as required, is preset in the system. It can be executed manually as well.

Through this function, the latest data is obtained from the host computer or other computers and it is reflected in COSMOS/AI. This is a very important function for this system, because a large volume of updated data is generated whenever the external environment changes, and the change frequently occurs. This function saves schedulers tremendous time and efforts. Otherwise they would have to gather the latest data and input or update by hand and the system would be of no practical use.

When developing a planning-type expert system, a prototype can be made with relative ease in general. But this attempt often fails at the stage of putting the system in practical use. As various causes may be conceivable for the failure, one of them is a lack of ability to keep up with oft-occurring changes in the external environment.

In many cases, the prototype is developed with limited data on the assumption that a change in external environment is seldom expected. However, once the system is placed for the field use, the system must keep up with the changes occurring in the real environment.

For example, in this scheduling work, flight delays caused by weather or other factors, and changes in the external environment such as schedule changes, must be kept up with quickly because various complex restrictions, such as flight route experience of crew within a certain period, must be observed.

It is conceivable to incorporate all changes of external environment using the user interface. However, when a work of which external environment changes largely and frequently is computerized, an expert must input a vast amount of data into his or her computer system by hand, and the workload of the expert is very heavy, even if the system has a somewhat superior user interface. The expert might complain that the previous manual technique was better because of the shorter work time and higher productivity.

In developing COSMOS/AI, solving this problem was the key to the success of developing a practical expert system. Fortunately, JAL has had fully developed computer systems which is able to feed necessary data for the scheduling work to COSMOS/AI. The data is incorporated via communication lines and LAN, and encoded through KB conversion.

Along with the changes in the external environment, contradictions often occur in schedules under preparation. When already-prepared parts of the schedules can be adjusted automatically in KB conversion, they are processed so as to solve contradictions. If it is impossible to adjust a crew member's schedule automatically, the person's schedule and the reason not to adjust are displayed on the warning list to call attention of schedulers for adjustment.

5.4. Tests and Evaluation

Running tests were performed in the form of actual scheduling on COSMOS/AI over a period of one year and a half using real data. A chain of action for evaluation and modification of the system was repeated, while paying attention to keeping up with the changes of external environment. We checked more than 3,000 test items in running test step and we completed all items eventually.

When the test result was able to be evaluated quantitatively, we used the tool which was prepared for evaluation of the test results. On the other hand, when the test results were not able to be evaluated quantitatively, schedulers evaluated the results with their expertise.

6. FEATURES OF THE SYSTEM

6.1. Distributed System

Distribution is a structural feature of this system. "Distributed system" has two meanings in this system. The first is that the system is

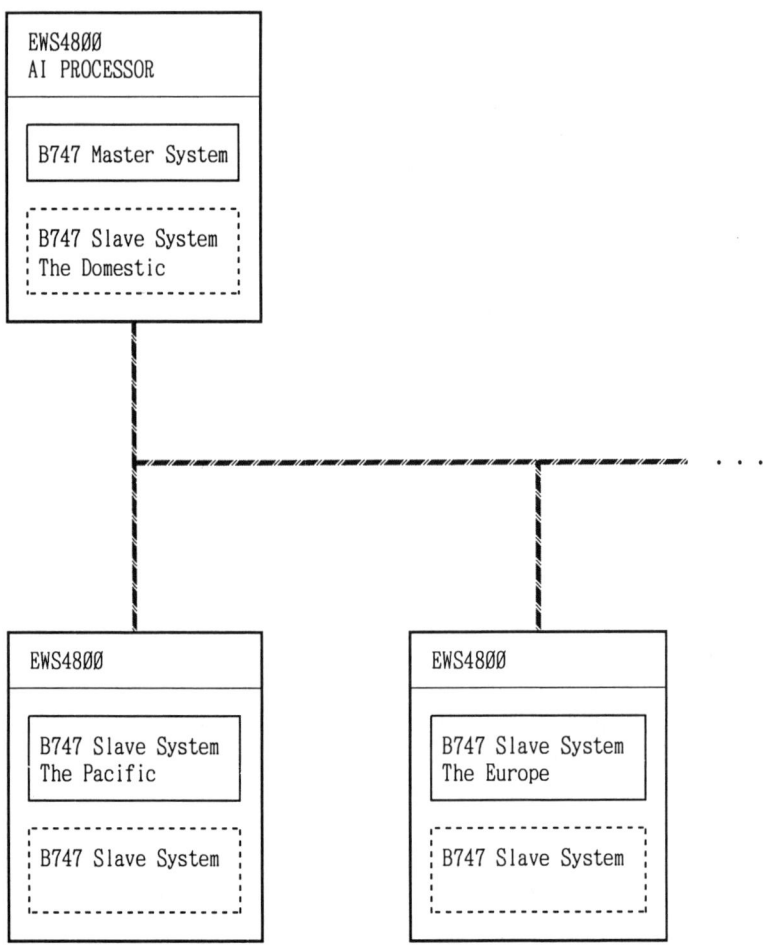

FIGURE 11.6. The Master and Slave systems.

independent of the host computer, JALFOS, and the second is that the system adopts the distributed expert system method.

The advantages of independence of the host computer are that loading and executing the expert system will by no means affect the host computer capability, and that the user-friendly interface with full functions can be provided using the mouse and multi-windows. Required data for this service by is fetched from the host computer via communication lines.

It may be easier to design a non-distributed system than a distributed system in some aspects. But, as a result of analysis of this work, the methods of distributed expert system were needed. The reasons are as follows.
- The job of schedulers contains not only preparing schedules, but providing the total support for cockpit crew. A certain number of schedulers are, therefore, required.
- Scheduling work can hardly be completed by only a scheduler. It requires cooperation and collaboration among the schedulers.

For these reasons, COSMOS/AI has a "master system" and some "slave systems". The master system is to assure data integrity among master and slave systems, to manage all cockpit crew schedules and other information within one aircraft type and one job title. The slaves are to serve several schedulers at the same time. Configuration of the master and the slave systems is shown in Figure 11.6. The system can be loaded freely either from the master system or slave systems up to the extent of hardware restrictions such as main memory. It is, therefore, possible for a scheduler to use a master system and a slave system, or, some slave systems on one EWS.

6.2. Cooperative Inference

JAL has so many flight routes and pilots, captains and co-pilots, for B747 aircraft that the assignment of flight crew is divided into flight route groups according to his section. There are four route groups such as the Pacific, Europe, Asia-Oceania and Domestic routes. Each captain has his own route qualifications, and quite a few captains have the route qualifications of his group and other groups as well. The route group which a pilot belongs to is called the Main Route Group and routes which are included in the route group are called the Main Routes. A pilot is, therefore, mainly assigned to the flight patterns which include some of his Main Routes.

When manning is tight it becomes necessary to do dynamic scheduling beyond each route group. As mentioned above, there are

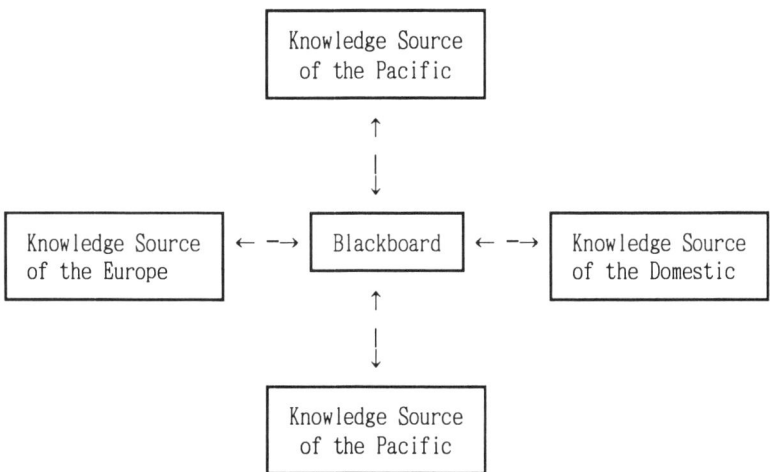

FIGURE 11.7. The image of cooperative inference.

constraints and rules specific to routes and route groups. When automatic scheduling for all the B747 captains is in process all at once, these rules and constraints are dynamically switched so as to meet with the requirement about the routes and the route group of flight patterns and captains. So, cooperative inference is adopted by using a common area inference called the "Blackboard." The cooperative inference was designed to resemble adjustment efforts among schedulers during previous manual scheduling. Now, schedulers do not have to discuss and adjust their schedules all together, unlike the previous scheduling. The image of the cooperative inference is shown in Figure 11.7.

6.3. Intelligent Backtrack

When the process of automatic scheduling hits a deadlock, for example, a if flight pattern is unable to be assigned though the constraints are loosened according to the availability of each crew, then the "Intelligent Backtrack" function is called in order to break the deadlock.

The intelligent backtrack has been created by incorporating the heuristics of schedulers who have several heuristic techniques and adjust the situation when their work comes to a deadlock. The techniques include several methods, such as exchanging parts of several crews' schedules, or, moving meeting dates, check-up dates, or other NOF dates on a certain crew's schedule.

7. IMPLEMENTATION

7.1. Deployment Process

The trial use of COMOS/AI started in the Fall of 1988. The trial use was targetted at the captains of the Pacific route group on B747 at first, and then gradually expanded over to other groups of crew. The trial use lasted for a year and a half. It was conducted in the same way as in practical use.

7.2. Maintenance

Two KEs manage the maintenance of COSMOS/AI. Their duties cover the maintenance of COSMOS/AI, as well as of a part of JALFOS.

Since COSMOS/AI was started for field use in February of 1990, a significant improvement has been made in operation of scheduling. The workload of schedulers has been reduced greatly.

The flexibility of the expert system has been fully exploited from the standpoint of the system maintenance. The merit of it may be proved by the fact that we have had no backlog left of user's requests for enhancement of the system. Much has been changed in the system itself and the surrounding environment since the prototype was first placed in operation three years ago. Yet, we have successfully met the challenges of improving and enhancing COSMOS/AI to keep up with user's new requirements and the changes of external environment.

8. CONCLUSION

The above techniques and features, which were rarely used in former expert systems from the view point of practical use, caused the success of the development of COSMOS/AI.

COSMOS/AI has contributed to the great reduction of schedulers' workload and to the good quality of monthly schedule. It is our sincere hope that the techniques and experiences acquired in developing COSMOS/AI will be instrumental in dealing with the difficulties of other systems to be developed in the future.

NOTES

1. SNA is a trademark of International Business Machines Corporation.
2. UNIX is a registered trademark of AT&T in the U.S.A. and other countries.
3. UTILISP is software developed at the University of Tokyo.
4. IBM 3090 is a product of International Business Machines Corporation.
5. NCR TOWER is a product of NCR Corporation.

Knowledge-Based Approach to Airport Staff Rostering

K. P. Chow and C. K. Hui

Department of Computer Science, University of Hong Kong, Hong Kong;
Computer Science Division, University of California, Davis CA

1. INTRODUCTION

SCHEDULING PROBLEMS are commonly found in servicing and manufacturing industries. In order to maximize the utilization of the supporting hardware and machines, machine operators are usually required to work on shifts so that machines remain running continuously without stopping. The construction of the shift duty assignment, usually called a *roster*, is a non-trivial task since many factors needed to be considered, such as the maximum number of hours an operator can work continuously and the minimum rest time between two consecutive duties. Since the construction of roster requires non-trivial intellectual skill, it is difficult to computerize roster scheduling using conventional data processing techniques. On the other hand, such roster planning processes have been performed by the human planner for years and experience has been collected to perform the planning task efficiently. The knowledge-based approach takes advantage of human expertise, and thus is used to automate the roster scheduling activities.

---

* Sun Workstation is a registered trademark of Sun Microsystems.
* PC Scheme is a registered trademark of Texas Instruments Incorporated.
* IBM Personal Computer is a registered trademark of International Business Machines Corporation.
* UNIX is a trademark of AT&T Bell Laboratories.
* IBM is a registered trademark and PC/AT is a trademark of International Business Machines Corporation.

We report here a case study on designing and implementing a computer rostering system for a group of airport servicing staffs for a local airline using a knowledge-based approach. Prototyping is used in the development process. Knowledge is represented in two different forms, namely forward chaining rules and constraints. Forward chaining together with iterative improvement are used as control strategies in the system. The first prototype was completed in less than a month. During the refinement process, a tool, called SHO, was constructed to simplify the modification process. The whole system was completed in approximately six months, of which most of the time was spent on knowledge and rules refinement. Initial implementation was developed using Common Lisp on a Sun Workstation*. It is then ported to PC Scheme*, a Lisp dialect, on an IBM Personal Computer*. The system has been used for roster planning at up to 500 airport servicing staffs by the airline for several years. As most knowledge and rules have been incorporated in the system, we are now in the process of rewriting the system so that the knowledge-based system can communicate with other systems in the organization and have a better performance.

1.1. The Knowledge-Based Schedules

Recent advances in knowledge-based systems allow us to use human expert knowledge and experience to tackle some difficult problems including scheduling problems (Fox, 1983; Fox & Smith, 1984). The case study we report here, the Knowledge-Based Scheduler (KBS), combines *forward chaining rule-based inference* and *constraints relaxation* techniques. KBS (Chow & Kui, 1987) is an experimental system which addresses the roster scheduling for airport servicing staffs of a local airline using a knowledge-based approach. It has been used for roster planning by the airline for the airport servicing staffs by a local airline for several years.

In this chapter, we shall discuss the problem, the problem solving methodology, a development tool which aids the construction of KBS, and the current status of the system.

2. DEVELOPMENT PROCESS

2.1. Problem Description

Roster scheduling is a constrained assignment problem. The problem of assigning m jobs to n machines is a kind of assignment problem. A job i when assigned to machine j incurs a cost c_{ij}. The objective is to assign the jobs to the machines (one job per machine) at the minimum total cost (Taha, 1982). Constrained assignment problem is the assignment problem subject to a set of constraints. The goal of roster scheduling is to assign n duties to n staffs subject to a set of constraints. Typical constraints are, for example, that some specific duties cannot be followed by other specific duties. Following is an example of the constrained assignment problem which is handled by KBS. It is a simplified version of the practical case. Figure 12.1 gives a visual illustration of an example problem when the number of staff equals 40. Following is the detail:

1. There are a total of n staff.
2. On each day of a week (say Monday), there are n duties (including OFF) to be performed. Excluding OFF, there are three kinds of duties, namely EARLY, LATE, and FLEX (FLEX duty is a stand-by duty, which lasts for eight hours and can start anytime of the day). Each duty has a label and a duration. A duration contains a starting time and a finishing time. One exception is that OFF duty has no starting and ending time. The nature and duration of an individual duty is fixed and different from each other. This means that two LATE duties may have different start time and end time.
3. Each staff member will start his or her shift duties in a different row of the roster. This ensures all duties in everyday of a week are performed. If a person s starts working from row i, one week later, he/she will perform duties from row $i + 1$, another week later he/she will perform duties in row $i + 2$,

Input of roster scheduling:
  Length of roster : 40 persons
  Distribution of duties :

	Sun	Mon	....	Sat
	10 OFFs	13 OFFs		9 OFFS
	9 EARLYs	9 EARLYs		7 EARLYs
	9 LATEs	10 LATEs		11 LATEs
	12 FLEXs	8 FLEXs		13 FLEXs

Output of roster scheduling:

	Sun	Mon	Tues	Wed	Thur	Fri	Sat
1	EARLY	FLEX	OFF	LATE	LATE	FLEX	OFF
2	OFF	LATE	EARLY	EARLY	OFF	LATE	FLEX
.							
.							
40	OFF	LATE	EARLY	FLEX	FLEX	OFF	LATE

FIGURE 12.1. Illustration of roster scheduling.

and so on. After performing duties from row n, s will perform duties starting from row 1. After n weeks, he/she will work on row i again.

4. At the very beginning, the duties from Sunday, Monday, to Saturday are all defined. The job is to fill the duties into the two dimensional table.

5. There are many constraints about the assignment of the duties. For example, for each week there must be two OFF duties; minimum rest time between two duties is twelve hours; some kinds of duties cannot be followed by some particular kind (i.e., a FLEX cannot be followed by a LATE); and total working hours are 42 per week.

6. There are other features that are preferred but not required. One of them is to distribute the different kinds of duties evenly in the roster, so that a staff will not need to perform several weeks of EARLYs, and then followed by several weeks of LATEs. Another example is that long weekends (Sat-Sun consequent OFF) should be as many as possible.

7. Sometimes, if some constraints are violated, they may be tackled by making minor changes in the previous stages prior to roster construction. Suppose the total working hours is 42.5 in some row. It may be possible to adjust the length of one shift duty in that week to satisfy the constraint, since each shift duty has preparation time ranging from 15 minutes to 45 minutes. Therefore, many constraints are relaxable because the constraints are about favorable features, or because they can be tackled somewhere else. A roster with some violated constraints may still be a good roster.

The goal of KBS is to construct a timetable for a group of staff subject to the above set of duties and requirements. The whole timetable is usually called the master roster.

The rostering problem can be modeled as the following constrained assignment problem:

1. There is a two dimensional **grid** ($n \times m$) to be filled with tokens.
2. There are m sets of tokens, each set has n tokens, and the tokens have some properties (the labels and durations of the shift duties). The tokens are stored in a $n \times m$ **token table**.
3. The job is to fill the ith set of tokens into the ith column of the grid.
4. There are constraints about the rows (the total number of working hours in a week; total number of OFF duties in a week).
5. There are constraints about neighbouring tokens (rest time between shift duties).
6. There are global measures about the degree of goodness of the filled grid (distribution of shift duties).
7. Some constraints are hard and others are relaxable.
8. The aim is to find a filled grid which satisfies a maximum number of constraints, if it cannot satisfy all of them.

We shall draw on this abstract formulation for the rest of the paper.

2.2. Knowledge Acquisition and Model Formulation

A problem can always be formulated in several ways and be solved by different problem-solving methods. Whether a formulation is considered to be good or not depends on:

- The ease of the formulation;
- Whether the formulated model can reflect the original conceptual problem; and
- The flexibility of the formulation

After discussion with the end users of the rostering system, we have formulated the problem in three different ways; namely integer programming, non-linear programming, and knowledge-based model. These three mappings are most straightforward and preserve most original meaning of the conceptual problem. We then studied the feasibilities of implementing the system with the three different formulations. They are discussed in the next three sections. Based on the above three criteria, we found that knowledge-based approach produces good solution, and produced a system easy to understand and maintain.

2.2.1. Integer Programming. We visualize the problem as putting an $m \times n$ table of tokens into empty slots of the $m \times n$ grid.

Suppose there is no constraint, the problem reduces to find a permutation of each column in the token table and put the permutation into the corresponding column of the grid. This is illustrated in Figure 12.2.

It can be formulated as integer programming by constructing an assignment variable matrix $X = \{x_{i,j,k}\}$ of dimension $m \times n \times n$. The first dimension corresponds to the column of the token table and the grid. The second dimension corresponds to the row in the token table. The third dimension corresponds to the row in the grid. Elements of X are variables of the integer program. They represent the assignment of tokens. Values of elements of X can only be 0 or 1.

$$x_{c,i,j} = \begin{cases} 1 & \text{token in the row } i, \text{ column } c \text{ of the token table is assigned to row } j, \text{ column } c \text{ of the grid.} \\ 0 & \text{token in the row } i, \text{ column } c \text{ of the token table is NOT assigned to row } j, \text{ column } c \text{ of the grid.} \end{cases}$$

Since a feasible solution is required, we can use a dummy objective function:

Minimize

$$z = 0$$

subject to

$$\sum_{i=1}^{n} x_{c,i,y} = 1 \quad \text{for all } c = 1 \cdots m,$$

$$y = 1 \cdots n.$$

$$x_{i,j,k} = 0 \text{ or } 1 \quad \text{for all } i = 1 \cdots m,$$

$$j = 1 \cdots n, \quad k = 1 \cdots n.$$

Other constraints can be constructed. If the constraint is about a property of the token, we can define another matrix $P = \{p_{i,j}\}$ of dimension $n \times m$, which characterizes the constraint.

For example in the master roster problem, the total number of days-off must be two in a week. This rule can be represented by a matrix $P = \{p_{i,j}\}$ of dimension $n \times m$ where

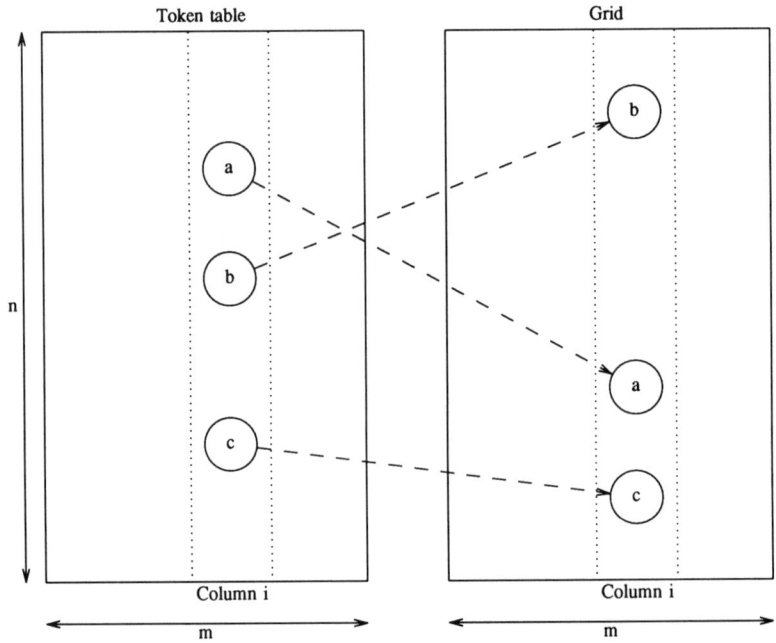

FIGURE 12.2. The constrained assignment process.

$$p_{i,j} = \begin{cases} 1 & \text{if token}_{i,j} \text{ is a OFF duty,} \\ 0 & \text{otherwise.} \end{cases}$$

and

$$\sum_{c=1}^{m}\sum_{i=1}^{n} x_{c,i,y} \times p_{i,c} = 2 \quad \text{for all } y = 1 \cdots n$$

Consider another constraint, that the total working hours must be 42 in a week.

Define $Q = \{q_{i,j}\}$, a matrix of dimension $n \times m$ where $q_{i,j}$ is the duration length of token in column j, row i of token table.

The new constraints will be:

$$\sum_{c=1}^{m}\sum_{i=1}^{n} x_{c,i,y} \times q_{i,c} = 42 \quad \text{for all } y = 1 \cdots n$$

Although we can formulate the problem as an integer program, the integer programming model cannot discriminate hard constraints and relaxable constraints. Also the integer program is NP-complete (Papadimitrou & Steiglitz, 1982) which is often not possible to be solved efficiently.

2.2.2. Non-linear Programming. We can modify the formulation slightly to allow violation of some constraints. For example, if the total working hours in a week does not necessary equal 42 hours but the total deviations should be minimized.

We can formulate the problem as

Minimize

$$z = \sum_{r=1}^{n} |(\sum_{c=1}^{m}\sum_{i=1}^{n} x_{c,i,r} \times q_{i,c}) - 42|$$

subject to

$$\sum_{i=1}^{n} x_{c,i,y} = 1 \quad \text{for all } c = 1 \cdots m,$$

$$y = 1 \cdots n$$

$$x_{i,j,k} = 0 \text{ or } 1 \quad \text{for all } i = 1 \cdots m,$$

$$j = 1 \cdots n, \quad k = 1 \cdots n$$

This can partially solve the problem of relaxable constraints, but it is no longer an integer programming. It is a non-linear programming formulation which is even more complex and intractable.

2.2.3. Knowledge-Based Approach. Artificial intelligence method emphasized a simulated human problem solving method on a computer. One advantage of the artificial intelligence method is it makes use of human expertise on a particular problem domain. For the rostering problem, the number of constraints is large, and many constraints are hard constraints which cannot be violated. The total number of ways of assigning the tokens in the grid is numerous, but only a portion of them can satisfy the constraints. There exist many heuristics to perform the assignment process which can reduce the size of the search space. As this problem has been performed manually for a long time, expert knowledge was used in the manual process. In addition, changes in the environment can be reflected by changing the rules and constraints (Grant, 1986).

KBS was developed using prototyping approach. The initial stage consisted of defining the problem, collecting the requirements from the user, and extracting the constraints of the rostering problem. The first few discussions were held with an expert who had performed the rostering planning for a few years. Only one expert was involved at the first stage, as there had been several attempts to implement the system before and all of them was unsuccessful. An initial prototype was completed in approximately two weeks. Planning results for small rosters were handed over to the users at the airport. Users were satisfied with the quick turnaround time and the rosters generated by the system. At the second stages, meetings were held with a group of experts. Comments for the roster generated by the prototype were collected. Problems in the roster identified and heuristic assignment rules were gathered from the experts. Refinements were then incorporated into the system and the system was then tested using larger rosters. The total system was completed upon several revisions and the total elapsed time for development was approximately six months.

2.3. Knowledge Representation

The rostering problem is different from diagnosis type rule-based systems because knowledge consists of set of constraints that need to be satisfied by the final roster, and a set of heuristic rules to guide the generation of the roster. Our research effort concentrates in deriving good representation techniques for control knowledge. The representation is then used to describe the heuristic assignment rules. In the next three sections, we describe the control strategies that we used in the rostering system and the constraints that were provided by the users.

2.3.1. Problem Solving Procedure. The goal of the roster problem is to arrange the tokens in such a way that all constraints are satisfied. The problem solving process divides into 2 stages: an *initial assignment stage,* and an *iterative improvement stage.* The initial assignment stage fills the empty grid with tokens, and allows violation of some of the constraints. Iterative improvement stage tries to resolve the violated constraints by swapping entries in the grid. It can also be viewed as optimizing the *goodness* of the grid, where goodness is a measure which is inversely proportional to the number of violated constraints.

The task of the first stage is to place different tokens into different slots to complete the grid. As we do not know the goal state, forward chaining is used in this stage. The initial solution generated will have some constraints violated. In this problem, we resolve those constraints by *swapping* the tokens. The second stage will use local improvement by swapping.

2.3.2. Initial Assignment Stage. The initial assignment stage is extremely important. Since in the improvement stage local swapping instead of global method is adopted to avoid combinatorial explosion, we are searching for local optimal solution instead of global optimal solution. The optimality of the solution is heavily dependent on the initial solution. Certainly, some ways of generating the initial solution are better than others. This is the best place to apply expert knowledge.

One important class of knowledge is the *ordering of assignment of different types of duties.* This ordering is discovered by the human expert through studying and performing the task over a long time. Another class will be the *assignment selection* knowledge. The ordering knowledge involves choices between what types of tokens should be assigned first, while the assignment selection knowledge deals mainly with whether a certain assignment is favorable or not. When the human expert performed the task long enough, he/she discovered some patterns of assignment which appear frequently in the completely filled grid. When the same task is performed again, he/she finds that if the same pattern is used, the final assignment will have less constraints violated. In this case, the pattern is called favorable. This is the expert assignment selection knowledge which is used in the system.

One simple way to represent the ordering knowledge is to embed them in the system. For selection assignment knowledge, they are coded as condition-action rules. For the KBS, selection knowledge are coded as forward chaining rules. They are divided into rule sets according to what duties are applicable. For each kind of duty there is an inference module to drive the corresponding rule set, and all modules are chained together by a global control which determines the ordering of the assignment.

Here are some example rules:

- IF   there is token with property A in a slot of the grid
  THEN assign a token with property B next to it.   (R1)

- IF   in the same row there are already 2 tokens with property X assigned
         AND the distance between the 2 tokens is between 2 and 4
  THEN   assign a token with property Y after the first X token. (R2)
- IF   there is a token with property M in a slot
  THEN   do not assign a token with property N in the previous slot. (R3)
- IF   there is no progress in the assignment
  THEN   remove rule R1, add rules R2 and R3 and retry. (R4)

Following are two KBS rules.

○ IF   the previous day is an off
  THEN   assign an early shift.

○ IF   the gap between two offs is 4
         AND the current day is the third working day
  THEN   assign a late shift.

2.3.3. Iterative Improvement Stage. This stage tries to reduce the number of violated constraints to minimum. The goal is to remove all violated constraints. Sometimes, it is impossible to attain the optimal solution within a reasonable time. We are employing the local method, iterative improvement, in the swapping stage. The local method we used is a hill climbing search strategy which tries to reduce the number of violated constraints by swapping entries in the roster. Instead of considering all possible swappings, a template of size four is used, i.e. we swap at most four entries in the roster for each trial. If the number of violated constraints is reduced by a swapping, the swapping is confirmed; otherwise, another set of entries will be considered. The process is continued until no improvement is achieved. The reason for using local method rather than global method is that using global method to perform optimization may lead to combinatorial explosion, and thus makes the solution impractical. This stage checks all constraints. If a constraint is violated, all feasible swapping actions that may resolve that constraint are enumerated, and KBS try to fire those actions until the constraint is resolved or all rules are fired. The process will stop if all constraints are resolved or no further improvements can be made.

Usually there are more than one kind of constraints. Some constraints are more difficult to satisfy. Therefore it is possible to further violate constraints that are easy to satisfy in order to resolve other constraints that are difficult to satisfy. In fact, we build a priority system for the constraints. We also adopt the following meta-knowledge:

The order of constraint resolution exactly match the priority of the constraints, and in the process of resolving constraints of priority i, we allows constraints of priority 1 to i − 1 to be further violated, but must not further violate constraints of priority i + 1 onwards.

Let us consider a concrete example. In KBS, since the initial assignment stage consists of expert knowledge rules, the initial solution has only two kinds of constraints prompt to violation. In that case we decide not to implement the priority system explicitly. The same effect is achieved by performing the swapping stage in two steps. In the first step, the harder constraints are resolved; in the latter stage, the easier constraints are resolved. In KBS, a concept called deviation is defined which maps the effects of violated constraints into a numeric measure. The problem is viewed as an optimization problem which minimizes the deviation.

2.4. Testing and Evaluation

2.4.1. The Prototype KBS. Since a development shell for constraint satisfaction techniques is not available at the time of prototype development (recently, constraint programming languages, such as CHIP and CHARMP, have been available commercially), KBS is implemented using Lisp (Winston & Horn, 1984). The first prototype, KBS 1.0, was developed on a Sun workstation running UNIX® using Common Lisp (Steele, 1984), and later transported to Scheme (Steele & Sussman, 1979) on an IBM PC/AT®. Common Lisp with UNIX provides a nice system development environment. The target system runs on personal computers since they are easily available in commercial environment. At the initial stage, we aimed at developing a prototype which can demonstrate the feasibility of knowledge-based approach for roster scheduling problems, fancy user interface is not constructed. We never expected that the prototype had been used for a few years. Input of the system is a data file containing the shift duties from Sunday to Saturday. Output of the system is a data file containing the master roster.

KBS represents the roster by an array. The main program controls the execution sequence of the system. Rules and constraints are separated from the main program, and are interpreted by the inference modules. In addition, some control is represented in procedural form and separated from the main program also. KBS allows a rule and a control procedure to combine and act as a new rule.

KBS logically consists of two components.

- initial solution generator
- solution improver

They are divided into the following modules.

- off-assignment module
- flex-assignment module
- shift-assignment module
- swapping module
- table-manipulation module
- main driver module

The off-assignment module, flex-assignment module, and shift-assignment module are rule-based modules correspond to the initial solution generator. The swapping module corresponds to the solution improver. The table-manipulation module is a set of functions supporting the manipulation of a set of global data structures. The main driver module chains up all modules (Chow & Hui, 1986).

The first prototype was completed in less than a month. Output from the prototype is considered satisfactory by the expert.

2.4.2. Evaluation. The input file format of KBS is shown in Appendix figure A-1. Each line corresponds to one shift duty. The row 'EARLY 7.5 16.5' indicates the shift duty is an early shift starts at 7:30 AM and ends at 4:30 PM.

Appendix figures A-2 through Figure A-4 give an illustration of a sample run for a roster of 20 staffs. Figure A-2 shows the roster after the initial assignment stage. The ideal total working hours per week is 42. The last column shows the deviations which have 21.5 hours in total. Figure A-3 shows the message from the iterative improvement stage and Figure A-4 shows the roster after the iterative improvement stage. After the iterative improvement stage the total deviation is greatly reduced. The final total deviation is 1.5 hours. The initial assignment stage takes 4,600 milli-seconds and the iterative improvement stage takes 14,600 milli-seconds on a Sun Workstation.

As the system was developed using prototyping approach, users actively participated in the development of the system. Problems in the roster were identified and changes were then immediately incorporated. Users were satisfied with the rosters generated by the system especially on attributes which were difficult to quantify, such as fairness. These attributes were not represented explicitly as a set of parameters, instead, they were implicitly handled by using the set of heuristic rules provided by users.

3. IMPLEMENTATION PROCESS

After completing the prototype KBS 1.0, we found that rostering problems have the following characteristics:
1. The process is forward chaining in nature: it starts from an empty roster to a completed one.
2. The problem is multiobjective in nature. The schedule planner requires the resulting roster to satisfy many objectives, some of them may be difficult to quantify such as fairness.
3. Some constraints are hard, and others are relaxable. It is possible to violate a few relaxable constraints in the whole roster.
4. Local method is adopted. We start with a roster and continually assign duties on it or modify the duties on it. Simultaneously working with two or more partially filled rosters is unusual.

Moreover, each roster problem can be tackled by considering:
1. Different arrangement of a similar set of procedures.
2. Different set of constraints to be considered in each stage.
3. Different stages to resolve the violated constraints.

The major difference between the rostering problem and a diagnosis type expert system application is that rostering problem uses *Heuristic Operators,* i.e., when the operator associated with a goal is executed, the resulting state may or may not achieve the goal, so the operators are 'heuristic' in nature. One needs to monitor the effects of the application of the operators. On the other hand, the human schedule planner usually has the knowledge of the overall skeleton of the roster construction process. Breakdown of the whole problem into sub-problems and the ordering of sub-problems are rather straightforward. In order to simplify the process for refining rules and constraints, we have designed and implemented a development tool called *SHO*, Schedule by Heuristic Operators. Moreover, we believe that the final system will eventually be handed over to the users. To make the system easier to maintain and understand, a development tool is needed. SHO is therefore designed with the goal to simplify the automation process for roster scheduling. In the next section, we give a brief overview of the SHO system and how KBS is implemented using SHO. A detail description of SHO is given in Hui (1988) and will not be repeated here.

3.1. Development Tool-Schedule by Heuristic Operators (SHO)

A good knowledge representation scheme should help the roster schedule planner to describe the problem easily. It should also be understandable by the expert schedule planner, who need not be a professional computer scientist. Following are some required properties:

- Direct mapping to user conceptual model;
- Small vocabulary;
- Feasible for a wide range of problems; and
- Easy mapping to current computing facilities.

SHO is a knowledge representation scheme designed for roster scheduling problems. It includes a set of heuristic operators which aims at achieving some goals, but the operators may or may not success in doing so. The roster scheduling process is represented as composition of operator instances. SHO operators consist of the following set of constructs:

- Heuristic operator diagram (hod);
- Different heuristic operators to achieve a common goal (relax-plan);
- Constrained forward chaining (try-forward-rules, rules, constraints);
- Priority subactions (priority-subaction); and
- Optimizing loop (try-loop).

Although there are only a few constructs, their combination of can tackle most rostering activities. We aim at finding a minimal set of constructs which are capable of expressing the necessary rostering activities. SHO constructs are implemented using frames. (This chapter only presents the essential properties of the SHO constructs. Engineering and implementational details are skipped and will be discussed elsewhere [Hui, 1988]. In particular, the priority-subaction and try-loop constructs have more than one form of implementation.)

3.1.1. Heuristic Operator Diagram (Hod).
Hod is a network-based construct adopted from Petri-net (Peterson, 1981) and non-deterministic finite state diagram (Hopcroft & Ullman, 1979). Intuitively, the idea of a hod is a state-operator diagram which aims to transform from a *start state* to an element of a set of *final states*. On the other hand, the destination state of the operator associated with each state does not always closer to the goal, the operator is kind of non-deterministic in nature. It only guarantees that the target state be within a set of possible states, but does not guarantee that the target state to be a particular one. The ideal of hod will be illustrated by an example from KBS (Chow & Hui, 1987).

Consider the task of assigning one kind of duty called OFF duty to the roster. At the start of this task, the roster is filled only with consequent Saturday-Sunday OFFs. It is a successful task when all OFF duties are assigned with some constraints being satisfied. The constraints are:

C1: there should be two OFFs in each row
C2: the distance between two OFFs cannot be more than four days

This is to prevent a staff to have consequent five or more working days. Furthermore, two OFFs with only one working day in between is not allowed, as the staff may find this kind of arrangement annoying. Corresponds to this task we have a procedure. This procedure, after executed, may fail in two ways: either leaving some OFF duties unassigned, or having some OFF pairs violating the constraint governing the distances between OFF pairs (C2). For these two fail cases, remedy procedures are constructed to amend the roster. Unfortunately the remedy procedures may also fail. For the remedy procedure unassigned OFF duties, it may assigned all unassigned OFF duties but making some OFF pairs violating C2.

All these tasks can be summarized using the hod shown in Figure 12.3. The goal of this hod is to transform the state from *state0* to *off-ok*, which corresponds to the planning goal of assigning OFF duties, *State0*, the start state, corresponds to a roster with only consequent Saturday-Sunday OFFs assigned; and *off-ok*, the only element in the final states, corresponds to the state of a roster where all OFFs are assigned and no constraints are violated. *Assign-off* is the operator associated with *state0*. It corresponds to the main OFF assignment procedure. *Unassigned-offs* and *invalid-conseq-offs* correspond to the roster after executing the main OFF assignment procedure of which some constraints are violated. *Reassign-off* is the remedy procedure of *unassigned-offs*, and *swap-offs* is the remedy procedure of *invalid-conseq-offs*. There is a link from *reassign-off* to *invalid-conseq-offs*. This corresponds to the fact that the remedy procedure of unassigned OFF duties may make some OFF pairs violating C2.

An hod instance *hod1* is represented using the following frame:

(*hod1*
   (ins-of *hod*)
   (states (. . .))
   (operators (. . .))
   (action-map ((*state op*) . .))
   (possible-states
      (*op state1 state2* . . .) . . .)
   (assume-start-states (*s*))
   (accept-states (. . .))
   (⟨*detail skipped*⟩)))

Each operator can be any function, procedures, SHO constructs or another hod.

Airport Staff Rostering

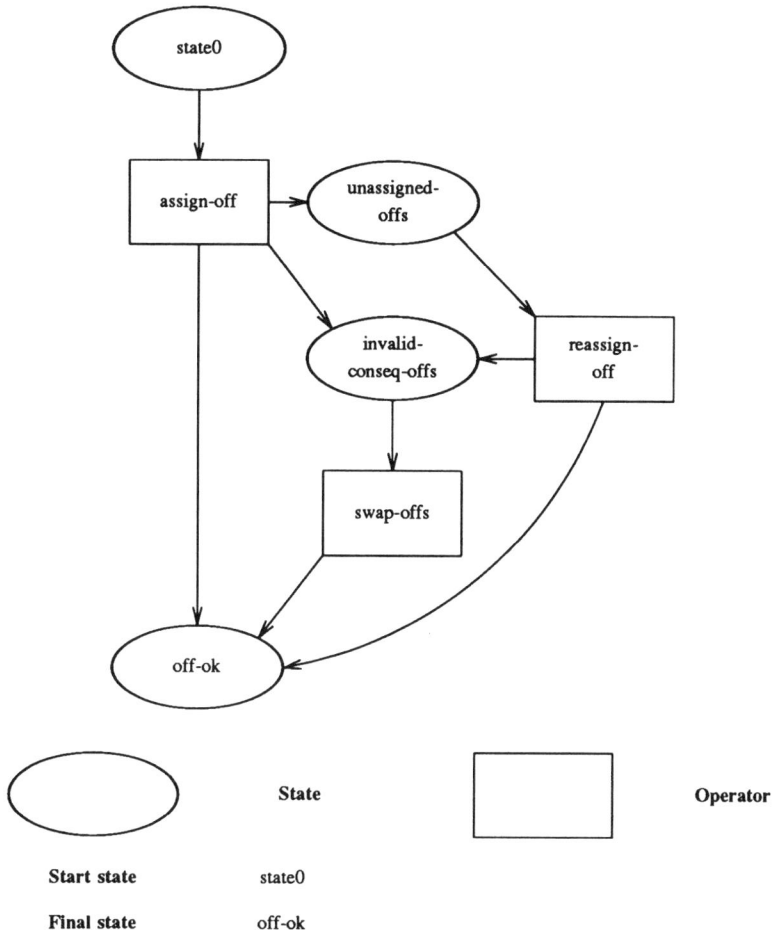

FIGURE 12.3 Example of hod.

A successful hod run has many possible paths. For the given example, a success run from *state0* to *off-ok* may follow one of the following paths:

- *assign-off*
- *assign-off, swap-offs*
- *assign-off, reassign-off*
- *assign-off, reassign-off, swap-offs*

Now we can see how the hod construct possesses grateful degradation property and facilitates prototyping. At first we need only to implement a prototype with *state0, off-ok,* and the operator *assign-off* only. This first prototype, usually fails to find a solution, can still be treated as a completed implementation, and we can integrate it with the other components of the whole system. The drawback of this first version is we need more trials to get a success run. On the other hand, we can quickly have a system for testing, and treat the implementation of other states and operators as later extensions.

The execution process of hod is summarized below. This process uses three local variables, namely cur_s (current state), cur_op (current operator), and D (set of already traversed states).

```
D ← { s }
cur_s ← s
loop
   cur_op ← a ( cur_s )
   execute ( cur_op )
   new_s ← new_state_after_exe-
      cution
   if ( new_s ∈ F ) return ( hod-suc-
      cess )
   if ( new_s ∈ D or new_s ∉ t
      ( cur_op ) ) return ( hod-fail )
   D ← D ∪ { new_s }
   cur_s ← new_s
endloop
```

3.1.2. Different Heuristic Operators to Achieve a Common Goal (Relax-Plan). Relax-plan is a simplified hod construct. It is commonly used in areas where a list of action operators are available for achieving a common goal. The operators have fixed priorities. The whole plan is just to try out the operators until the goal is achieved.

Each relax-plan instance associates with a list of operators and a goal. When executing the instance, the operators in the list will be tried out from the head of the list one by one until either (1) the goal is achieved, or (2) all operators are tried but the goal is not yet achieved. In case (1) happens, it is considered a success; in case (2) happens, the instance execution is considered a failure.

The frame representation of a relax-plan instance is:

(*relax-plan1*
  (ins-of *relax-plan*)
  (goal *test1*)
  (ops (*op1 op2 . . .*)))

3.1.3. Constrained forward chaining (try-forward-rules, rules, constraints). Constrained forward chaining is a standard forward chaining inference engine (Harmon & King, 1985). It contains three kinds of constructs: *try-forward-rules, rules,* and *constraints.* After a try-forward-rules operator is activated, it checks for the constraints. If all constraints are satisfied then it fires the rules until the goal is achieved. This operator is considered success if and only if the goal is achieved. The frame representations for a try-forward-rules instance, a rules instance, and a constraints instance are:

(*try-forward-rules1*
  (ins-of *try-forward-rules*)
  rules-list (. . .))
  (constraint-list (. . .))
  (goal-test *test1*)
  (quit-test *test2*)
  (⟨*detail skipped*⟩))

(*rules1*
  (ins-of *rules*)
  (condition *test3*)
  (action *action1*)
  (⟨*detail skipped*⟩))

(*constraints1*
  (ins-of *constraints*)
  (violate-cons *test4*)
  (⟨*detail skipped*⟩))

3.1.4. Priority subactions (priority-subaction). The third construct is called priority-subaction. Each priority-subaction associates a set of candidates (or objects), a goal, a priority function and a subaction. Once a priority-subaction is selected, the subaction is applied to the candidates in the candidate set until the goal is achieved. The priority function determines which candidate in the candidate set will be used by the next application of subaction. If the goal is achieved during the execution, then the whole priority-subaction operator is considered a success, otherwise it fails.

The frame representation of a priority-subaction instance is:

(*priority-subaction1*
  (ins-of *priority-subaction*)
  (candidates (. . .))
  (goal *test1*)
  (priority-function *fcn1*)
  (subaction *operator1*)
  (⟨*detail skipped*⟩))

When a priority-subaction is entered, the priority-function is applied to all candidates. The candidates will be sorted in descending order according to the result of priority-function. The subaction will then be applied to the candidates in the sorted list one by one, starting from the candidate with the highest priority. It stops when the goal is satisfied and returns success, otherwise it returns fail.

Referring to the example in Figure 12.3, the procedure to assign OFF (the *assign-off* operator) is a priority-subaction construct. The procedure to assign OFF constitutes of assigning the OFF duties week by week. For each week, the schedule planner tries to assign two OFFs in it. For each day of the week, the planner has a score about the suitability of assigning an OFF. He/she will try to assign the OFF to the day with the highest score. On the other hand, the assignment needs to satisfy the set of constraints. The knowledge of the schedule planner corresponds to a nesting of two priority-subaction and one try-forward-rules. The *assign-off* is a priority-subaction whose candidates are the different rows in the roster which corresponds to different person, the goal is to assign all OFF duties, and the subaction is an operator called *assign-off-in-row*. Since there is no particular preference among the weeks, there is no priority function. *Assign-off-in-row* is also a priority-subaction whose candidates are different days of the week, the goal is to assign two OFFs in a row, the subaction is an operator called *assign-off-at-entry*, and the priority function is the score of suitability. *Assign-off-at-entry* is a try-forward-rules which determines an OFF assignment is possible or not, and the goal is to assign an OFF duty. The relationship of the above three operators is illustrated in Figure 12.4.

Reassign-off and *swap-offs* are operators associated with states *unassigned-off* and *invalid-conseq-offs*. They are also composed of priority-subaction and try-forward-rules instances. Both of them aim at transforming the state to *off-ok*. These transitions amend to roster so that no constraints are violated. When *reassign-off* is used, it may move to the state *invalid-conseq-offs*, and *swap-offs* will then be invoked in this case.

3.1.5. Optimizing loops (try-loop). The hod construct does not allow any state to be reached twice. Optimizing loops are intended for handling the iterative feature which is difficult to be represented in hod. When a try-loop operator is entered, it will continue executing the operator described in the loop-detail until the goal is achieved and returns

Assign-off
   is-a : priority-subaction
   goal : assign all OFF duties
   candidates : all rows
   subaction : **Assign-off-in-row**

Assign-off-in-row
   is-a : priority-subaction
   goal : assign two OFF duties
   candidates : all days
   priority-function : score-of-suitability
   subaction : **Assign-off-in-entry**

Assign-off-in-entry
   is-a : try-forward-rules
   goal : assign an OFF duty
   (function is to assign an OFF in an roster entry)

FIGURE 12.4. Nesting of SHO constructs.

success, or until the continue-test is false and returns fail. Try-loop is good for representing the optimization process.

The frame representation of a try-loop instance is:

(*try-loop1*
  (`ins-of` *try-loop*)
  (`goal-test` *test1*)
  (`carry-on-test` *test2*)
  (`loop-detail` *operator1*)
  ($\langle$*detail skipped*$\rangle$))

For the KBS, after all duties are assigned to the roster, the last stage is to minimize a numerical parameter of the roster named *deviation*. The schedule plannner uses a hill-climbing approach. He/she repeatly uses a procedure called *swap-shifts* which tries to swap duties in the roster to reduce the *deviation*, until no further improvement can be found. Without try-loop, the above piece of knowledge cannot be represented by SHO. The try-loop representation of the above problem is shown in Figure 12.5.

In general, knowledge of all rostering problems can be represented using different combinations of hod, priority-subaction, try-forward-rules, and try-loop.

3.2. Technology Transfer and Maintenance

The second version of KBS was implemented by both the partially implemented SHO constructs and Lisp using the frame representations discussed above. Lisp is used where the SHO constructs are not yet implemented, but the algorithms of those Lisp functions follow the logic of the constructs.

The second version was developed on a Sun workstation running UNIX using Common Lisp (Steele, 1984). The system contains about 3000 lines of source codes. The partially implemented SHO scheme involves about one-third of the coding. This system produces a 174 person roster within ten minutes. The quality of the roster was considered satisfactory by the expert.

The final KBS, KBS 2.0, was implemented using SHO. The resulting system contains about 2000 lines of Lisp codes and 46 Sho objects. It also produces a 174 person roster within ten minutes. Finally, the system was delivered to the users at the airport and the source codes for the whole system was handed over to the MIS Department of the airline. The maintenance and support of the system was then taken care of by the airline's computer staff.

We were told that the system had been ported to support roster planning for other departments at the airport of the airline.

3.3. KBS Maintenance and Rewriting

KBS has been running for a few years and has been ported to support other department's rostering within the organization. It is basically a standalone PC system, user unfriendly, and roster is the only output from the system. Moreover, it is slow for a large roster, e.g. it takes 30 minutes to generate a 400 staffs roster.

Recently, we started investigating the feasibility of developing a complete and integrated system which would take the flight information as input and generate the roster with staff names attached. Moreover, the system has to reassign duties of those staffs that have annual leaves and trainings.

The new system has three modules, namely manpower planning module, weekly roster generation module, and daily roster maintenance module. The manpower planning

Optimize-deviation
  is-a :   try-loop
  goal-test :   deviation cannot be further reduced
  carry-on-test :   always true /* hill climbing */
  loop-detail :   **swap-shifts**

FIGURE 12.5. Try-loop example.

module automates the shift generation process from the detail flight information. The problem can be viewed as a variation of the bin-packing problem and is described separately. The weekly roster generation module, KBS 3.0, is a complete rewrite of the previous KBS system, including some additional features, such as collecting some statistics about the roster. Basic inference and processing mechanism is the same as in KBS.

The system has been rewritten in C running on PC 386. There is an observable improvement in performance. A roster of 400 staffs which requires 30 minutes by KBS 2.0 can now be completed in less than 1 minute by KBS 3.0. On the other hand, the flexibilities of modifying rules and constraints easily in KBS under SHO is lost in return for the improvement in speed since many constraints and rules are coded as C functions. Some constraints which depends on parameters, like minimum rest between two duties is twelve hours, can be modified through a parameter definition file. As the system has been running for several years, the rules and constraints have become stable and the lost in flexibilities is not important.

4. CONCLUSION

We presented here a complete report on developing a knowledge-based system for rostering for a local airline. The system has gone through the phases of problem definition and formulation, prototype development, tool implementation and prototype refinement, and complete rewriting to integrate the system into the organization. The system has been stable and is now used for daily operation.

As pointed out by one of the referees, the other major problem for staff rostering is to recommend proper actions when there are sudden changes in flight arrival and departure times. The new system has a daily maintenance module which supports daily adjustment of the roster. On the other hand, we believe that artificial intelligence techniques can be used to provide better recommendations which is now under investigation.

ACKNOWLEDGEMENT

We would like to thank Alan Wong of Cathay Pacific Airways for his ideas and helpful comments throughout the whole project, David Liu, Nelson Lee, Mabel Cheung, John Cheng, and Florence Chin of Cathay Pacific Airways for their cooperation in the first version of KBS, Lily Chan and David Ho of Cathay Pacific Airways and Herman Law of Firmware Design Company for their help during the rewriting of the system.

REFERENCES

Chow, K.P., & Hui, C.K. (1987). Knowledge-based approach to scheduling problems. *Proceedings of the IEEE Asian Electronic Conference (September 1987)*, 404–409.

Chow, K.P., & Hui, C.K. (1986). *Check-In staff roster planning*. Computer studies working paper.

Fox, M.S. (1983). *Constraint-directed search: A case study of job-shop scheduling*. PhD Thesis.

Fox, M.S., & Smith, S.F. (1984). ISIS-a knowledge-based system for factory scheduling, *Expert Systems* 1(1) 25–49.

Grant, T.J. (1986). Lessons for O.R. from A.I.: a scheduling case study. *Journal of the Operational Research Society* 37(1) 41–57.

Harmon, P., & King, D. (1985). *Expert systems*. New York: John Wiley & Sons.

Hopcroft, J., & Ullman, J. (1979). *Introduction to automata theory, languages, and computation*. Reading, MA: Addison-Wesley Publishing Company.

Hui, C.K. (1988). *Knowledge-based approach to roster scheduling problems*. M. Phil. Thesis.

Papadimitriou, C. & Steiglitz, K. (1982). *Combinatorial optimization: Algorithms and complexity*. New Jersey: Prentice-Hall Inc.

Peterson, J.L. (1981) *Petri net theory and modeling of systems*. New York: Prentice-Hall.

Steele, G.L. (1984). *Common LISP: the language*. Digital Press.

Steele, G.L., & Sussman, G.L. (1979). *The revised report on SCHEME: A dialect of LISP, AI Memo 452*. Cambridge, Massachusetts: MIT Artificial Intelligence Lab.

Taha, H.A. (1982). *Operations research: An introduction (third edition)*. New York: MacMillan Publishing Co. Ltd.

Winston, P.H., & Horn, B.K.P. (1984). *Lisp (second edition)*. Reading, MA: Addison-Wesley.

APPENDIX

SUNDAY
    EARLY 7.5 16.5
    EARLY 8 17.5
    EARLY 8 17.5
    EARLY 9 18.5
    EARLY 9 18.5
    LATE 13.5 23
    LATE 14.5 23
    LATE 16.5 23.5
    LATE 17.5 23.5
    FLEX
    OFF
    OFF
    OFF
    OFF
    EARLY 7 16.5
    EARLY 7 16.5
    OFF
    LATE 14 23
    EARLY 6.5 12.5
    EARLY 7.5 16.5
MONDAY
    EARLY 6.5 14
    EARLY 7 15.5
    EARLY 7 15.5
    LATE 12.5 21.5
    .
    .
    .

TUESDAY
    .
    .
    .

FIGURE A-1. KBS input file format.

```
> (initial-assignment)
No slot satisfying all rules, relax!
NIL
> (print-all-info)
```

Sun	Mon	Tue	Wed	Thu	Fri	Sat	Hours	Deviation
7.5-16.5	13.5-23	OFF	FLEX	16-23.5	16.5-23.5	OFF	/42.0	0
OFF	9-18.5	7-16	15-21	OFF	7.5-16.5	15-23	/41.5	0.5
14-23	OFF	7-15.5	FLEX	OFF	6.5-12.5	7-16.5	/42.0	0
8-17.5	16-23.5	OFF	OFF	6.75-15.25	9-16.5	8.5-17	/41.5	0.5
FLEX	OFF	6.5-15.5	7-16.5	12.5-21	12.5-21.5	OFF	/45.0	3
OFF	FLEX	15.5-23	OFF	7-16.5	7.5-16.5	16.5-23.5	/42.0	0
14.5-23	OFF	9-18.5	11.5-21	OFF	7-16.5	FLEX	/46.0	4
17.5-23.5	12.5-21	OFF	OFF	FLEX	13.25-22.75	12.5-21.5	/42.0	0
16.5-23.5	OFF	7.5-16.5	7.5-16.5	9-18.5	FLEX	OFF	/43.5	1.5
OFF	7-16.5	16.5-23.5	16-23.5	OFF	6.75-16.25	8.5-17	/42.0	0
7.5-16.5	13.25-21.25	OFF	6.5-11.5	13-22.5	OFF	7-16.5	/41.0	1
9-18.5	13-21.5	OFF	OFF	6.5-11.5	7-16.5	13.5-23	/42.0	0
13.5-23	OFF	6.5-15	6.5-11.5	14-23.5	13.5-23	OFF	/42.0	0
OFF	FLEX	13.25-22.75	15-22	OFF	6.75-16.25	8-15	/42.0	0
8-17.5	12.5-21.5	OFF	6.5-12.5	FLEX	OFF	9-18.5	/43.0	1
9-18.5	7-15.5	13-22.5	OFF	OFF	7-16.5	6.5-11.5	/42.0	0
7-16.5	OFF	6.5-15	6.5-14	9-17.5	13.5-23	OFF	/43.5	1.5
OFF	7-15.5	8.5-16.5	12.5-20.5	14-23	OFF	6.75-12.25	/39.0	3
7-16.5	6.5-14	OFF	OFF	6.5-11.5	13.25-22.75	13.25-22.75	/41.0	1
6.5-12.5	8.5-17.5	17-23	13-22.5	OFF	OFF	16.5-23.5	/37.5	4.5

FIGURE A-2. Sample KBS run after initial assignment.

```
> (iterative-improvement)
  ..attempting rule #<RESOLVE-RULE-1 374877>
Con-4 violated in 19 4
Con-1 violated in 20 7
Rule fired #<RESOLVE-RULE-1 374877>
  ..attempting rule #<RESOLVE-RULE-1 374877>
Con-1 violated in 20 7
Rule fired #< RESOLVE-RULE-1 374877>
  ..attempting rule #<RESOLVE-RULE-1 374877>
Con-1 violated in 20 7
swap early-late duty 1 of rows 19  20
swap early-late duty 3 of rows 17  18
swap early-late duty 6 of rows 17  2
swap early-late duty 4 of rows 15  7
swap early-late duty 3 of rows 13  20
swap early-late duty 4 of rows 13  18
swap early-late duty 5 of rows 13  18
swap early-late duty 3 of rows 9  18
swap early-late duty 5 of rows 9  4
swap early-late duty 7 of rows 5  2
  ..attempting rule #< RESOLVE-RULE-1 374877>
Con-1 violated in 20 7
                        .
                        .
                        .
```

FIGURE A-3. KBS iterative improvement message.

Airport Staff Rostering

> (print-all-info)

	Sun	Mon	Tue	Wed	Thu	Fri	Sat	Hours	Deviation
	7.5-16.5	13.5-23	OFF	FLEX	16-23.5	16.5-23.5	OFF	/42.0	0
	OFF	9-18.5	8.5-16.5	6.5-11.5	OFF	13.5-23	13.25-22.75	/41.5	0.5
	14-23	OFF	7-15.5	FLEX	OFF	6.5-12.5	7-16.5	/42.0	0
	8-17.5	16-23.5	OFF	OFF	9-18.5	9-16.5	8.5-17	/42.5	0.5
	FLEX	OFF	OFF	6.5-14	12.5-21	12.5-21.5	15-23	/42.0	0
	OFF	FLEX	15.5-23	OFF	7-16.5	7.5-16.5	16.5-23.5	/42.0	0
	14.5-23	OFF	7-16	6.5-12.5	OFF	7-16.5	FLEX	/42.0	0
	17.5-23.5	12.5-21	OFF	OFF	FLEX	13.25-22.75	12.5-21.5	/42.0	0
	16.5-23.5	OFF	6.5-15	7.5-16.5	9-17.5	FLEX	OFF	/42.0	0
	OFF	7-16.5	16.5-23.5	16-23.5	OFF	6.75-16.25	8.5-17	/42.0	0
	7.5-16.5	13.25-21.25	OFF	15-21	13-22.5	OFF	7-16.5	/42.0	0
	9-18.5	13-21.5	OFF	OFF	6.5-11.5	7-16.5	13.5-23	/42.0	0
	13.5-23	OFF	17-23	12.5-20.5	14-23	13.5-23	OFF	/42.0	0
	OFF	FLEX	13.25-22.75	15-22	OFF	6.75-16.25	8-15	/42.0	0
	8-17.5	12.5-21.5	OFF	6.5-11.5	FLEX	OFF	9-18.5	/42.0	0
	9-18.5	7-15.5	13-22.5	OFF	OFF	7-16.5	6.5-11.5	/42.0	0
	7-16.5	OFF	9-18.5	7-16.5	6.5-11.5	7.5-16.5	OFF	/42.5	0.5
	OFF	7-15.5	7.5-16.5	11.5-21	14-23.5	OFF	6.75-12.25	/42.0	0
	6.5-12.5	8.5-17.5	6.5-15.5	OFF	6.75-15.25	13.25-22.75	OFF	/42.0	0
	7-16.5	6.5-14	6.5-15	13-22.5	OFF	OFF	16.5-23.5	/42.0	0

FIGURE A-4. Sample KBS run after iterative improvement.

Practical Application of a Connectionist Expert System—The INSIDE Story

H. C. Lui, A. H. Tan, J. H. Lim and H. H. Teh

*Institute of Systems Science, National University of Singapore,
Heng Mui Keng Terrace, Kent Ridge, Singapore 0511*

1. INTRODUCTION

TRADITIONAL RULE-BASED expert systems typically require a time consuming knowledge acquisition phase. Neural networks technology, also known as the connectionist approach, offers learning algorithms whereby knowledge bases can be trained from examples. A connectionist diagnostic expert system has been developed for Singapore Airlines (SIA) to assist technicians in diagnosing a critical piece of avionic equipment. The system, known as Inertial Navigation System Interactive Diagnostic Expert (INSIDE) is designed to reduce diagnostic time. The diagnostic software consists of an Example module, which captures the knowledge of technicians based on past diagnostic cases and a Flowchart module, which implements the troubleshooting flowcharts faithfully. These two modules complement each other to achieve fast diagnosis and extensive coverage of all cases. During consultation, the system first activates the Example module to check if the set of symptoms observed is similar to any previous cases. If so, then the system quickly reports its finding and pinpoints the defective part. Otherwise, the system passes control to the Flowchart module, which prompts the technician to execute a sequence of tests as recommended by the manufacturer's flowcharts. A unique feature of this system is that after the Flowchart module finds the fault, it will formulate the result as a new case for the Example module to learn. With this kind of incremental learning capability, the knowledge base of the Example module can expand as the system is being used.

Besides its diagnostic capability, INSIDE can also be used to keep repair records and generate management reports. A user-friendly interface is also provided so that minimum training is required for technicians to use. The entire system can be run on low-cost microcomputer. It is also written in a modular fashion so that it can be easily adapted to new applications.

1. Expert Systems

There have been many successful applications of rule-based expert system technology over the past 15 years. To develop an expert system, the knowledge engineer will undergo a time consuming knowledge acquisition process. Typically, he interviews domain experts to extract relevant knowledge and then encodes it as rules in the expert system. This requires much of the experts' valuable time. Moreover, the expert may not be able to articulate his knowledge clearly and concisely enough. Hence, it is not straightforward to translate the expert's knowledge into rules. When several experts are involved, their opinions may differ or even contradict, which will further complicate the knowledge engineer's task. In addition, it is very difficult to check whether the knowledge is complete or consistent. As a result, knowledge acquisition is typically an iterative process and the knowledge base will be modified until the performance of the system is satisfactory.

In recent years, a new approach of designing expert systems has emerged. It is based on neural networks technology and is commonly known as the Connectionist Expert System (CES). In essence, this approach attempts to build intelligent systems by modelling the information processing aspect of the biological brain. Such a system typically consists of a set of nodes (or neurons). Nodes are interconnected among themselves. Each node receives information from others, performs some simple calculations, and then passes the result to others. As such, knowledge is distributed across the entire network, and is represented by the connection weights between nodes. Powerful learning algorithms, such as the pocket algorithm (Gallant, 1988; 1990), the construction algorithm (Chan et al., 1989), and the back-propagation algorithm (Rumelhart et al., 1986), exist so that the knowledge base can be trained from a set of examples. Thus the tedious effort of knowledge acquisition can be greatly reduced. After training, the system behaves as though it follows rules. Sejnowski calls it rule-following as opposed to rule-based (Sejnowski & Rosenbert, 1987). In (Bradshaw et al., 1989), the performance of the connectionist approach is compared with that of the rule-based method. It took the developer one man-year to build the rule-based system (with 700 rules), whereas the connectionist approach was developed in less than one week using a simple simulator. Yet both systems performed as well as the human expert. In addition, the time for inferencing was also greatly reduced from five minutes to a few milliseconds.

In this chapter, we describe an application of the Connectionist Expert System to assist technicians in diagnosing a piece of avionic equipment for Singapore Airlines (SIA). It is generally observed that a new technician will rely more on the troubleshooting manual to assist him in locating the failure. However, after he gains a few years of experience, he gradually develops his own expertise and relies more on his own knowledge rather than the manual. In particular, he can quickly recognize the symptom pattern and identify the failure in a few steps. Moreover, technicians can perform accurate diagnosis, even without fully understanding how the equipment works. They do so mainly by matching symptom patterns with previous familiar cases which they have encountered before. Only in rare occasions do they need to refer to the diagnostic flowcharts again. This phenomenon of novice-to-expert shift has been well studied by psychologists in areas such as chess (Chase & Simon, 1973), physics (Larkin et al., 1980) as well as computer programming (Bateson et al., 1987). This is our attempt to build an expert system which behaves in a similar way. The system must be able to learn while it is being used, and its knowledge base must be able to expand as new information becomes available.

Section 2 briefly describes the equipment and the diagnostic procedures. Section 3 describes an overview of the expert system operations. Sections 4 and 5 give a more detailed description of the algorithm while sections 6 and 7 discuss the implementation and experimental results.

2. THE PROBLEM DOMAIN

The expert system developed here is used to diagnose a piece of equipment known as the Inertia Navigation System (INS), which is used in commercial aircraft to determine the exact bearing and location of the plane. The equipment consists of about 25 electronic circuit boards, a power supply and an inertial platform. The technician's task is to repair the faulty unit by identifying and replacing those cards which cause problems. The INS unit has been in production for a long time and comes with a set of diagnostic flowcharts which can help the technicians in the course of troubleshooting. Typically, when a unit is removed from the aircraft, a reason-of-removal form is filled out and the initial set of faulty symptoms are registered. The unit will then be placed on a testbed. Its internal memory will be examined and the malfunction codes (MC) retrieved. The MC codes are unique to this equipment and provides further information on the fault. In general, this set of initial information is not sufficient to pinpoint the faulty component. Hence the technician will perform additional tests to isolate the fault. He may rely on his instinct, his past experience, or the diagnostic manual. After the faulty card(s) are replaced, the unit will then undergo calibration tests before it is returned to the aircraft.

It has been found that the mean-time-between-removal of this piece of equipment is dropping. Hence the technicians are overwhelmed with their workload. The airline workshop is therefore looking for an expert system which can help the technicians to reduce the diagnostic time. In particular, they want a system which can give a fast response time and can also expand its knowledge base as the system is being used. After careful consideration, the Connectionist approach has been chosen. The following sections describe in detail such an expert system, which we call INSIDE—(Inertia Navigation System Interactive Diagnostic Expert).

3. APPROACH AND STRATEGY

As the INS is an established piece of equipment, the set of flowcharts has extensive coverage of all the failure modes and is therefore an invaluable knowledge base for troubleshooting. However, if the technician follows the flowchart faithfully, he will need to go through many steps to arrive at a conclusion. On the other hand, it is observed that 80% of the failures concentrates on about 20% of the components. Hence if an experienced technician is familiar with the failures of those 20% of the components, he can repair the equipment 80% of the time. For the remaining 20%, he has to refer to the manual. The experienced technician solves the familiar cases mainly by performing pattern matching—comparing the symptoms with similar cases in his internal memory. In this way, he can bypass the flowchart completely and arrive at a solution in only a few steps, thus shortening the diagnostic time. This kind of example-based heuristic knowledge is therefore very useful in equipment diagnosis. It is interesting to note that these two knowledge sources complement each other very well—the rule-based (flowchart) knowledge offers extensive coverage, but leads to long diagnostic time, while the example-based knowledge can quickly arrive at a solution. However, it cannot handle unfamiliar cases.

Having observed this, we have built a system which incorporates both kinds of knowledge sources. The system thus has two modules—a flowchart module which captures the rules from flowcharts, and an example module which captures the heuristic knowledge of familiar cases. The two modules share a common user interface, which interacts with the user in a question and answering mode. Figure 13.1 shows the basic block diagram of the entire system. When the technician enters a new diagnostic case to the system, control is first passed to the example module. This module will check if the new case is similar to any of the old cases in its knowledge base. As mentioned before, the initial set of symptoms, consisting of the malfunction codes and warning lights information only, may not be sufficient to arrive at a conclusion. The example module will then enter into a dialog session with the technician, prompting him to do additional tests one by one. Such consultation will continue until either one of the following conditions arrive: (1) The new case is similar to an old one. Hence the example module recommends that the technician replace the card found faulty for the old case. (2) The new case is not close to any of the old cases and the example module fails to give any recommendation. When this happens, control is passed to the flowchart module. This module will follow the diagnostic path set by the flowcharts to find the failure component. It does so by prompting the technician to perform additional tests.

The knowledge base of the example module can be constructed in two ways. The air-

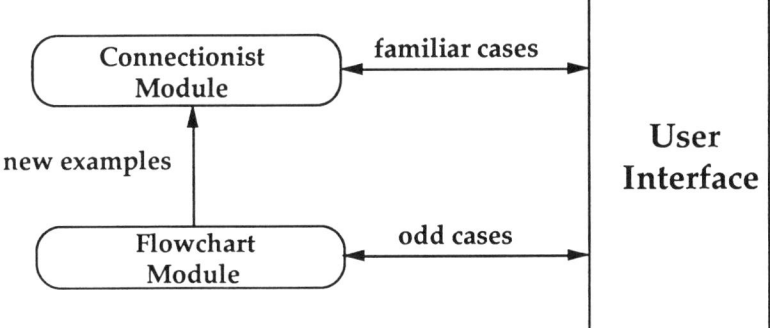

FIGURE 13.1. INSIDE block diagram.

line workshop has kept excellent repair records on these INS units over the years. Each record details the initial symptoms, the additional tests performed and the faulty component card replaced. This information can then be translated into symptom-fault association pairs and incorporated into the knowledge base. Notice that this knowledge captures indirectly the experiences of technicians as they are making shortcuts to solve problems. Another alternative to acquire knowledge is to extract it from the flowchart module. When the example module fails but the flowchart module finds the fault, the system can formulate a new case based on the findings of the flowchart module and send it to the example module to be incorporated to its knowledge base. In this way, the knowledge base of the example module will grow as the system is being used. It will then be able to solve future cases similar to the present one.

4. EXAMPLE MODULE

The purpose of the example module is to capture the technicians' expertise based on past successfully diagnosed cases so that during consultation, they can be recalled when similar symptom patterns are observed. Hence, the primary function of this module is pattern matching. We adopt the connectionist approach to implement this module because it has been demonstrated that this approach is more robust in dealing with incomplete and ambiguous information. Another important factor is that powerful learning algorithms exist so that the knowledge base can be built automatically from a given set of examples.

There are basically two types of pattern matching networks—feature-based and prototype based (Hecht-Nielson, 1989). The former makes use of modifiable functional forms to classify patterns. The popular backpropagation algorithm (Rumelhart et al., 1986) falls into this category. Prototype based networks operate by first grouping examples into representative prototypes (or cluster centers). During the matching process, the network attempts to find the closest prototype that matches the input pattern. Many neural network models such as Counterpropagation (Hecht-Nielson, 1989), Kohonen Net (Kohonen, 1988) and the RCE algorithm (Scofield et al., 1988) are in this category. Since it is possible to add more prototypes or cluster centers even when the system is being used, the latter approach is chosen for this implementation.

The prototype approach is similar to traditional pattern classifiers—namely the nearest neighborhood approach or its variances. Moreover, our approach shares some similarities with the case-based-reasoning (CBR) method (Morgan Kaufman, 1989). When a new case is being entered, both approaches attempt to retrieve an old case in their respective knowledge bases which are most similar to it. And both approaches learn by remembering, i.e., to store new, unseen cases back to enlarge their knowledge bases. However, the CBR approach will modify the retrieved case in order to adapt it to the current situation, while the connectionist approach attempts to form cluster centers from examples. Moreover, for the connectionist approach, the basic computation is numerical evaluation. Thus the response time is fast.

4.1. Network Representation

Conceptually, the example module can be thought of as a 3 layer network as shown in Figure 13.2. Nodes in each layer are connected to the next layer as depicted in the diagram. But within the same layer, nodes do not communicate among themselves. The first layer is the input layer. It consists of two kinds of nodes. The first group represents symptoms such as the MC codes and warning lights. The second set denotes the results of additional tests to be performed by the technicians during the course of consultation. All input nodes can assume values $\{1, 0, -1\}$, representing TRUE, UNKNOWN and FALSE respectively. They are all initialized to the UNKNOWN state at the beginning of the consultation. The nodes in the second (hidden) layer are representative diagnostic cases. Each hidden node receives information from all the input nodes. Internally, it computes a similarity measure between the input attributes and the case it represents. If the match is close enough, then the node will "fire" and elicit an output to the third (output) layer. Each node at the output layer corresponds to a fault and a recommendation on which circuit card should be replaced. Notice that a single hidden unit can cause multiple output nodes to "fire," thus suggesting to the technician that more than one faulty component have to be replaced.

There are primarily two ways to compute the similarity measures. When both cluster centers and the input pattern can be expressed as vectors in a high dimensional space, then the distance between two vectors is a good measure of similarity. Alternatively, if all vectors are normalized to the same length, then the angle between them also indicates how similar they are. In the latter case, a popular choice is to measure the cosine of the angle, which can be evaluated by computing the inner product of two vectors. Both simi-

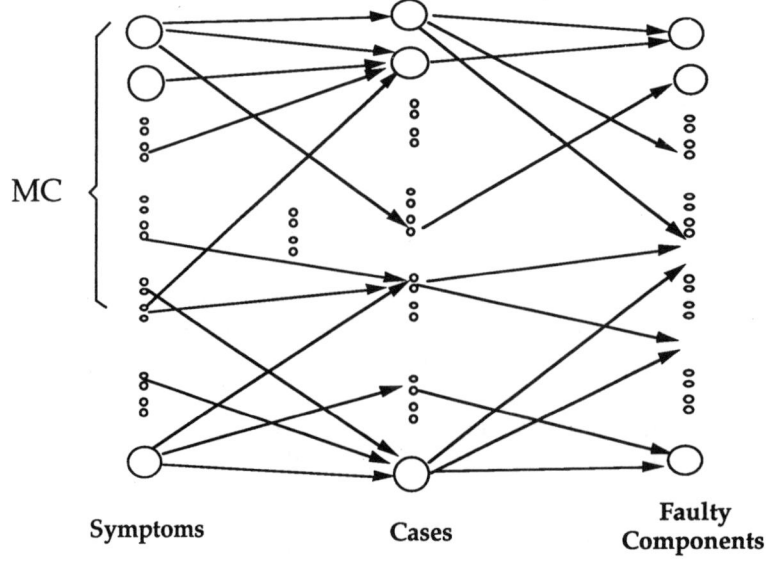

FIGURE 13.2. Example module.

larity measures are widely used in neural network literature.

In an earlier implementation (Tan, 1990) the inner product measure was adopted and each hidden node corresponds to each past diagnostic record. Obviously, the number of hidden nodes will become very large after the system has been in use for some time. In this implementation, we use a clustering procedure to group similar cases together, and the clustering algorithm chosen makes use of a distance type similarity measure. The detail algorithm will be explained in subsequent sections.

4.2. Inference Engine

After the initial set of symptoms such as warning lights and MC codes are entered into the input layer of the example module, the information will propagate forward to the hidden layer. Each hidden node computes a distance score between the cluster point it represents and the input vector. Thus the shorter the distance, the more similar they are. Typically, the initial set of symptoms is not sufficient to lower the distance measure to an acceptable level. If this is the case, additional information in terms of new test results is needed. At this point, the signal flows backward from the hidden layer to the input layer to solicit test results. This is achieved by prompting the technicians to conduct certain tests. The system employs an algorithm to decide the most appropriate test to be performed. This will be described later. When the test result becomes available, the respective attribute of the input vector is filled with either the TRUE or FALSE value and the signal flows forward again from input to hidden layer. Distance scores are recomputed and the cycle repeats itself until one of the following conditions are satisfied: (1) One of the distance measures is lower than the acceptable threshold. In this case, the example module declares that it has found a previous case which is similar to the present situation, and recommends that the technician replaces the faulty card corresponding to the previous case. (2) All cluster points fail to yield a distance lower than the threshold. Thus the example module fails to find a solution and the flowchart module is invoked.

It is noted that the forward-backward signal flow described above is reminiscent of the forward-backward chaining control mechanism in traditional expert systems.

4.2.1. Distance Computation.
We adopt the weighted Euclidean distance as a similarity measure between the input vector and cluster points. So for input vector X and cluster point C_j, the distance D_j is,

$$D_j = \sum_{i=1}^{N} W_i \cdot (X_i - C_{ji})^2 \qquad (1)$$

Where N is the dimension of the input vector and W_i denotes the weight of the ith attribute. All of the weights take on positive values and reflect the importance of attribute i. These values are assigned by domain experts based on their heuristic knowledge.

4.2.2. Determination of Query Question.
To select the most appropriate question to ask, the system first finds a set of "promising" cluster points which are relatively close to the input vector. The set of possible cluster points S is found by first identifying the cluster point j^* which yields the minimum distance,

$$D_{j^*} = \min_{j} [D_j] \quad \forall j \qquad (2)$$

then S consists of all those cluster points C_k whose distance measures are not too far away from D_{j^*}, i.e.

$$S = \{C_k | D_k \leq D_{j^*} + \delta\} \qquad (3)$$

After obtaining such a set of possible cluster points, the next step is to choose the attribute A_i in the input vector X which has a value UNKNOWN and is most important. To select such an attribute, we consider many factors, such as the importance of the attribute (the weight W_i as discussed in the previous section), the cost V_i of conducting such a test, as well as the "effectiveness" E_i of that attribute. The cost V_i measures the difficulty of obtaining attribute i and includes such items as the time required, the man-power involved and the material needed to conduct such a test. All these considerations are lumped together into a number. Its value is specified by the domain expert familiar with the equipment and the test procedures. The effectiveness E_i computes the weighted frequency counts of attribute A_i for all cluster point C_j in the set S as follows,

$$E_i = \sum_{j \in S} \frac{1}{(p + D_j)} \cdot A_i^{(j)} \qquad (4)$$

where p is a positive constant to prevent divide-by-zero error and $A_i^{(j)}$ is the nonzero attribute in cluster point C_j.

Finally, the attribute i^* to be selected is the one which maximizes the following quantity,

$$B_i^* = \max_i [E_i + W_i - V_i] \quad \forall i \qquad (5)$$

Once i^* is selected, the question corresponding to i^* will be prompted to the technician, asking him to perform the corresponding test.

4.3. Knowledge Acquisition

Knowledge acquisition has been a tedious task in developing expert systems. For the connectionist approach, powerful learning algorithms exist which can automatically construct the knowledge base from a set of training data. In our case, the training data are the historical records of successful diagnoses. These records are organized as symptoms-fault associative pairs. Since one of the requirements of the example module is that the knowledge base will grow as the system is being used, the learning algorithm must be able to support both batch and incremental learning. The former is needed to create the initial knowledge base from a set of historical records, while the later is employed to update the knowledge base when new diagnostic cases are available. Although there are many learning algorithms available for the connectionist approach, not all of them support these two modes of learning with reasonable learning time. The popular back-propagation algorithm, for example, can form very compact knowledge representation. However, its learning time is too long to make it feasible for incremental updating. The procedure we have adopted here is a clustering-based learning algorithm similar to the Reduced Coulomb Energy (RCE) method (Scofield et al., 1987). The algorithm is outlined as follows:

In this algorithm, each training record is an associative pair (X, Y), where X is the input symptom vector and Y corresponds to the faulty component index. Each cluster point has a radius of attraction R_j, whose value lies between its allowable maximum and minimum values. When a new training vector X is entered, the algorithm computes distance scores D_j for all existing cluster points C_j. If D_j is less than R_j for any j, it means that the input pattern is covered by C_j. Then the algorithm checks if the faulty class of C_j is the same as Y in the training record. If they are the same, then the training record is marked "covered" and nothing else needs to be done. Otherwise, it means that the radius R_j is too large and has to be reduced.

The above procedure is repeated until all the cluster points are exhausted. If it is found that the input record is not covered by any cluster point, then a new cluster point is created. Its center will be at the input vector coordinates, its radius of attraction is equal to the maximum allowable value and its faulty class corresponds to the fault of the training record.

If the radius R_j has already been reduced to its allowable minimum, and yet Y in the training vector is different from the faulty class of C_j, then the cluster point C_j is made to represent more than one faulty class. This means that the set of symptoms does not uniquely identify the fault and hence the example module recommends multiple possible fault components. The user will then need to verify each of these suggestions.

Notice that when the radius of a cluster point is reduced, the previously covered training records may become exposed again. Thus, whenever the radius is decreased, the system is marked "unstable," and all the training data will be presented for another iteration, until the system finally becomes stable.

With this learning algorithm, there is actually no distinction between incremental and batch learning. Whenever a training record is available, the system can invoke the learning algorithm to incorporate the new record into the existing knowledge base. In this way, the knowledge base can expand as the system is being used. Moreover, the learning time is relatively fast and it does not require many iterations for the system to become stable.

5. FLOWCHART MODULE

The flowchart module is invoked when the example module fails. This module converts all the flowcharts in the manufacturer's troubleshooting manual into electronic form. The main functions of this module are described as follows:
1. According to the Malfunction Code (MC) given, find the available flowchart automatically.
2. Give the definition of the Malfunction Codes and the limits of the relevant parameters.
3. Display the maintenance instructions and conditions for checking, monitoring, verifying and replacing.
4. Provide information on test-points, range of parameters and some detailed specification of action to be taken.
5. For exceptional cases, offer suggestions for reference.

In our software implementation, each decision point in the flowchart is represented by a node. Each node has multiple output links to the following nodes. When each node is visited, a text is displayed to the user, explaining in detail the maintenance instructions and prompting the user to enter the test result. Depending on the outcome of the test, different output paths will be followed and the next node is visited. This sequence is repeated until finally the fault is found.

6. IMPLEMENTATION

INSIDE is designed to run on inexpensive IBM PC or compatible microcomputers under the DOS environment with minimum hardware requirements. A math. coprocessor chip is used in the current system but otherwise no special hardware is needed. Where possible, commercial software packages are purchased to shorten the implementation cycle. However, the connectionist approach is a relatively new concept so the whole diagnostic software is written by our staff. The software is also written in a modular and data-driven manner so that it can be easily adapted to troubleshoot other equipment.

To further enhance the functionality of the system, INSIDE is extended to provide also the record keeping facility for the workshop. Thus, the entire software consists of two subsystems—the History subsystem for record keeping and report generation, and the connectionist diagnostic expert subsystem as discussed above. Figure 13.3 shows the system level data flow diagram of the whole system.

6.1. System Organization

The History subsystem is implemented using dBASE4 Program. It is completely manual driven and provides the workshop technicians with an easy and user friendly environment to handle past records. It offers functions for users to search for a case, enter a new case, edit and update an existing case, and finally, to confirm a case in which the diagnosis has been successful. In additions, for supervisory purposes, the History subsystem also performs analysis on past cases and produces

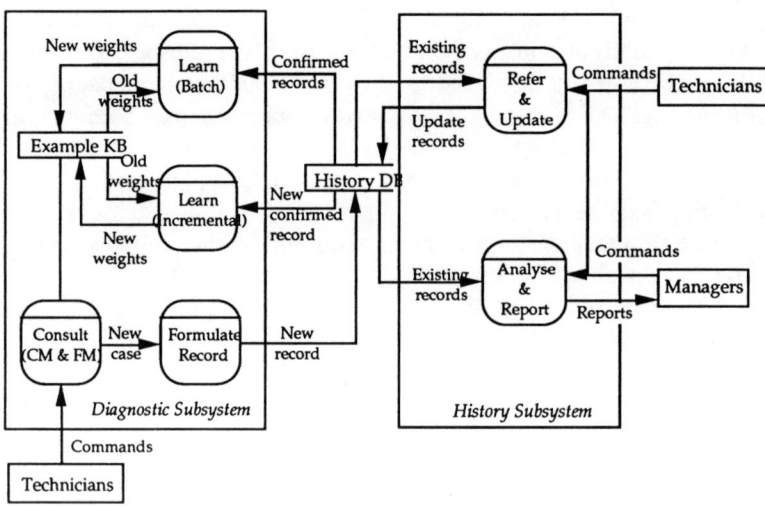

FIGURE 13.3. System level data flow diagram.

various statistical reports to the authorized supervisors for auditing. To protect the database, security measures like password protection and periodic backup are also included.

The Diagnostic subsystem is written in C programming language and hence the system response is quite fast. We employ a piece of commercial software CODEBASE4 to interface with the dBASE history database. This package provides C function library to access the database records. Thus the history database serves as a communication interface between the two subsystems (Figure 13.3). Each history record includes many fields such as date-of-removal, serial-number and staff-id who works on the unit, ..., etc for administrative information. For diagnostic purpose, they can be categorized into two groups—confirmed and unconfirmed cases. The former represents those successfully diagnosed instances, while the latter consists of cases whose findings still need to be verified. In our system, only confirmed cases will be incorporated to the example knowledge base as shown in Figure 13.3.

The technician can either invoke the History or the Diagnostic subsystem. He can also troubleshoot a new case, or to continue to work on a partially diagnosed, unconfirmed record. In the latter instance, all the previously diagnosed steps are retrieved so that the technician can proceed from where he left off. With this facility, the user can terminate the diagnostic session halfway, and continue with it at some later point of time. After the diagnostic session, all the relevant information will be saved to the common history database.

When a new, confirmed record is generated, it will trigger the incremental learning automatically so that the new record can be incorporated into the example knowledge base. On the other hand, batch learning is manually invoked by the operator. It will search for all the confirmed cases in the history database when constructing the knowledge base.

6.2. Man-Machine Interface

The entire software is written with strong emphasis on providing a friendly user interface for technicians to use. Standard techniques such as menu-directed-selection, pop-up windows, data entry by mouse or cursor keys are employed throughout different software modules in a consistent manner. Help functions such as text explanation and consultation log are also included during the diag-

Connectionist Expert System

```
AC 01  ☐    ADI GYRO FLAG on    ☐    DISTANCE ERROR        ☐
AC 02  ☐    HEADING FLAG on     ☐    RADICAL ERROR         ☐
AC 03  ☐    HSI on              ☐    WIND DISPLAY ERROR    ☐
AC 04  ☐
AC 05  ☐    ADI ATT UNSTABLE    ☐    ATT INOPERATION       ☐
AC 06  ☐    ADI ROLL UNSTABLE   ☐    NO DME UPDATE         ☐
AFG LT ON ☐ GRD SPEED ERRATIC   ☐    NO REMOTE DATA INSERT ☐
WARN LT ON ☐ MILES IND ERRATIC  ☐    BATT CHARGE FAILS     ☐
```

| Malfunction | 1 | 2 | 3 | 4 | 5 | 6 |
| Code | 0123456789012345678901234567890123456789012345678901 23 |

```
DISPLAY BLANK           ☐   ALIGN TO MODE 7 FAILS   ☐   SWITCH OFF fails  ☐
DISPLAY FROZEN/         ☐   ALIGN TO MODE 8 FAILS   ☐   UNIT DIRTY        ☐
MEMORY SCRAMBLED        ☐   IRUG TUMBLED            ☐   WATER CONDEMN     ☐
DISPLAY FROZEN AT 0     ☐   IRUG TILT PITCH AXIS    ☐
BATT & WARN LT FLASH    ☐   VE VN WXSH WYSH UNSTABLE ☐
```

FIGURE 13.4. Input panel.

nostic session. As a result, technicians can learn to use the system with minimum training time. The following paragraphs are a brief outline of the main user interface design of the system.

When the History module is invoked, a menu is displayed for user to select his action. Where text information is required, the field width is highlighted and its entry is immediately validated against possible errors.

As for the Diagnostic module, a panel as shown in Figure 13.4 will be displayed at the beginning of the consultation. The technician, while reading from the reason-of-removal form, can use the mouse to select those symptoms registered in the form. Then the system enters into a question-and-answer mode. The screen will display a few lines of text as shown in Figure 13.5, suggesting that the technician perform certain tests. A dialog box also appears on the screen. The user can enter the test result by selecting the appropriate field. If "HELP" is selected, the user can further use the special function keys to

```
┌─────────────────────────────────────────────────────────┐
│ Inertial Navigation System Interactive Diagnostic Expert │
├─────────────────────────────────────────────────────────┤
│  CONSULTATION                                            │
│                                                          │
│    Is action code 03 reported ?                          │
│                    ┌───────────┐                         │
│                    │ YES       │                         │
│                    │ Don't Know│                         │
│                    │ No        │                         │
│                    │ Help      │                         │
│                    └───────────┘                         │
│                                                          │
│    examine cluster(s) 37                                 │
│                                                          │
│    ... pursue question 3                                 │
│                                                          │
└─────────────────────────────────────────────────────────┘
```

FIGURE 13.5. INSIDE screen: consultation.

display the current consultation log or to obtain an explanation of why such a test is needed.

When the example module arrives at a conclusion, the user can also seek an explanation. The reason is usually because the input symptom pattern is similar to a previous case. Figure 13.6 shows a typical response. If the example module fails and the flowchart module is invoked, all the initial diagnostic information is passed to the flowchart module. Since the latter makes use of the MC codes as basis for diagnoses, the system can automatically prioritize the MC codes according to their relative importance. However, the technician can still select his own choice. The flowchart module then guides the technician to follow the diagnostic path set forth by the manufacturer until all MC codes are cleared. Again, explanation texts are displayed and dialog box is created for the user to enter his choice.

7. SYSTEM DEPLOYMENT AND EVALUATION

This system was jointly developed by staff from the Institute of Systems Science (ISS) and Singapore Airline (SIA). The project started in August, 1989. In the first phase of the project, knowledge engineers consulted the domain experts (technicians) quite frequently in order to understand the problem domain and requirements, and also to determine the symptoms and faults classifications. A research prototype, consisted of the example and flowchart diagnostic modules, was developed in December of that year to test the feasibility of the approach. After evaluating its effectiveness (see Tan et al., 1990, for more detail), both parties agreed to enhance its capability and to make it a record-keeping cum diagnostic system. A project team was thus formed, comprising researchers from ISS and software staff from SIA. By November 1990, a final working system was successfully developed and delivered to SIA workshop. All in all, about 36 man-months of effort was spent on this project.

After the system was deployed, several visits were made to the workshop to (1) obtain feedback on the usage of the system and (2) to gather the most up-to-date performance statistics.

The technicians reported that they had been using the system regularly. The performance was satisfactory but was not evaluated in a scientifically way. Because of this, a database of 640 useful cases was collected and a formal performance evaluation was carried

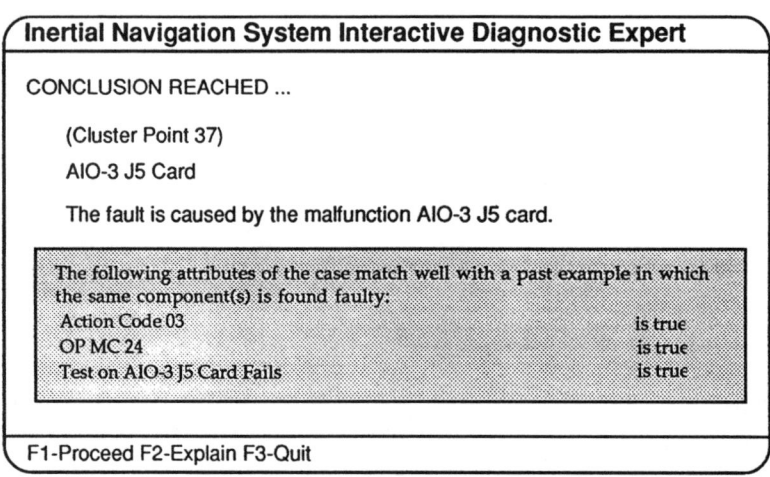

FIGURE 13.6. INSIDE screen: conclusion.

Connectionist Expert System

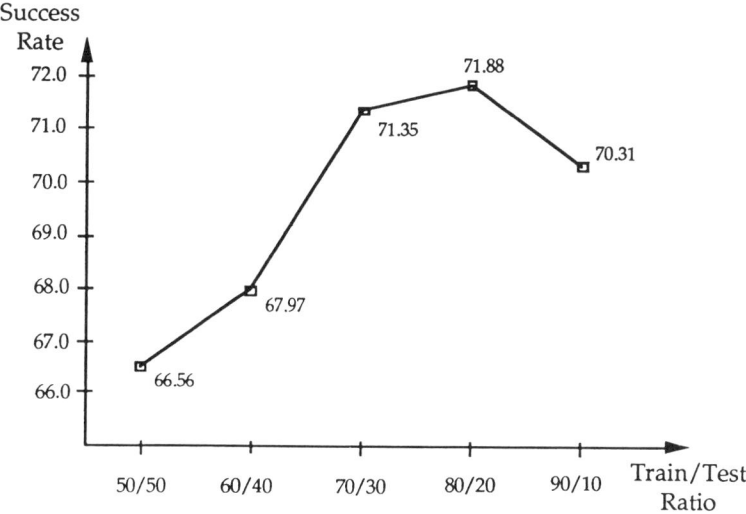

FIGURE 13.7. Success rate against train/test ratio.

out on the example module at ISS. The database was further partitioned into two portions—one to train the connectionist knowledge base while the other to test its accuracy. The performance was evaluated against two parameters: (1) the success rate—the percentage that the connectionist module provided the correct answer from the test database and (2) the number of cluster points generated from the training database.

Five experiments were conducted, corresponding to five different ratios of training vs testing database sizes, namely, 50/50, 60/40, 70/30, 80/20 and 90/10. Figure 13.7 shows the general trend that the success rate improves as the training data size increases. Although the number of cluster centers increases accordingly (Figure 13.8), the rate of increase is slowing (Figure 13.9). Notice that when only 10% of the database is reserved for testing, the number of testing data is relatively small to give statistically meaningful result. This may account for the slight drop of success rate in Figure 13.7. However, these general trends are expected to hold when more data is used. In fact, as the system is being

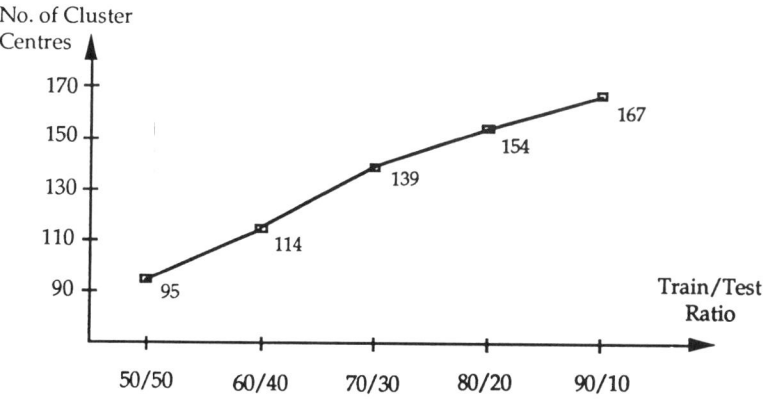

FIGURE 13.8. Number of cluster centers against train/test ratio.

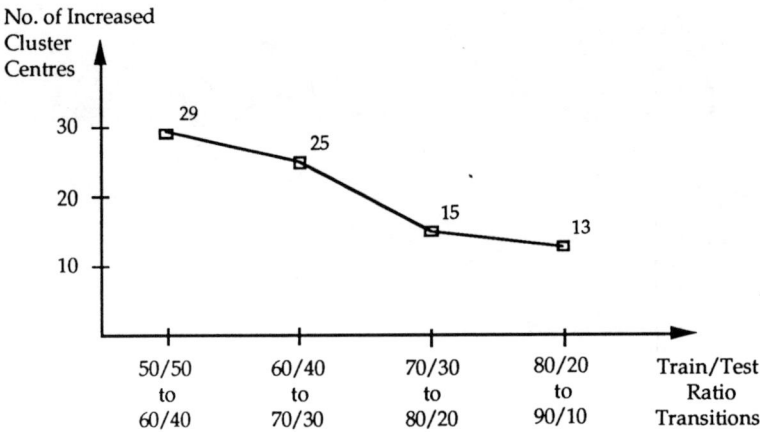

FIGURE 13.9. Number of increased cluster centers against train/test ratio transitions.

used, the chance that an incoming case is similar to a previous one becomes higher and higher, so the success rate improves. Since new, unfamiliar cases occur less often, the need to generate new cluster centers decreases, as indicated in Figure 13.9.

8. CONCLUSION

A connectionist diagnostic expert system, known as INSIDE, is described. In addition to assisting technicians in troubleshooting, it also keeps track of repair records and generates management reports. For the diagnostic subsystem, the connectionist approach is adopted so that the knowledge base can expand as the system is being used. Moreover, INSIDE is implemented on a low-cost microcomputer. Nonetheless, it offers fast response time and a user-friendly interface. Although the system is designed for the INS equipment, the approach is generic for other diagnostic applications. In fact, the software is implemented in such a way that it can be easily adapted to troubleshoot other pieces of equipment in the workshop.

ACKNOWLEDGEMENT

We greatly appreciate the management support from both the Singapore Airlines (SIA) and the Institute of Systems Science (ISS). Special thanks go to Mr. Lim Yeow Khee and the workshop personnels of SIA for their invaluable time and insightful advices. We are also grateful to Mr. Loi Thye Heng for his dedicated effort and support. Ms. Loh Wan Leen and Mr. Leong Kin Meng wrote the History subsystem. Mr. Pan Qiang wrote the initial version of the flowchart module and Mr. Low Boon Toh assisted in the final testing. Without their contributions, this project would not have been successful.

REFERENCES

Bateson, A.G., Alexander, R.A., & Murphy, M.D. (1987). Cognitive processing differences between novice and expert computer programmers. *Int. J. Man-Machine Studies, 26*, 649–660.

Bradshaw, G., Fozzard, R., & Ceci, L. (1989). A connectionist expert system that actually works. *Advances in Neural Information Processing Systems I*, 248–255.

Case-Based Reasoning. In *Proceedings: Case-Base Reasoning Workshop, DARPA: Machine Learning Program Plan*, pp. 1–13, Morgan Kaufmann, May 1989.

Chan, S.C., Hsu, L.S., Brody, S., & Teh, H.H. (1989). Neural three-valued-logic networks. *In Proceedings, Inter-faculty Seminar on Neuronet Computing, June 1989, National University of Singapore*, pp. 54–75.

Chase, W.G., & Simon, H.A. (1973). The mind's eye in chess. In W.G. Chase, (Ed.), *Visual information processing*. New York: Academic Press.

Gallant, S.I. Connectionist expert systems. *Communication of the ACM February 1988*.

Gallant, S.I. (1990) A connectionist learning algorithm with provable generalization and scaling bounds. *Neural Networks,* **3**(2), 191–202.

Hecht-Nielsen, R. (1989). *Neurocomputing,* Addison-Wesley.

Larkin, J., McDermott, J., Simon, D.P., & Simon, H.A. (1980). Expert and novice performance in solving physics problems. *Science,* 208, 1335–1342.

Kohonen, T. (1988). *Self-organization and associative memory,* 2nd edition, Springer-Verlag.

Rumelhart, D.E., Hinton, G., & Williams, R. (1986). Learning internal representations by error propagation. In D.E. Rumelhart and J.L. McClelland (Eds.), *Parallel distributed processing: Explorations in the microstructure of congition.* MIT Press.

Scofield, C.L., Reilly, D.L., Elbaum, C., & Cooper, L.N. (1987). Pattern class degeneracy in an unrestricted storage density memory. In Conference on Neural Information Processing Systems–Natural and Synthetic, IEEE Nov 1987, pp. 674–682.

Segnowski, T.J., & Rosenbert, C.R. (1987). Parallel networks that learn to pronounce english text. *Complex Systems,* 1, 145–168.

Tan, A.H., Pan, Q., Lui, H.C., & Teh, H.H. (1990). INSIDE: A neuronet based hardware fault diagostic system. *Proceedings of IJCNN '90,* June 17–21 1990, San Diego, USA.

Development of Expert Systems Supported Construction Planning for Shield Tunneling Method

SATOSHI OKUIDE,* YASUHIRO KITAGAWA,** MINORU HARADA, AND ZENICHI IGARASHI***

*Hitachi Ltd., **Hitachi Seibu Software Co. Ltd., Chuo-ku Osaka, Japan;
***Okumura Corp., Abeno-ku Osaka, Japan

1. INTRODUCTION

OUR EXPERT SYSTEM was developed aimed at optimum and fast planning for shield tunneling works. It is an expert system for applied design problems that integrates technologies such as relational databases, AI, and computer-aided design (CAD).

This expert system is able to design and draw a suitable shield machine with an automatic output of design calculations, and also specify an optimum control range for the operation of shield tunneling works. It is possible for a user to quickly make a construction plan for the shield tunneling works, taking full advantage of the expertise stored in the expert system.

The shield tunneling method is a tunneling method in which ground is excavated by a shield machine with a segment lining. In recent years, this method has been widely used in areas where the ground is soft or the site is in a densely populated area.

For shield work, a shield machine and construction plan must be considered for various ground conditions, such as soft ground, gravel, sand layers, and so on, along with other conditions such as high water pressure or curved alignment. In addition, the growing regulations concerning environmental protection for ground settlement, vibration, etc., has made it more difficult to apply the shield tunneling method.

Conventionally, a construction plan was jointly drawn by experts from the specialized fields, but this approach consumed large amounts of time and labor. Our expert system makes optimum specifications for the shield machine. We can input construction conditions such as tunnel diameter, design alignment and contract period as well as the condition of the ground soil and the status of underground water. This automatically leads to the drafting of an optimal shield machine based on its knowledge base. The system also analyzes ground settlement using the finite element method and selects an optimal code of construction and supplementary construction methods. It then outputs design specifications and design calculations.

2. BACKGROUND

In shield tunneling projects, a higher degree of planning is required because of the advanced construction technology. Such planning is usually done by experienced specialists. However, their know-how is individualized and not systematized; and planning depends on the collaboration of individuals from civil engineering to those in mechanical and analytical fields.

Therefore, there are always differences in opinion on the part of specialists, resulting in much lost time.

Shield Tunneling Method

FIGURE 14.1. Photograph of shield machine.

We developed our expert system to eliminate these problems and enable planning that could be done quickly and reasonably. In other words, the objective of systematization is to bring together all the expertise and varied experiences into a knowledge base, so that definitive design programs and construction methods can be realized.

3. APPLICABLE RANGE

Our expert system applies to tunneling work using the Earth Pressure Balanced Shield, which is one of the close-face type shield machines, as shown in Figure 14.1, and to the design of a shield machine (outside diameter of 2000 to 6200 mm). The reason we selected this method is because of increased usage. It is new and is standardized in its code of construction.

4. COMPOSITION OF HARDWARE

The expert system can move on a 32-bit workstation (HITACHI 2050/32). The hardware is shown in Figure 14.2. Because of the

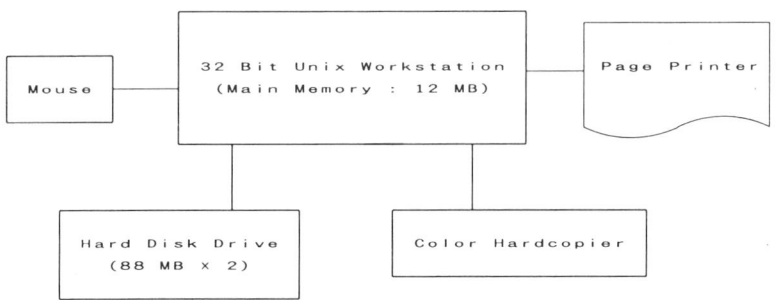

FIGURE 14.2. Hardware architecture.

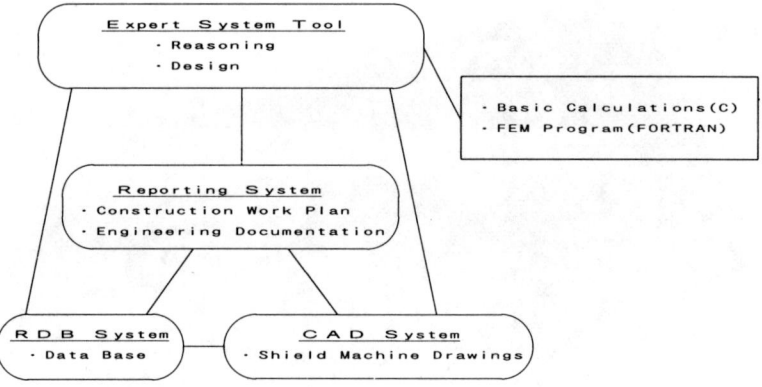

FIGURE 14.3. Software architecture.

software, the main memory has to have 12 megabytes. The operating system is equivalent to a UNIX SYSTEM V (HITACHI HI-UX). We adopted a workstation approach because of its convenience at the site or in a branch office.

5. COMPOSITION OF SOFTWARE

As shown in Figure 14.3, the software combines a relational database system (EXCEED2), an expert system building tool (HITACHI ES/KERNEL), a CAD system (HITACHI HICAD), and a documentation system (HITACHI OFIS/REPORT).

The systems are assigned the following functions. The relational database keeps the specialist's knowledge in graph form and develops only the knowledge required for reasoning. This function, as shown in Figure 14.4, is dynamically executed in reasoning, reducing the reasoning time and improving storage capacity. The expert system building tool performs forward reasoning on the basis of given information and the facts extracted from the relational database. The calculating process that cannot express frame knowledge or production rules is written in the C language. The CAD system automatically drafts the shield machine and various drawings based on the results after reasoning. The documentation system outputs the results of the reasoning as a configuration of design specifications or calculations. For complex engi-

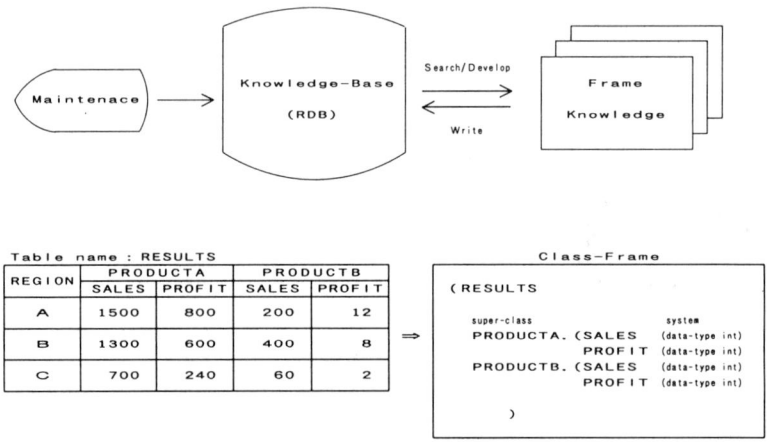

FIGURE 14.4. Utilization of relational database.

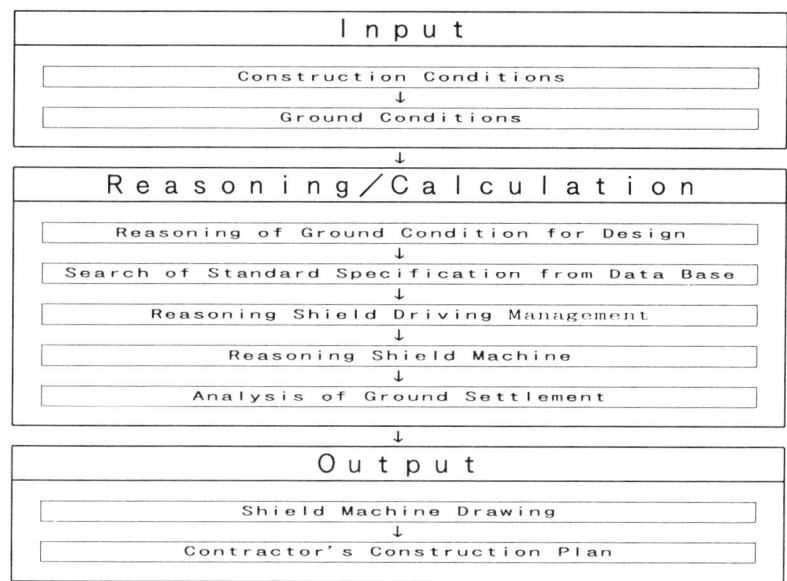

FIGURE 14.5. Process flow.

neering calculations, C and FORTRAN are used.

6. GENERAL ASPECTS OF THE APPLICATIONS

The expert system, as shown in Figure 14.5, comprises 3 phases; input, reasoning and calculation, and output. The phases are summarized as follows.

6.1. The Input Phase

During input, data about construction and ground conditions are entered. To input construction condition data, three input screens

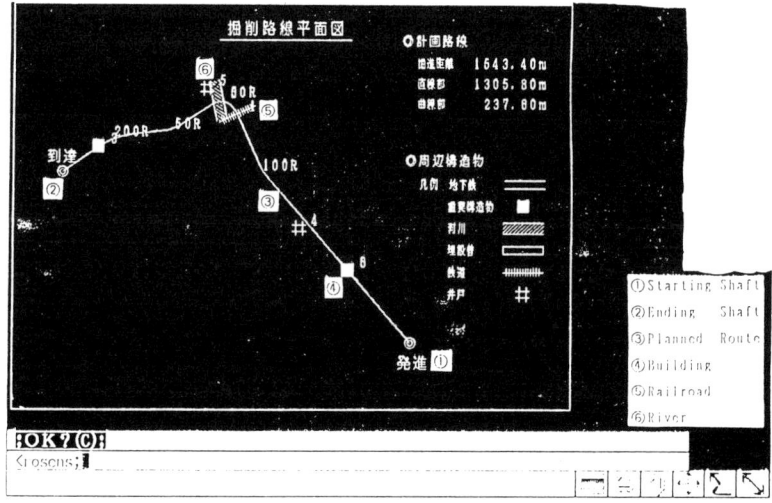

FIGURE 14.6. Drawing of planned tunnel route.

containing construction conditions, configuration of the planned route, and conditions around the planned route are prepared.

The construction condition data include the project's name, the shield machine diameter, the period of construction, and segment types. The configuration of the planned route by distance, curve radii, and inclines from the beginning to the end of the tunnel are input. Data for the surrounding area, the location of important buildings, the existence of railroads, the condition of crossed rivers, and so on, are also input. These data are used to forecast the influence of tunneling. The CAD system can draw the surrounding area and planned route configuration from the information input and check for input mistakes, as shown in Figure 14.6.

For the ground condition data, the composition of the ground layer, underground water levels, and loading weights are fed into the computer based on the data achieved during the boring investigation. The input condition is immediately drawn by the system in order to assure the layer composition and ground pressure, as shown in Figure 14.7. This process is repeated for each boring investigation.

6.2. The Reasoning/Calculation Phase

In this phase, 3 reasonings are executed to help make decisions about ground conditions, design the shield machine, and determine the construction method. Also, calculations for forecasting the ground settlement are performed.

During ground condition reasoning, the ground conditions are determined to aid in designing the shield machine and in managing construction. Figure 14.8 shows the results of reasoning for determining ground condition. The upper part of the screen shows the ground condition aspects used for shield machine design, and the lower screen shows those used for construction management. Each set of results has three proposals, ranked from first to third.

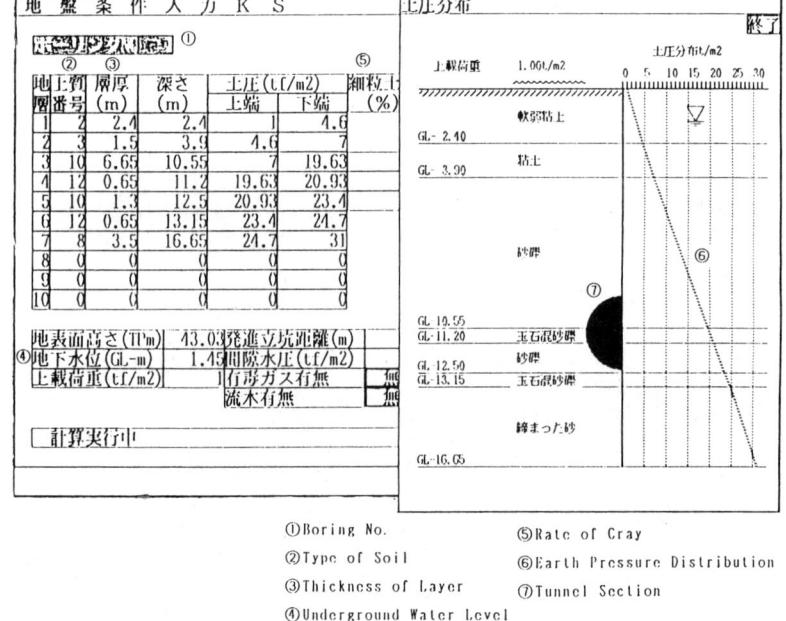

FIGURE 14.7. Input screen of ground conditions.

Shield Tunneling Method

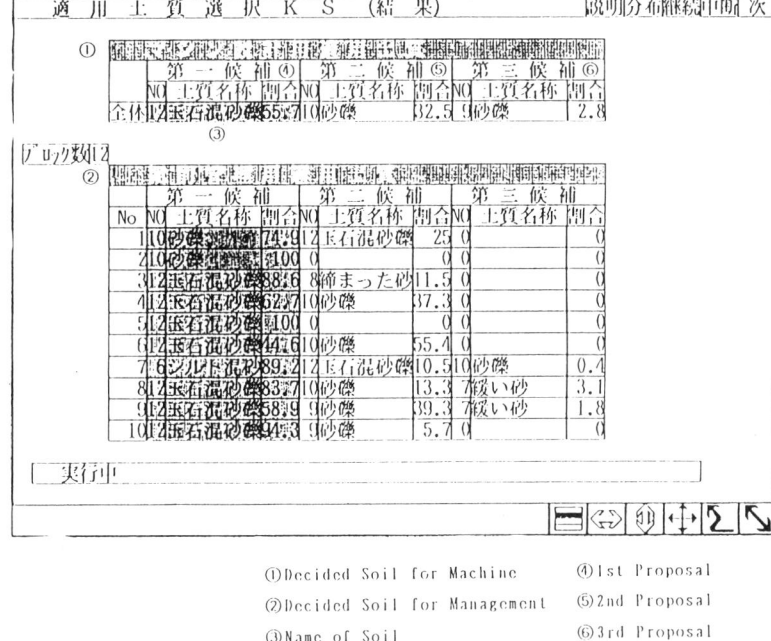

FIGURE 14.8. Screen of decisions for ground conditions.

Users can change the results of reasoning with the system by using the ground condition distribution chart shown in Figure 14.9 and their own experience. With these changes, various ground conditions are easily examined.

To look up standard specifications, various shield machine designs and construc-

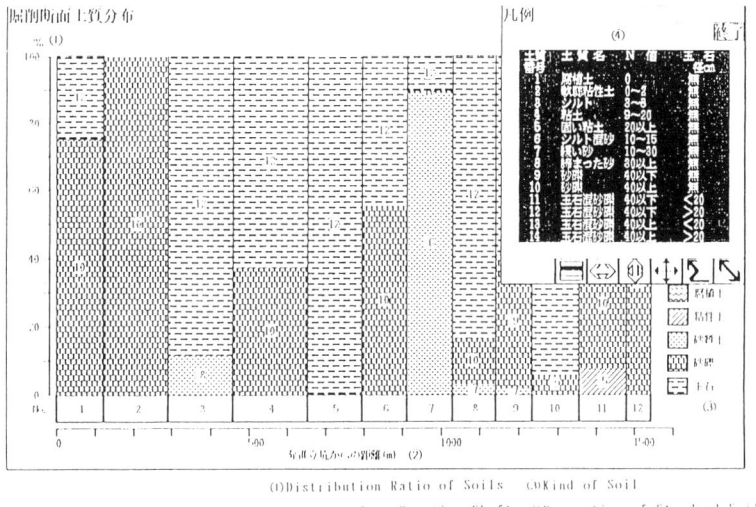

FIGURE 14.9. Distribution chart of ground conditions.

TABLE 14.1
Control Items for Tunneling

Items	Remarks
Mud Injection	Material, Volume, Grouting Method
Earth Pressure at Excavation Chamber	Control Code
Backfill Grouting	Material, Volume, Pressure
Schedule of Tunnel Driving	Required Schedule for Shield Driving
Supplementary Construction Method for Shaft	Method, Scale, Volume
Ground Settlement	Analyzing Settlement
Ground Water	Assessment for Environment

tion management possibilities, automatically based on determination of the ground condition and input conditions, are referenced within the database and are converted to frame knowledge by the system.

During construction management reasoning, an examination is automatically done of management items for the tunneling shown in Table 14.1.

During reasoning for shield machine design, examinations are automatically done on items shown in Table 14.2, and the compositions of the cutter head and the main body of the shield machine are automatically designed.

Figure 14.10 shows an example of the knowledge (production rule) used during reasoning.

During the calculation of ground settlement, it is possible to do a detailed analysis using the finite element method at the location where there is a high possibility of ground settlement after the construction management reasoning.

These input data for the analysis are automatically created by the system based on the ground condition data. Figure 14.11 shows the contour chart of ground settlement.

6.3. Output Phase

The drawing of the shield machine is automatically done by the CAD system. Three drawings are made: the cutterhead, the main body, and the support equipment. These are drawn with correct dimensions, and it is possible to modify them manually with the CAD system. Figure 14.12 contains examples of cutterhead and main body drawings.

When making the construction planning sheet, it is possible to output the final plan, including various specification forms and calculation forms, as shown in Figure 14.13.

Also during this phase, information can be output, for example, about what procedures were taken under what conditions that could affect the reasoning of the system. This capability makes it possible to easily evaluate the propriety of the reasoning results.

7. SIZE OF THE SYSTEM

The number of rules, frames and program steps used in the expert system are shown in Table 14.3.

TABLE 14.2
Design Item of Shield Machine

Items	Remarks
Excavation	Cutter Head, Cutter Teeth, Cutter Drive Motor, Mud Injection Pipeline
Mucking System	Screw Conveyor, Rotary Feeder, Belt Conveyor
Thrust Force	Shove Jacks
Water Tightness	Cutter Head, Bulk Head, Tail Seal
Curve Alignment	Over Cutter, Shove Jacks, Articulate Shield Body
Segment Lining	Segment Erector, Segment Adjuster

```
[`発進部A型粘性土`]                              ・・・・・ group name of rules
(発進部A1タイプ設定_rule_1                        ・・・・・ name of rule
if
(発進部坑口    の  @`坑口タイプ名`      が    "A"     であり
                  @適用土質番号        が    1       以上であり
                  @適用土質番号        が    5       以下である)
then
施工管理検討中  0.1。
(send      `A型粘性土`    assign(`補助工法タイプ`,`A型粘性土`))
(send      `A型砂質土`    delete_frame)
(send      `B型発進坑口`  delete_frame)
(send      `C型発進坑口`  delete_frame)
explain 発進部坑口の補助工法は、適用土質番号が粘性系である`
ためA型粘性土タイプとする
)
(A型粘性土発進坑口_rule_1                         ・・・・・ name of rule
if
(`ブロック1`  の  @土被り           を    ?x1       とし
                  @地下水位         を    ?x2       とし
                  @間隙水圧         を    ?x3       とし
                  @上載荷重         を    ?x4       とし
                  @地層数           を    ?x5       とする)
(?frame       の  @class            が    発進部坑口     であり
                  @`補助工法タイプ` が    `A型粘性土`    であり
                  @`シールド土被り` が    0              である)
(発進部坑口  の  @`シールド外径`   を    ?x             とする)
then
(send    ?frame    assign(`シールド土被り`,?x1))
(send    ?frame    assign(地下水位,        ?x2))
(send    ?frame    assign(間隙水圧,        ?x3))
(send    ?frame    assign(上載荷重,        ?x4))
(send    ?frame    assign(地層数,          ?x5))
(send    ?frame    assign(`下端深さ`,      ?x1+real(?x*0.001)))
)

comments;
* Rules are written in Japanese in this system.
* Literals with @ mark are slot name in frame.
* Literals with ? mark are variables.
```

FIGURE 14.10. Example of production rules.

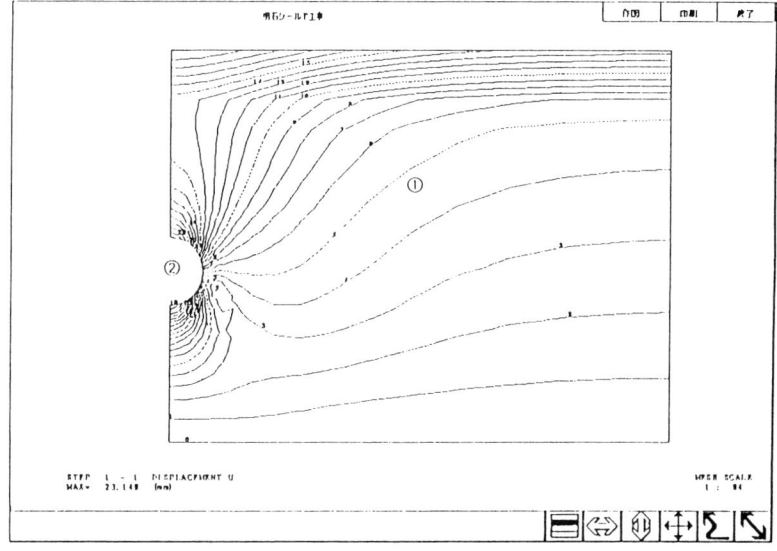

①Curved Line of Ground Settlement
②Tunnel Section

FIGURE 14.11. Displacement of ground settlement.

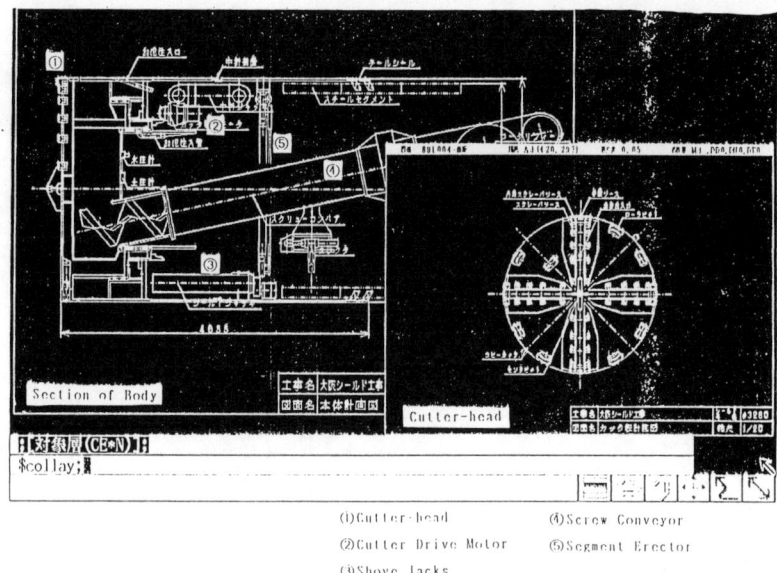

FIGURE 14.12. Drawing of shield machine structures.

8. DEVELOPMENT REALM

Three knowledge engineers, 4 system engineers, and 3 to 4 specialists developed the expert system. The time required for the development of the prototype was about 18 months and the time for rearrangement of a practical system took about 6 months. Total personnel time was about 60 person-months.

The costs incurred were about 100,000 US dollars for hardware and about 350,000 US dollars for software. The expert system was jointly developed by Hitachi Ltd. and Okumura Corporation.

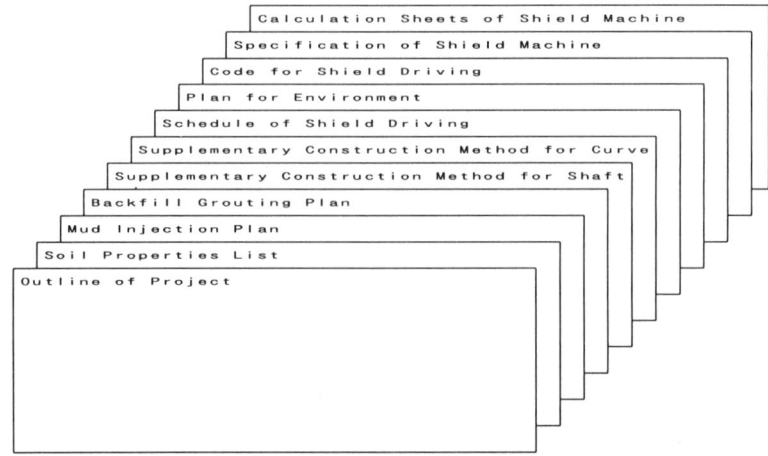

FIGURE 14.13. Output list for construction plans.

TABLE 14.3
Size of System
Specification of Shield Machine, Method of Construction, Standard Soils

Items	Number of Data
Data Base Items	15,000
Kind of Frames	100
Number of Rules	850
Calculating Program Steps	9,000
Drawing Program Steps	5,000
Parts of Shield Machine	250
Commands	A Large Number

9. USE AND EFFECT OF THE SYSTEM

This system is used when construction technicians at design divisions or construction sites have shield tunneling construction operations to present to government offices or construction consultants.

Construction technicians only have to input the basic construction and ground conditions to have the system return a detailed construction planning sheet. It is possible that work that was previously done by a number of experienced special technicians can be done by a not-so-experienced construction technician.

This system offers judgment at important points of the users' data in reasoning steps such as determining ground condition and the basic specifications of the shield machine, and also asks users for their judgment. The system continues reasoning based on these judgments, so that the user's thoughts are reflected in the reasoning. Thus, this system becomes more human in character.

Also, this system lets technicians other than specialists easily calculate and judge ground settlement, which previously was only done by analytic specialists, so savings in personnel are also large.

Moreover, the automatic drawing of shield machines and the documentation functions for computing specifications and calculation forms, lightens the workload of the technician in charge and results in higher quality design for the customer.

This system has been used for actual construction plans since October, 1989 and has executed 15 construction plans. It is difficult to evaluate the payoff in using this system, but it has received the following comments from the technicians who used it:

(1) Standardized construction planning became possible when plans were formed by various people.
(2) Construction planning could be quickly done and work that used to take at least 1 week now takes only a couple of days.
(3) It is now easy to make alternative construction plans.
(4) Detailed examinations can be done by non-experts.
(5) Even a technician with little experience can make detailed construction plans.
(6) The persuasion of customers has been more effective.

10. CONCLUSION

The expert system supporting a shield tunneling plan was developed based on an experience of shield tunneling exceeding 250 km. We are confident that it can help in such plans.

In the future, we intend to expand the functions to include cost estimation and the planning of shaft construction, plant facilities, and secondary lining. The knowledge base will also be made applicable to a wider range of sites.

REFERENCES

Harada, M., Igarashi, Z., Okuide, S., & Kitagawa, Y. (1990). Development of expert system supported construction planning for shield tunneling method. *Proceedings of Second Annual Conference on Innovative Applications of Artificial Intelligence,* IAAI90.

Harada, M., & Okuide, S. (1988). *Okumura Corp. and Hitachi Ltd., expert system supported shield tunneling plans,* volume 1988.11, Hitachi Hyoron.: 53–57.

Igarashi, Z. (1989) Development of expert systems supported construction planning for shield tunneling method. *Proceedings of The 44th Annual Conference of The Japan Society of Civil Engineering.*

Application of K-FOLIO at Lucky Securities: BRAINS

JAE KYU LEE*, HYUN S. KIM*, SEOK C. CHU**, JUNG C. SHIN***,
SUHN B. KWON*, WOO J. KIM*, AND KEE Y. GWAG****

*Department of Management Science, Korea Advanced Institute of Science and Technology, Korea;
**Department of Management Information Systems, Kyonggi University, Korea;
***Department of Investment Technology & Research, Lucky Securities Co., Korea;
****Administration Section, Semiconductor Business, Samsung Electronics Co., Korea.

1. INTRODUCTION

SINCE 1985, WE HAVE attempted to integrate an optimization model with an expert system by developing a system called the Intelligent Stock Portfolio Management System (ISPMS). In ISPMS, the integration is performed by interpreting the knowledge as a part of the formulation of the optimization model (Lee, Chu, & Kim, 1989). A prototype K-FOLIO was implemented to visualize the concept of ISPMS (Lee et al., 1990). K-FOLIO consists of a knowledge base, an inference engine, a knowledge acquisition system, a preference revelation system, a data base management system, a machine learning system, a quadratic programming (QP) model, and an interpreter which associates knowledge and preferences with the QP model. A proprietary frame-based tool, UNIK-FRAME, was used to develop K-FOLIO. The first version of K-FOLIO was installed at the Lucky Securities Company (Lee et al., 1989) using their own knowledge, and is named BRAINS. This paper describes the features of K-FOLIO, and the implementation process and performance test results of BRAINS.

2. FEATURES OF K-FOLIO

2.1. Problem Description and Architecture of K-FOLIO

The selection of an optimal stock portfolio has been a long concern of investors. In seeking an optimal stock portfolio, financial theorists have developed several optimization models such as the Markowitz model (Markowitz, 1952), and equilibrium models such as the single-index model, the multi-index model (Sharpe, 1963), and CAPM (Fama & Risk, 1968; Mossin, 1966; Sharpe, 1970).

Although these models are very valuable, they are not sufficiently realistic for investors, because they risk overlooking a large portion of up-to-date information. To overcome such limitations, expert systems have been developed recently. PMIDSS (Intelligent Decision Support System of Portfolio Management Decision Making; Lee & Stohr, 1985), FOLIO (Cohen & Lieberman, 1983), Le Courtier (Cognitive Systems, Inc., 1985), and Portfolio Management Advisor (The Athena Group, 1987) are several examples.

Although the financial models and expert systems have their own advantages, none of them is theoretically complete by itself. The financial models alone cannot incorporate up-to-date expert knowledge and investor's preferences; expert systems alone cannot support normative decisions based on the given information (Lee et al., 1990). Combining the advantages of both sides is therefore desirable. For this purpose, an architecture that we call the Intelligent Stock Portfolio Management System (ISPMS) is developed to associate the expert system with Markowitz's quadratic programming model (see Figure 15.1). To realize the concept of ISPMS, the prototype K-FOLIO was developed. The key features of K-FOLIO are explained under the following subheadings:

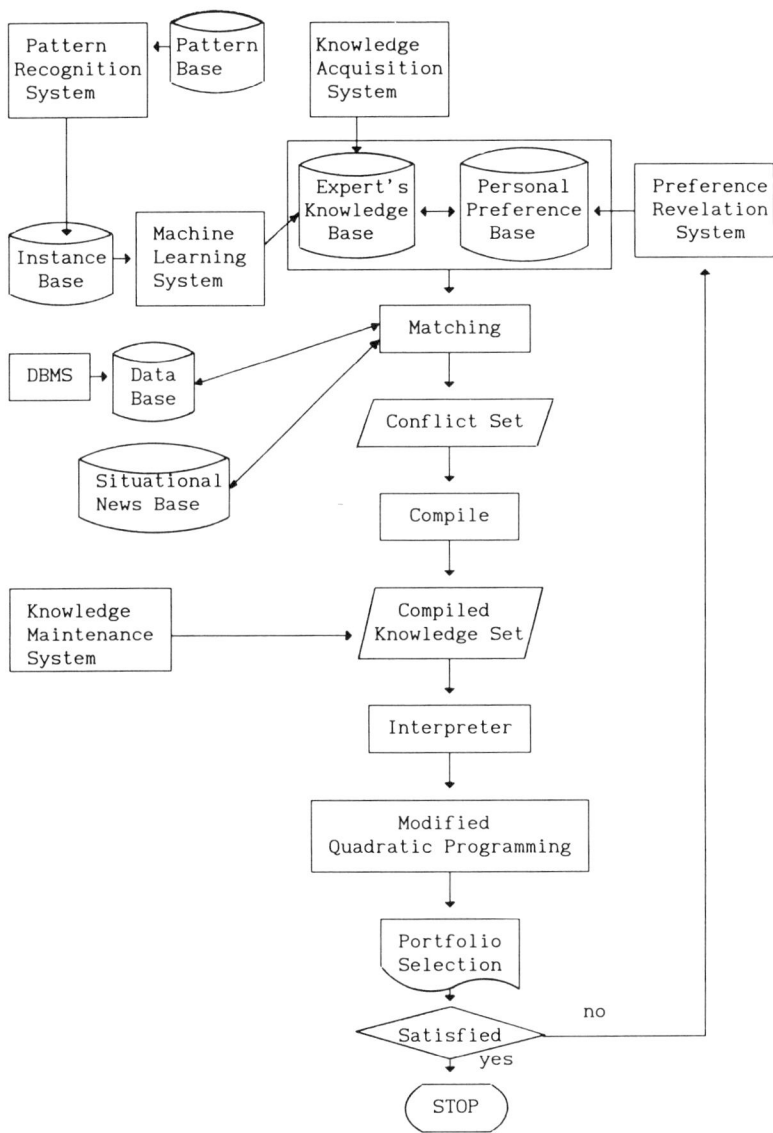

FIGURE 15.1. Architecture of K-FOLIO.

```
{{ Rule-frame
    IF :  statement A
          (AND statement B)
          (OR statement C)
          .....
    THEN : ⌈ statement ZZ         ⌉
           ⌊ GRADE = a grade      ⌋
    CR : percentage-1 percentage-2 percentage-3
    EXCEPT : ⌈ company-A (company-B ...)   ⌉
             ⌊ industry-A (industry-B ...) ⌋
    BECAUSE : statement
    USAGE : [ EVAL  BUY/SELL ]
    RELEVANT-FACTOR : knowledge-frame-1 knowledge-frame-2 ...
    SPECIFICATION : knowledge-frame-1 knowledge-frame-2 ...
    PERIOD : [ LONG MEDIUM SHORT ]
    SOURCE : a name
    DATE : a date      }}
```

Legend

```
Capital letters : reserved words
( ) : optional statement
[ ] : one of the statements should be chosen
```

FIGURE 15.2. Overall syntax of rule.

1. Knowledge Representation
2. Inference and Explanation
3. Integration with Optimization
4. Machine Learning

2.2. Knowledge Representation

The syntax of rules is shown in Figure 15.2. A rule has the reserved words IF, AND, OR, THEN, CREDIBILITY(CR), GRADE, BECAUSE, EXCEPT, USAGE, RELEVANT-FACTOR, SPECIFICATION, PERIOD, SOURCE, DATE and the arithmetic operators. When the IF statements are matched with the database, the conclusion in the THEN part is put into effect. In the conclusion part, either of the following two types of statements appears: the descriptive statement or the GRADE statement. If the matched rule includes a descriptive statement, the conclusion statement will be added to the working memory of relevant companies (or indus-

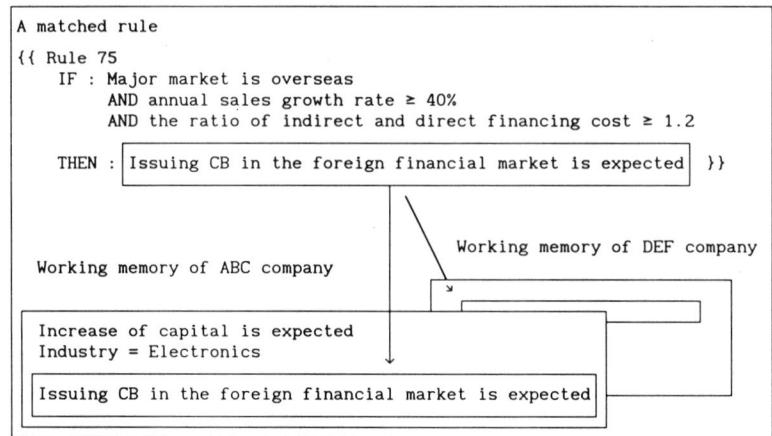

FIGURE 15.3. Generated working memory in the matching process.

ABC company

```
RULE   rule 10
CR  =  0.7
IF     Company = ABC
THEN   GRADE A
       BECAUSE  the company ABC has developed a new compact
       disk player in July 1991.

RULE   rule 12
CR  =  0.6
IF     Industry = Electronics
AND    Issuing CB in the foreign financial market is expected
THEN   GRADE = AA

RULE   rule 13
CR  =  0.6
IF     PER ≥ 10
AND    Debt Ratio ≥ 200%
THEN   GRADE = C
```

FIGURE 15.4. Rules in conflict set of company ABC.

tries), as in Figure 15.3. On the other hand, if the conclusion is the GRADE statement, the rule will be added to the conflict set of relevant companies (or industries), as illustrated in Figure 15.4. For the purpose of computation, the symbolically represented grades from AAA to D are internally transformed into corresponding real numbers between -1 and 1, as shown in Table 15.1.

CR stands for the credibility of the rule as a percentage. BECAUSE statements are used purely for explanatory purposes and are not used during the matching process. The BECAUSE statement is therefore particularly useful when the conditional part of the rule consists of company or industry names. The EXCEPT statement is used to handle exceptional companies within a certain industry or a set of companies that satisfy certain criteria. The other reserved words concern knowledge usage and maintenance. USAGE declares the usage purpose of the knowledge, either stock evaluation or investment timing. Knowledge for the first purpose is usually composed of fundamental knowledge. This knowledge is used to assign individual stocks a composite grade with a corresponding explanation. After having evaluated the composite grade, the timing of the stock buying/selling should be decided. For the timing decision, technical knowledge that can be obtained from the charts is used. RELEVANT-FACTOR and

TABLE 1
Grades and corresponding real numbers

Grade	Real Number	Median	Description
AAA	$0.8 < n \leq 1.0$	0.9	Highly Recommendable
AA	$0.6 < n \leq 0.8$	0.7	↑
A	$0.4 < n \leq 0.6$	0.5	
BBB	$0.2 < n \leq 0.4$	0.3	
BB	$0.0 < n \leq 0.2$	0.1	Unknown
B	$-0.2 < n \leq 0.0$	-0.1	
CCC	$-0.4 < n \leq -0.2$	-0.3	
CC	$-0.6 < n \leq -0.4$	-0.5	
C	$-0.8 < n \leq -0.6$	-0.7	↓
D	$-1.0 \leq n \leq -0.8$	-0.9	Highly Prohibited

SPECIFICATION stand for the relationships among rule frames. PERIOD, SOURCE and DATE indicate the purpose of the investment period, the author of the knowledge, and the date in which the knowledge is prepared, respectively. In addition to the expert's knowledge, the investor can also reveal his own preferences and private knowledge. Personal preferences include the amount (or percentage) of investment in a specific stock or industry. Conflicts between private and expert knowledge may hinder their incorporation. To reconcile these conflicts, a predefined priority may be applied.

2.3. Inference and Explanation

The main purpose of inference is to match the rule base with the data base and the unstructured descriptions. After the match, the conflict set of the grades and explanations for each individual stock and industry are organized as shown in Figure 15.4. We call this process a compilation. Since the compilation is a very time-consuming task, we have developed a partial compiling technique to accommodate minor changes in knowledge and data. Explanatory statements are synthesized out of the conflict set, as shown in Figure 15.5.

2.4. Integration of Knowledge with the Optimization Model

According to Markowitz (1952), portfolio selection can be optimized by the following quadratic programming model:

Notation

x_i : the fraction of the portfolio held in stock i

$X = [x_1, x_2, \ldots, x_n]$

R_i : the return on stock i

R_p^* : some given level of expected return on the portfolio

$E(\cdot)$: the expected value

σ_{ij} : the covariance of returns for stocks i and j

Var (R_p) : the variance of the portfolio's return

$$\text{Min} \quad \text{Var}(R_p) = \sum_{i=1}^{n} \sum_{j=1}^{n} \sigma_{ij} x_i x_j \quad (1)$$

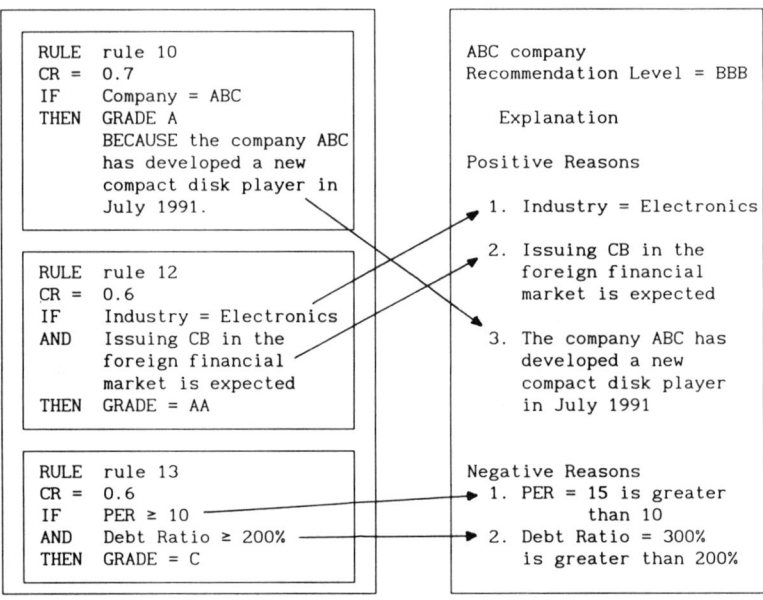

FIGURE 15.5. Process of explanation synthesis.

subject to

$$\sum_{i=1}^{n} E(R_i) x_i = R_p^* \quad (2)$$

$$\sum_{i=1}^{n} x_i = 1 \quad (3)$$

$$x_i \geq 0 \quad i = 1, \ldots, n \quad (4)$$

The purpose of QP models (1) – (4) is to minimize the portfolio's risk (variance) while satisfying the minimally expected return condition. Since the objective function is a quadratic form with linear constraints, a modified simplex method like the one developed by Wolfe (1959) can solve the problem efficiently. To obtain the coefficients $E(R_i)$ and σ_{ij} for all i and j, the single index model or the multi-index model can be used. The QP model can also support the tradeoffs between the risk and the expected return by changing the level of R_p^* parametrically. The QP model may also be modified to a quadratic goal programming model (Ignizio, 1976) if the targeted return and risk can be predefined. The QP model is integrated with the expert system by interpreting the knowledge in the expert system as constraints and algorithmic modifications of the QP model. A typical interpretation can be seen in the following examples:

[Example 1]
{{ Rule-70
    CR : 0.7
    IF : Company = C_1
        OR Company = C_2
    THEN : GRADE = AA
        AMOUNT ≤ 100,000
        AND PERCENTAGE = 10% }}

From Rule-70, we can derive constraints (5) and (6).

$$M \cdot (x_1 + x_2) \leq 100,000 \quad (5)$$

$$x_1 + x_2 = 0.1 \quad (6)$$

where x_1 and x_2 are the shares of a portfolio held by stocks C_1 and C_2, respectively, and M is the amount of total investment.

[Example 2]
{{ Rule-71
    CR : 0.8
    IF : Industry = I_1
    THEN : Amount ≤ 500,000
        OR PERCENTAGE ≤ 20%
    EXCEPT : C_3, C_4 }}

The constraints derived from Rule-71 are the mixed 0-1 integer model, as shown in (7)–(10).

$$M \cdot \sum_{\substack{i \in I_1 \\ i \notin C_3, C_4}} x_i - B y_1 \leq 500{,}000 \quad (7)$$

$$\sum_{\substack{i \in I_1 \\ i \notin C_3, C_4}} x_i - B y_2 \leq 20\% \quad (8)$$

$$y_1 + y_2 \leq 1 \quad (9)$$

$$y_1 + y_2 = 0, 1 \quad (10)$$

B is the coefficient representing a very big number.

[Example 3]
{{ Rule-72
    CR : 0.9
    IF : PER ≤ 7
        AND Annual Sales Growth Ratio
        ≤ 70%
    THEN : AMOUNT = 400,000 }}

To interpret Rule-72, we need to identify the companies that satisfy the condition. The desired constraint is (11).

$$M \cdot \sum_{i \in D} x_i = 400{,}000 \quad (11)$$

where D is the company set that satisfies the conditions of Rule-72. Figure 15.6 shows an example of the investment plan obtained from the QP model reflecting the knowledge.

2.5. Pattern Recognition and Machine Learning for Chart Analysis

To decide the timing of the investment, we have adopted technical analysis to extract

```
K-FOLIO                                        Optimization Model

Your Investment Amount is 10,000,000 (won).
Your Annual Average Expected Return of Portfolio is 10.00 (%).
Your Risk of Portfolio is small (standard error 0.888368).

              **** Solution of Optimization Model ****

        Company         Invest Ratio(%)   Invest Amount   Average volume(3days)

    Samsung Electronics      3.83          3,830,000          120,130
    Goldstar                29.18         29,180,000          221,200
    Daewoo Electronics       3.91          3,910,000          159,670
    Shinkwang Dyeing         7.80          7,800,000            2,310
    Korea Computer          22.86         22,860,000           11,340
    Jungpoong Products       3.86          3,860,000            9,970
    Kuckdong Electric       18.23         18,230,000           21,900
    Yeonhab Electric        10.33         10,330,000           84,120

F1:DOS  F3:Modify  F5:Before Modi  F7:After Modi  F9:Grade  F10:Result Save
```

FIGURE 15.6. Percentage of portfolio acquired by QP model.

knowledge from charts. Chart analysts use the charts that visually represent stock prices and trading volumes data to grasp important symptomatic patterns and to predict the impact of the occurrences. However, the pattern recognition and prediction of the stock's behavior are very difficult and time-consuming tasks, even to veteran chart analysts. It is therefore desirable to automate such processes. In K-FOLIO, investors can define pattern primitives using pattern description language. K-FOLIO then automatically detects patterns, and generates rules based on the detected patterns. Figure 15.7 is a sample pattern definition screen. The upper window shows the list of pattern names defined by investors, and the lower window shows the description of the pattern indicated by "GC." The pattern GC is composed of two primitives in sequence. The first primitive indicates that the 6-day moving average line is *below* the 25-day moving average line for 2 to 4 days. The succeeding primitive means that the 6-day moving average line (*s*hort-term *m*oving *a*verage line) is *inc*reasing and stays *above* the 25-day moving average line, while the gap be-

```
Options   Target    Pattern   Time-Interval   Execute   Result   DB   Instance

  XY-IN    XY-DE     IG-S       IG-B       PL-S
  PL-B     VL-S      VL-B       PV-S       PV-B
  GB-IN    GB-DE     GC         DC         TR-INC
  TR-DEC




      ((moving-average 6 25 (2 4 below) (1 4 inc_sma above wider)))



F1:Add  F2:Delete  F3:Change  F4:Select  F5: Save  F10:Select-Done  Esc:End
```

FIGURE 15.7. An example of pattern definition.

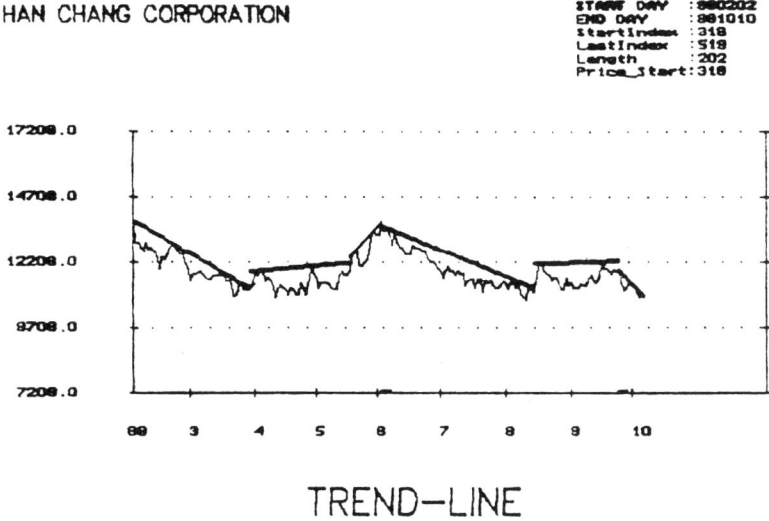

FIGURE 15.8. Chart of upper supporting line of stock price.

tween the two lines has been *wider* for 1 to 4 days. Two sample charts are shown in Figures 15.8 and 15.9.

3. THE KNOWLEDGE ACQUISITION PROCESS

To construct BRAINS for Lucky Securities Co., we collected knowledge from diverse sources, and entered it into K-FOLIO.

3.1. Sources of Knowledge

Brains' knowledge is collected from the following sources.

3.1.1. Expert's Heuristic Knowledge. Most of the heuristic knowledge is obtained from investment experts. Such knowledge resembles the following examples:

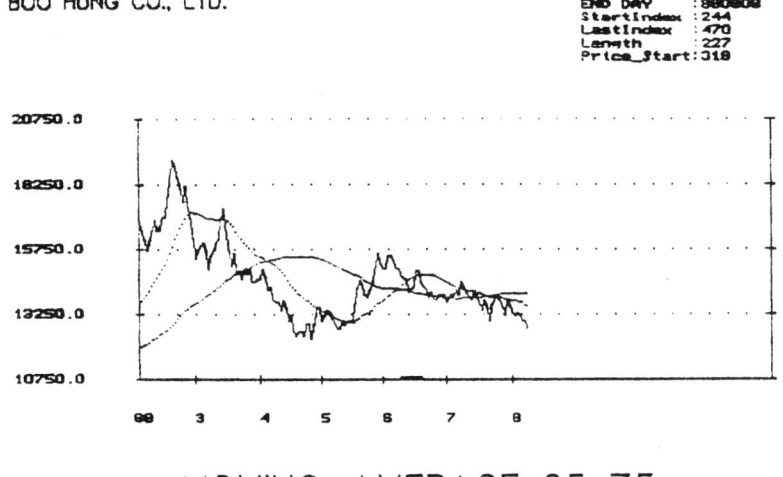

FIGURE 15.9. Chart of moving average lines of stock price.

IF oil prices decrease,
THEN the paint, plastic, chemical fiber industry will improve.
IF trading with the Communist bloc opens,
THEN the electric home appliance industry will improve.

3.1.2. Formal Periodical Reports. Periodical reports provide bi-annual financial statements. The information is stored in the database, and selected ratios from reports can be used for stock evaluation.

3.1.3. Informal Information about Companies and Industries. Informal information such as increases in capital, introduction of a new product by a certain company, and government support for a specific industry are examples of important informal knowledge.

3.1.4. Formula Definition. Formulas constitute another type of knowledge. Formulas can be defined using the attributes in the database. Formulas allow us to define rules with the attributes derived from the database and formulas. For example,
*Ratio of the Net_Profit_Increase_Rate to the Sales_Amount_Increase_Rate = Net_Profit_Increase_Rate / Sales_Amount_Increase_Rate * 100. Maximum trading volume during 10 days since April 1, 1991 = MAX (volume 040191 10). The day when the price is highest during April 1–10 in 1991 = WHENMAX (price 040191 10).*
The sum of trading volume during April 1–30, 1991 = SIGMA (volume 040191 30).

3.1.5. Patterns in Charts. As mentioned earlier, patterns in charts can be detected automatically. We can pair the pattern with its impact on stock price. Such instance pairs can be used to generate rules by an inductive learning scheme (see Figure 15.10).

3.2. Knowledge Acquisition Method

To help the knowledge acquisition process, a knowledge base editor and an automatic rule generator are used.

3.2.1. Direct Input via the Knowledge Base Editor. Experts and investors can create and edit a knowledge base via a knowledge base editor. The knowledge base is organized in a tree structure as shown in Figure 15.11. One can move the cursor to select, insert, delete, and modify the knowledge represented in frames. If we select a rule frame, we can modify its contents as shown in Figure 15.12.

3.2.2. Automatic Rule Generation by Machine Learning. Pattern-based rules are automatically generated from the instances of patterns detected in the charts. An instance is composed of a pattern and a grade with regard to the price change following the oc-

```
K-FOLIO                                                        GRADE

 1) IF pattern = XY-IN THEN GRADE = AA, CR = 0.55
 2) IF pattern = XY-DE THEN GRADE = C,  CR = 0.48
 3) IF pattern = IG-S  THEN GRADE = C,  CR = 0.57
 4) IF pattern = IG-B  THEN GRADE = AA, CR = 0.71
 5) IF pattern = PL-S  THEN GRADE = C,  CR = 0.58
 6) IF pattern = PL-B  THEN GRADE = AA, CR = 0.78
 7) IF pattern = VL-S  THEN GRADE = C,  CR = 0.69
 8) IF pattern = VL-B  THEN GRADE = AA, CR = 0.45
 9) IF pattern = PV-S  THEN GRADE = C,  CR = 0.56
10) IF pattern = PV-B  THEN GRADE = AA, CR = 0.67
11) IF pattern = GB-IN THEN GRADE = AA, CR = 0.63
12) IF pattern = GB-DE THEN GRADE = C,  CR = 0.56
13) IF pattern = GC    THEN GRADE = AA, CR = 0.68
14) IF pattern = DC    THEN GRADE = C,  CR = 0.49
15) IF pattern = TR-INC THEN GRADE = AA, CR = 0.67
```

FIGURE 15.10. Pattern-based rules.

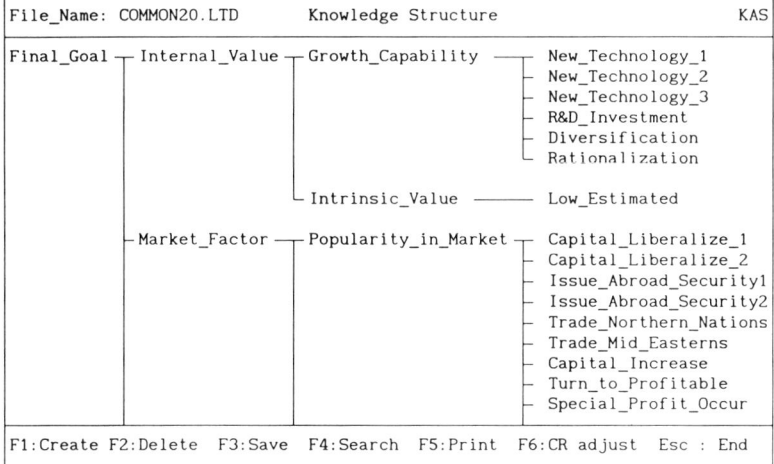

FIGURE 15.11. Knowledge base structure.

currence of the pattern. An instance looks like (12).

$$\{\{ \text{ Instance-1}$$
$$\text{pattern : GC}$$
$$\text{grade : AA } \}\} \qquad (12)$$

The grade of a pattern is defined by the range of the price change between the days of pattern occurrence and evaluation. For example, the grade "AA" in (12) means that the price has increased more than 3% after 25 days from the pattern occurrence. The CR in Figure 15.10 stands for the ratio of instances that supports the class.

4. IMPLEMENTATION PROCESS

4.1. Development Stages

The following stages preceded the implementation of BRAINS:

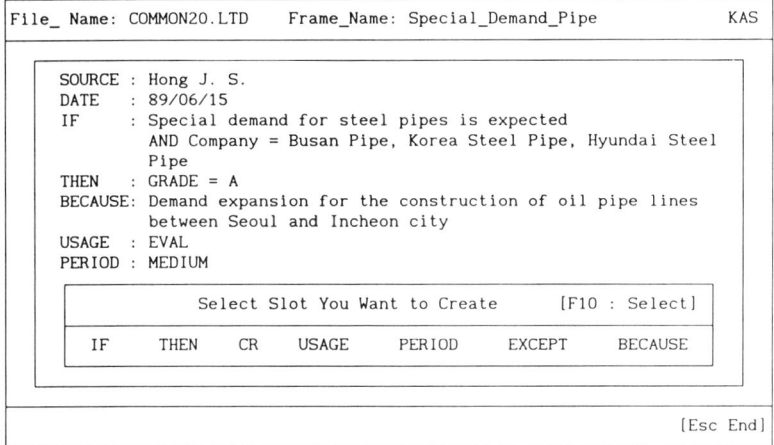

FIGURE 15.12 Knowledge input mode.

4.1.1. Theoretical Research. Basic research on the expert system's approach to stock investment began in 1985. Since then, three master's theses (Akan, 1986; Gwag, 1990; Kim 1987) and one doctoral thesis (Chu, 1988) have been submitted on the topic. They are published in (Lee et al., 1989; Lee et al., 1990; Trippi & Turban, 1990; Turban & Watkins, 1988).

4.1.2. Prototype Development. A prototype named K-FOLIO was developed on a PC/AT using LISP and PASCAL. K-FOLIO has been demonstrated at conferences and some securities companies. K-FOLIO is also reported in nationwide newspapers and magazines.

4.1.3. Cooperation with a Securities Company. In 1988, Lucky Securities Co., one of the leading securities companies in Korea, approached KAIST to utilize K-FOLIO for the company's investment consultants. The K-FOLIO incorporating Lucky Securities Co.'s knowledge is named BRAINS. A project team (4 persons) at Lucky was organized, and its first task was learning to use the system from KAIST's development team. Hardware was upgraded to PC/386 with 8MB of main memory.

4.1.4. Enhancement of the System. Additional user's requirements emerged as we installed the system at Lucky. Typical additional features are sensitivity analysis from the individual stock evaluation window in Figure 15.13, selection of the investment period, dynamic knowledge maintenance, interface with databases including formula derived from the database's attributes, and networking between the mainframe database and users' workstations.

4.2. Technology Transfer Process

To transfer the expertise of KAIST to Lucky, the following education is conducted.

4.2.1. Education and Training. In the beginning, members of the Lucky project team were not familiar with expert systems. Therefore, education on both concepts and software was necessary. A three-hour lecture was held once a week for three months. The topics covered are as follows:

- Principles of expert systems and stock investment
- Manipulation of uncertainty in stock investment
- Knowledge engineering and machine learning in stock investment

```
Type the company name

ABC company

Grade of ABC company = BBB


Explanation

  Positive Reasons

       (1) GRADE = AA with CR = 0.6 for Industry = Electronics
           AND issuing CB in the foreign financial market is expected

       (2) GRADE = A with CR = 0.7
           BECAUSE: the company ABC has developed a new compact disk
                    player in July 1991

  Negative Reasons

       (1) GRADE = C with CR = 0.6 for PER = 15 is greater than 10
           AND Debt Ratio = 300% is greater than 200%
```

FIGURE 15.13. Individual stock evaluation.

- Development strategies and tools for the stock investment system
- Financial market and expert systems
- The architecture of K-FOLIO
- Knowledge acquisition aid
- Automatic knowledge generation system
- Quadratic programming
- LISP: introduction and practice
- UNIK-FRAME: a frame-based system
- Source code reading of K-FOLIO

Source codes of K-FOLIO were open to the project team, enabling it to expand the system in the future according to their needs.

4.2.2. Locus of Project Team. The project team organized for the development of BRAINS is located in the R&D section of the company. The team was strategically supported by the top management. Members of the team visited Japan and the United States in order to evaluate BRAINS in comparison to other currently existing systems.

4.2.3. Communication. Seminars and project meetings were held regularly. User manuals and technical manuals written by the KAIST development team were handed over to the project team. A graduate student from KAIST was employed at the Lucky Securities Company as a team member, and played a key role in the management of the system. Owing to this liaison, technology could be transferred easily to Lucky. A Lucky project member in turn resided at KAIST for closer communication and technology transfer.

4.3. Operation and Maintenance

4.3.1. Building the Knowledge Base. The project team built BRAINS' knowledge base through the following survey:

1. The project team interviewed ten members of the market and corporate research department. After the interview, formal questionnaires were prepared to discover the relevant decision variables in the stock investment decision and their impact. Another interview group was assembled to evaluate the opinions of the research department. Regular reports about the market, along with the questionnaire results, were used to build the knowledge base.

2. A part of the knowledge was automatically extracted from charts using stock price, trading volume, and market index data from April 1, 1989 to January 31, 1990.

3. The initial knowledge was revised after the presentation of BRAINS to branch managers.

4. The knowledge base underwent final refinement during April 1990–June 1990. During this period, the knowledge from technical analysis was supplemented and the knowledge credibilities (CR) were adjusted. BRAINS has been in continuous operation since July 1, 1990.

4.3.2. Knowledge Maintenance. The rules from machine learning are regenerated whenever the data are updated. Data such as stock price, trading volume and market index are updated daily, financial statements are updated biannually or annually, and expected returns and covariances of individual stocks are calculated every month. Heuristic knowledge and informal information about individual companies and industries are added as they become available. Any knowledge whose life span has expired is identified using meta-knowledge.

4.4. USAGE OF BRAINS

Listed stocks are evaluated every day, and the output results are distributed to 50 branches of the Lucky Securities Company through their computer network. The technical analysis knowledge is used mainly for short-term investment, while the fundamental knowledge is used for mid-term and long-term investments. BRAINS plays a role in decision support for investors as well as consultants. However, it might take time to convince other investors of the benefits and popularity of BRAINS.

5. KNOWLEDGE TESTING AND EVALUATION

After implementing BRAINS, we attempted to evaluate the system's benefits in terms of the number of customers, sales volume, consultant's satisfaction, consultant's time saving, etc. The first advantage was that consultants could explain their opinions to investors more systematically. Investors could also review the reasons for a consultant's recommendation. Thus, they could reach a decision more efficiently. The contribution to increased sales was very difficult to measure because there are many other factors that influence sales. Moreover, the quality of knowledge also influences performance. Since the knowledge should be updated dynamically, manual knowledge maintenance was very expensive. Thus, the machine learning mechanism was the most favored source of knowledge.

To evaluate the performance of knowledge from machine learning, we conducted a series of experiment. The stocks were evaluated after 30 days, and classified into two categories: relatively "risen" or "fallen." The training data set was collected from the period of April 1987 to October 1987. The generated rules were then tested for the period of November 1987 to October 1989. The rules that supported "risen" for the training period were able to classify the test stocks under the same category with an accuracy of 72.2%. The rules for "fallen" were able to perform with an accuracy of 74.9%. According to these experimental results, the performance of machine-learned knowledge alone is still very promising.

6. CONCLUSION

Developing expert systems for investment decisions is very difficult due to the diverse sources of knowledge, uncertainties, dynamic knowledge changes and the necessity of integration with optimization models. The architecture of K-FOLIO has remedied such difficulties to some extent.

ACKNOWLEDGMENT

The authors are grateful for the assistance of the Lucky Securities Company researchers S.J. Youn, H.C. Kim and Y.J. Yoon.

REFERENCES

Ahan, S.M. (1986). Design of an expert system for stock portfolio management. M.S. thesis, Department of Management Science, Korea Advanced Institute of Science and Technology.

The Athena Group, Portfolio management advisor. *Expert Systems*, 1987, **4**(1), 54.

Braun, H., & Chandler, J.S. (1987). Predicting stock market behavior through rule induction: an application of the learning-from-example approach. *Decision Sciences*, **18**, 415–429.

Chu, S.C. (1988). *Intelligent stock portfolio management system*. Ph.D. dissertation, Department of Management Science, Korea Advanced Institute of Science and Technology.

Cohen, P.R., & Lieberman, M.D. (1983). A report on Folio: an expert assistant for portfolio managers. In *Proceedings of the Eighth International Joint Conference on Artificial Intelligence*, 212–214.

The Courtier System, Cognitive Systems Inc., 1985.

Fama, E.F. (1968). Risk, return and equilibrium: some clarifying comments. *Journal of Finance*, 29–40.

Granville, J.E. (1976). *A strategy of daily stock market timing for maximum profit*. Englewood Cliffs: Prentice-Hall.

Ignizio, J.P. (1976). *Goal programming and extensions*. Lexington Books.

Gwag, K.Y. (1990). *Dynamic management of knowledge-based stock investment advisory system*. M.S. Thesis, Department of Management Science, Korea Advanced Institute of Science and Technology.

Kim, H.S. (1987). *Generating rules by inductive machine learning: exploratory application to stock investment*. M.S. Thesis, Department of Management Science, Korea Advanced Institute of Science and Technology.

Lee, J.B., & Stohr, E.A. (1985). Representing knowledge for portfolio management decision making. In *Proceedings of the Second Conference on Artificial Intelligence Applications*, Miami.

Lee, J.K., Chu, S.C., & the Associates. (1987). *Integration of expert systems with quantitative methods*. Technical Report, N203-2720-4, KAIST.

Lee, J.K., Chu, S.C., & the Associates. (1988). *Development of UNIK for the integration of knowledge and optimization models*. Technical Report, N324-3078-7, KAIST.

Lee, J.K., Chu, S.C., & Kim, H.S. (1989). Intelligent stock portfolio management system. *Expert Systems*, **6**, 74–87.

Lee, J.K., Chu, S.C., Kim, H.S., Kwon, S.B., Kim, W.J., & Gwag, K.Y. (1989). *K-FOLIO ver. 2.0 user manual.* Department of Management Science, Korea Advanced Institute of Science and Technology.

Lee, J.K., Suh, M.S., & the Associates. (1989). *Development of UNIK for the integration of knowledge and optimization models and its application to petroleum industry.* Technical Report, N486-3509-7, KAIST.

Lee, J.K., & Kim, H.S. (1990). Syntactic pattern-based inductive learning for chart analysis. Working paper, Department of Management Science, Korea Advanced Institute of Science and Technology.

Lee, J.K., Trippi, R.R., Chu, S.C., & Kim, H.S. (1990). K-FOLIO: integrating the Markowitz model with a knowledge-based system. *Journal of Portfolio Management,* **17**, 89–93.

Markowitz, H. (1952). Portfolio selection. *Journal of Finance,* 77–91.

Michalski, R.S. (1983). A theory and methodology of inductive learning In R.S. Michalski, Carbonell, J.G. & Mitchell, T.M. (Eds.). *Machine learning: An artificial intelligence approach.* Palo Alto: Tioga Publishing.

Mossin, J. (1966). Equilibrium in a capital asset market. *Econometrics,* 768–783.

Pring, M.J. (1985). *Technical analysis explained.* New York: McGraw-Hill.

Quinlan, J.R. (1979). Discovering rules by induction from large collection of examples. In Michie, D. (Ed) *Expert systems in the micro-electronic age,* Edinburgh University Press.

Quinlan, J.R. (1986). Induction of decision trees, *Machine Learning,* 1, 81–106.

Sharpe, W.F. (1970). *Portfolio selection and capital markets.* New York: McGraw Hill, 65–75.

Sharpe, W.P. (1963). A simplified model for portfolio analysis. *Management Science,* 277–293.

Trippi, R.R., & Turban, E. (Eds.) (1990). *Investment Management: Decision support and expert systems.* Boston: Boyd & Fraser Publishing.

Turban, E., & Watkins P.R. (Eds.) (1988). *Applied expert systems.* North-Holland.

Wolfe, P. (1959). The simplex method for quadratic programming. *Econometrica,* **27**, 382–398.

Author Index

Aoki, T., 1
Chow, K.P., 64,143
Chu, S.C., 186
Chui, K., 64
Gwag, K.Y., 186
Hara, H., 122
Harada, M., 176
Hirata, T., 11
Hong, Y.-S., 34
Hui, C.K., 143
Igarashi, Z., 176
Inaba, M., 1
Kaneko, T., 54
Katsuyama, T., 43
Kim, H.S., 186
Kim, I.K., 96
Kim, W.J., 186
Kitagawa, Y., 176
Kojima, S., 122
Kwon, S.B., 186
Lee, H.-K., 34
Lee, J.K., 109,186
Lim, J.H., 162
Lo, S.S., 64
Lui, H.C., 162
Matsuda, N., 122
Matsui, S., 79
Minami, E., 11

Mori, A., 133
Mori, Y., 122
Naito, A., 43
Nakamura, H., 79
Nishimura, M., 122
Ohnishi, K., 43
Okuide, S., 176
Onodera, K., 133
Sakurai, M., 1
Shin, J.C., 186
Song, Y.U., 109
Suh, M.S., 109
Sumigama, T., 1
Takatsuto, H., 54
Taki, H., 43
Tan, A.H., 162
Teh, H.H., 162
Terano, T., 79
Terunuma, S., 54
Tsuji, H., 43
Yamamoto, H., 54
Yamamoto, K., 79
Yasuda, Y., 122
Yi, S.-H., 34
Yoo, S.I., 96
Yoshida, M., 43
Yoshida, M., 54
Yun, H.S., 109

Subject Index

air conditioning, 64
airline, 133, 143, 162
airport staff roster, 143
alarm based, 54
automobile, 96
blast furnace operation, 1, 34
blast pressure, 35
BRAINS, 186
case-based reasoning, 165
Central Research Institute of Electric Power Industry, 79
certainty factor, 17
China Light and Power Co., 64
cockpit crew scheduling, 133
connectionist expert system, 162
construction planning, 176
COSMOS/AI, 133
crude oil delivery schedule, 109
design, 43, 176
DGDA, 79
diagnosis, 59, 64, 79, 96, 162
DIAS2, 96
electronic control unit, 96
elevator design, 43
ESTO, 11
fault diagnosis, 11
fuzziness, 6
gas turbine, 64
hierarchical scheduling, 125
Hitachi Ltd., 176
Hitachi Seibu Software Co., Ltd., 176
HSDS, 79
hydro power stations, 79
Hyundai Motor Co., 96
inertia navigation system, 162
INSIDE, 162
integration, 176, 190
investment, 186
ISPMS, 186
Japan Airline, 133

JOYO, 54
Korea Advanced Institute of Science and Technology, 109, 186
Kyonggi University, 186
K-FOLIO, 186
learning, 8
Lucky Securities Co., 186
Mitsubishie Electric Corporation, 43
National University of Singapore, 162
NEC Corp., 133
Nippon Steel Corporation, 11
NKK Fukuyama Work, 1
Oji Paper Co., 122
Okumura Corp., 176
operational guidance, 54
optimization, 190
paper production, 122
POSCO, 34
POSDATA, 34
Power Reactor and Nuclear Fuel Development Corp., 54
PSDA, 79
RCM pilot project, 64
real time process control, 1
RIST, 34
rule generation, 194
Samsung Electronics Co., 186
scheduling, 109, 122, 133, 143
Seoul National University, 96
shield tunneling method, 176
Singpore Airline, 162
steel, 11, 34, 79
steel manufacturing, 11
steel structure, 79
Toshiba Corp., 54, 122
UNIK-PCS, 109
University of California, Davis, 143
University of Hong Kong, 64, 143
University of Tsukuba, 79
Yukong Ltd., 109